T0320131

The Dynamics of Entrepreneurial Contexts

Frontiers in European Entrepreneurship Research

Edited by

Ulla Hytti

Research Director, University of Turku, Finland

Robert Blackburn

Professor, Kingston University, UK

Silke Tegtmeier

Associate Professor, University of Southern Denmark, Sønderborg, Denmark

IN ASSOCIATION WITH THE ECSB

 Edward Elgar
PUBLISHING

Cheltenham, UK • Northampton, MA, USA

Published by
Edward Elgar Publishing Limited
The Lypiatts
15 Lansdown Road
Cheltenham
Glos GL50 2JA
UK

Edward Elgar Publishing, Inc.
William Pratt House
9 Dewey Court
Northampton
Massachusetts 01060
USA

A catalogue record for this book
is available from the British Library

Library of Congress Control Number: 2017950441

This book is available electronically in the **Elgar**online
Business subject collection
DOI 10.4337/9781788110990

ISBN 978 1 78811 098 3 (cased)
ISBN 978 1 78811 099 0 (eBook)

Typeset by Servis Filmsetting Ltd, Stockport, Cheshire

Contents

Contributors

Satu Aaltonen, University of Turku, Finland

Elisa Akola, University of Turku, Finland

Karin Axelsson, Mälardalen University, Sweden

Robert Blackburn, Kingston University, UK

Francesca Maria Cesaroni, University of Urbino Carlo Bo, Italy

Linda Höglund, Mälardalen University, Sweden

Ulla Hytti, University of Turku, Finland

Anders Isaksson, Chalmers University of Technology, Sweden

Trevor Jones, University of Birmingham, UK

Tanja Lepistö, University of Turku, Finland

Hans Löfsten, Chalmers University of Technology, Sweden

Maria Mårtensson, Stockholm University, Sweden

Marie Pospíšilová, Institute of Sociology of the Czech Academy of Sciences, Czech Republic

Monder Ram, University of Birmingham, UK

Heikki Rannikko, Metropolia University of Applied Sciences and Ramboll Management Consulting, Finland

Hanna Rydehell, Chalmers University of Technology, Sweden

Annalisa Sentuti, University of Urbino Carlo Bo, Italy

Silke Tegtmeier, University of Southern Denmark, Sønderborg, Denmark

Erno Tornikoski, Grenoble Ecole de Management, France

María Villares-Varela, University of Southampton, UK

Daniel Yar Hamidi, University of Borås, Sweden

Preface

As President of the European Council for Small Business (ECSB), I am delighted to introduce the 12th volume in the Frontiers in European Entrepreneurship Research series. This latest volume contains chapters selected from among the 153 papers presented at the 29th Research in Entrepreneurship and Small Business (RENT) Conference held in Zagreb. The RENT Conference, jointly organized by ECSB and EIASM (The European Institute for Advanced Studies in Management), is the most significant annual gathering of entrepreneurship scholars, policy makers and experts in Europe. We are very proud of how ECSB and EIASM have been able to develop this event into one of the most influential entrepreneurship conferences worldwide. The RENT conference provides a forum for researchers and interested parties to come together, share ideas and network in a friendly environment. Whilst the ECSB also runs the 3E Conference and co-brands numerous other activities all year round, the life of our association still culminates in our annual signature event.

By way of context, the ECSB is a non-profit organization that strives to contribute to the development of understanding entrepreneurship and small businesses. The organization has around 400 full members and a growing network in excess of 2,000 friends from nearly all European countries. Thus, ECSB is the largest European association of researchers, educators and practitioners in entrepreneurship. It is this strong membership base that provides the backbone of the ECSB and helps drive forward the frontiers of research in this significant field of human endeavour. The Board of ECSB and EIASM work hard at making the RENT conference more attractive to its members. The event is supplemented by several pre-conference activities, including doctoral and post-doctoral workshops, the former assisting doctoral students in improving their research, the latter providing post-docs with an opportunity to strengthen their publications and dissemination activities. We provide professional development workshops, designed to share expertise and foster the intellectual skills of participants. We also continue to hold a policy forum around topical issues in entrepreneurship and linking up with the local organizers of the conference. In addition we offer special interest groups (SIGs) for our members and a mentoring programme to assist in career development, which links up seasoned scholars with junior members who can benefit from the experience and advice of their peers.

Now turning to this book, the aim of the Frontiers series is to disseminate the latest scientific insights to a community of stakeholders that extends beyond the academic network, generating engagement, impact and shaping future academic and policy agendas. It provides a tangible legacy for our current and future members and shows what people working together, across Europe, can achieve. The chapters in this volume are selected from a long list of the best papers presented at the conference upon nomination from the Scientific Committee and the session Chairs. The selected papers then go through a developmental review process, of a minimum two stages, until they have achieved the high-quality standard required to be included in this volume. I would like to thank those authors and reviewers who have contributed to this volume.

In sum, the Frontiers series offers a selection of the latest, cutting-edge research in entrepreneurship and small business in Europe. It has become a key resource for all those interested in understanding entrepreneurship and how this knowledge can be exploited to create a more entrepreneurial and sustainable Europe. This volume, however, presents the tip of the iceberg in terms of the excellent work the ECSB community undertakes. Could I encourage you to visit our website for the most up-to-date developments and initiatives from the ECSB, www.ecsb.org. On behalf, of the ECSB, I look forward to your engagement with us.

Robert Blackburn
ECSB President
2017

Acknowledgements

We would like to thank Edward Elgar Publishing for their encouragement and support in the development of this book. We are also grateful for the reviewers listed below who helped in the selection and development of the chapters:

List of reviewers
Levent Altinay, Oxford Brookes University, UK
Michael Anyadike-Danes, Aston University, UK
Norin Arshed, Heriot-Watt University, UK
Janice Byrne, IESEG, School of Management, France
Leo Paul Dana, Montpellier Business School, Montpellier, France
Per Davidsson, Queensland University of Technology, Australia
Susanne Durst, University of Skövde, Sweden
Kerstin Ettl, University of Siegen, Germany
Mark Freel, University of Ottawa, Telfer School of Management, Canada
Jörg Freiling, University of Bremen, Germany
Urs Fueglistaller, University of St Gallen, Switzerland
Mats Hammarstedt, Linnaeus University, Sweden
Matthijs Hammer, Saxion University of Applied Sciences, Germany
Nola Hewitt-Dundas, Queen's University Belfast, UK
Lena Högberg, University of Linköping, Sweden
Sally Jones, Manchester Metropolitan University, UK
Rita Klapper, Leuphana University of Lüneburg, Germany
Magnus Klofsten, Linköping University, Sweden
Eddy Laveren, University of Antwerpen, Belgium
René Mauer, ESCP Europe Business School, Germany
Esra Memili, University of North Carolina-Greensboro, USA
Kostas Pitsakis, Kingston University, UK
Tommi Pukkinen, University of Turku, Finland
Reinhard Schulte, Leuphana University of Lüneburg, Germany
Jonathan Scott, Northumbria University, Newcastle Business School, UK
David Smallbone, Kingston University, UK

Pekka Stenholm, University of Turku, Finland
Lex van Teeffelen, Nyenrode University, Netherlands
María Villares-Varela, University of Birmingham, UK
Paul Westhead, Durham University, UK

1. Introduction: establishing new frontiers for European entrepreneurship research

Ulla Hytti, Robert Blackburn and Silke Tegtmeier

INTRODUCTION

The Frontiers in European Entrepreneurship Research series aims to contribute to and extend discussions within entrepreneurship research with the idea of consolidating, questioning and testing conventional wisdom and knowledge. In addition, the goal is to create room for new ideas to help the entrepreneurship research field to evolve into new directions. Finally, the series allows knowledge transfer from previously insular national research communities to a burgeoning wider international entrepreneurship research community (Welter and Lasch, 2008).

In past years, research reviews have been conducted to make sense and highlight what is distinctive about European entrepreneurship research, compared with other regional approaches and specifically in the US (for example, a special issue edited by Welter and Lasch in 2008). In this introduction our aim – both through the chapters included in this volume and by revisiting some of the earlier volumes – is to take stock and elaborate on the possible future directions for European entrepreneurship research. We acknowledge this is an ambitious task and that we are not able to offer a pre-emptive review, or a list of suggestions, but merely act as a starting point for future activities.

In this introductory chapter we will first summarize the chapters in this volume. Then, we discuss the key features of European entrepreneurship research as we understand them, based on existing reviews, as well as what can be seen through this series. The key features are: *contextual embeddedness, methodological diversity* and *distinctive clusters* that, in combination, have resulted in versatile contributions that characterize the European entrepreneurship research field. Finally, we suggest avenues for future contributions that we would like to see from the research community and,

1

ultimately, published in upcoming volumes in the Frontiers in European Entrepreneurship Research series.

INTRODUCING THE CHAPTERS

Jones et al. (Chapter 2) take stock on research on migrant entrepreneurship and develop suggestions for future directions. First, they point to the need for comparative studies that would enable understanding how the institutions and policies impact on migrant entrepreneurship. They also highlight that the celebratory discourses depicting the single, heroic migrant entrepreneur (Ogbor, 2000) need to be balanced by deeper understanding of racism and social exclusion. In addition, they envision that migrant entrepreneurship should benefit from more in-depth analyses of gender and generate understanding from gendered arrangements in the household and in the firm. Finally, the authors propose a way forward by focusing on the non-economic, social outcomes from migrant entrepreneurship. Jones et al. underline that the mixed embeddedness theory *'has brought the impact of structures back to the analysis of migrant entrepreneurship, and their interplay with personal networks'*.

It is therefore appropriate that Aaltonen and Akola, in Chapter 3, apply a mixed embeddedness framework to investigate, empirically, the role of trust and bridging social capital in immigrant business owners' start-up processes in Finland. The authors argue for the particular case of the Finnish context to investigate the topic since significant immigration is a relatively new phenomenon in Finland. Thus, in contrast to many other contexts, the role of bridging social capital and trust building between immigrant entrepreneurs and the surrounding society are, arguably, more immediate in Finland. Through a qualitative methodology and presenting short vignettes – stories – the study analyses the development of trust, or otherwise, relationships between business owners and their clientele, the entrepreneurship community, authorities and employees. Both occasions of trusting and distrusting were recognized. The findings also reveal the overlapping and interdependent dimensions of social capital. Personal trust between the entrepreneur and clientele becomes important when lacking collective or institutional trust. Shared codes and language strengthen the trust between actors. Trust building can be viewed as a process but it is far from linear. Thus, time needed for trust building may become somewhat a surprise for the immigrant entrepreneurs.

A novel stance is taken by Axelsson, Höglund and Mårtensson in Chapter 4 to contextualize entrepreneurship in a wider context of political and programmatic discourse. The authors rely on a discourse approach, drawing upon governmentality and through the concepts of programme and technology to investigate the interpretations of entrepreneurship in a school setting. In particular, they analyse how the strategy for entrepreneurship education (programme) is made operable in practice by a competence development initiative (technology). Governmentality is understood '. . .as a method of governing that encourages action of the self, by the self, rather than through formal institutions' (Axelsson et al., Chapter 4) and '. . .the concept of technology refers to a particular method to analyzing the activity of governing' (ibid.). The findings highlight shifts in time: schools initially privileged the entrepreneurship discourse but moved gradually towards the enterprising discourse. Later, a new entrepreneurial-approach discourse emerged. The authors suggest that this approach develops the initiative from isolated initiative within the school to one encompassing the whole school and the entire educational system. It is seen as natural and positive for everyone, both accessible and necessary to all pupils and teachers. The authors highlight how the schools seem to be stretching and surpassing the initial ideas of the programme. Hence, they can be seen to become entrepreneurial in themselves, making the programme to better fit their own ideas and to avoid working with entrepreneurship in the narrow economic understanding. Axelsson et al. also critically reflect on the possible unintended consequences of the new 'entrepreneurial approach', and identify three sources of potential tensions: between political and societal needs and the freedom of the individual, between entrepreneurship as a tool for democracy and exclusion, and between inclusion and norms of entrepreneurship. The authors suggest that widening the discourse from entrepreneurship, in the economic sense, to the entrepreneurial approach may produce unwanted outcomes: the enterprising self as someone mastering their own faith and producing good for society evokes the core of the economic and market-oriented neo-liberalistic ideal of entrepreneurship.

In Chapter 5, Pospíšilová investigates co-preneurship from a family embeddedness perspective with a particular emphasis on its gendered nature. Co-preneurs are defined as partners who share their responsibilities both in business and family spheres. In the study, the analysis focuses on discourses about the division of tasks at home and work. By studying co-preneurs in the specific context of Slovakia, the author also wishes to shed light on the social aspects of entrepreneurship in post-Communist societies and to highlight how the Communist past and present are reflected in the norms, values and attitudes. The research is based on in-depth interviews conducted with each of the partners separately, totalling 21 interviews (one potential participant declined to be interviewed). In the analysis, the focus was directed on identifying cultural repertoires for talking about roles in work and home spheres. The author applied the analytical steps suggested by Gioia et al. (2012) to identify patterns in arguments supporting a certain arrangement of division of work. It also aimed at identifying the combination of different repertoires and potential conflicts. The analysis produced five different repertoires: traditional, function-based, responsibility, collective and competence-based repertoires. The traditional repertoire emphasized the 'natural' division of women's care-taker and men's breadwinner roles. Here, also, the contributions of the partners were valued differently, often undermining those of women. In the competence-based repertoire the division of tasks is argued based on individual abilities, will and enthusiasm. The findings highlight that these preferences are also gendered: women expressing an interest for the tasks at home was applied to explain men's lower participation at home. The functional repertoire was based on formal functions in the business, whilst the responsibility repertoire emphasized a strong sense of responsibility for the business. In the collective repertoire the enterprise is understood as a collective that necessitates everyone's contribution. Interestingly this repertoire was mainly linked to the business sphere, while the domestic sphere was related to the traditional repertoire. The analysis also highlights how the combination of some repertoires can lead into conflicts.

Cesaroni and Sentuti in Chapter 6 contribute to the research on gender and family business by investigating how daughters' career ambitions and expectations influence their actual role in the family business and if this role is aligned with their goals. They highlight that previous research addresses daughters' motivations to join and the different roles available in the family business, as well as the conditions that facilitate or hinder the daughters' ability to take over the family business. They suggest a gap in understanding the relationship between daughters' goals with the actual roles they achieve in the family business. Their study is based on a qualitative, multiple case study involving interviews with the daughters and other family members (where possible) as well as secondary data from business documents and media. The research materials were analysed to identify daughters' professional expectations before entering the family business. This information was cross-checked with their actual role in the family business. This led to a second phase in the analysis, in order to make sense of what led some participants to accept a role that is inconsistent with their original goals. The analysis produced a typology of four profiles: leaders by choice, compelled leaders, managers by choice and compelled managers. Leaders by choice are daughters who are able to take over the family business and fulfil their goals. The authors note that in these family businesses there were no sons, and daughters taking over the firm was thus considered natural. Compelled leaders are daughters who take over the family business not because of their own desire but mainly because of a sense of responsibility towards their family and parents. Managers by choice represent daughters who work in the family business in limited managerial roles and have left the leadership to their siblings. Compelled managers are daughters who had a goal of taking over the firm but were forced to settle for a minor role. They settle with this role as they feel that they cannot question the role of their brothers in the leadership of the firm and that they feel strongly attached to the family and family business.

Yar Hamidi, in Chapter 7, focuses on a neglected area of board leadership in small and medium-sized enterprises (SMEs) by investigating the effects of chairperson leadership, knowledge and experience on firms' abilities to build dynamic capabilities. As opposed to many studies in this area that rely on archival or secondary data, the study applies first-hand survey data. In contrast to existing studies considering boards from an external perspective, this research assumes the agency theory by using the resource-dependency perspective to investigate the effect of board leadership. The data set is derived from the Norwegian value-creating board surveys collected in 2005 and 2006 and the final sample consists of 315 cases of SMEs with boards of at least two members. Multiple linear regressions were conducted to develop three models. The findings offer support for two of the hypotheses, indicating that there is a strong positive association between the chairperson's leadership efficacy and the formation of dynamic capabilities (H1) and between the chairperson's firm-specific knowledge and the formation of dynamic capabilities (H2). However, the third hypothesis is not supported since findings indicate a moderate reverse relationship between chairperson's industry experience and the formation of dynamic capabilities in SMEs. The author suggests that this may indicate that extensive industry experience may lead to conformity of the industry rules and norms that are taken for granted by the chair, and therefore less likely to aim at strategic change.

In Chapter 8, Lepistö, Aaltonen and Hytti investigate how strategy is constructed in a dialogue between independent consultants in a partnership. The authors argue for the need to understand strategies in a network context comprising different stakeholders, and not only in connection to a single firm. They also argue the need for more empirical research in co-creation and strategy in a micro firm context. Current research has mainly been undertaken in the marketing context, investigating the co-creation between the firm and its customers but neglected in the area of strategy work in micro and small firms. The analysis relies on the strategy-as-practice approach, which views strategy as something people do with people from inside and outside an organization. The interest lies in practices comprising understandings, procedures and engagements. The chapter utilizes a case methodology, where the case is the strategy dialogue in workshops consisting of the partnering consultants in two different micro firms. Research materials consist of observational, recorded and transcribed materials from two workshops. The findings highlight five different practices of co-strategizing: dialoguing 1) about the customer; 2) who we are and what we do; 3) use of experience and knowledge in customer co-operation; 4) required steps in the future; 5) need for a customer perspective. Hence, the chapter suggests that decisions about the customer are not only important in the start-up phase, but a dialogue about the main customer is a relevant ongoing practice in co-strategizing. Varied expertise and experience of the partners participating in the strategizing is regarded as both a challenge and opportunity: it opens up new commercial avenues but the different expectations need to be managed and reconciled. The strategy is viewed as an outcome of social construction involving the multiple partners, and as an iterative and ongoing process. Finally, the chapter highlights the opportunities of dialogue and workshops as tools for micro firms in strategy development, working together with the various stakeholders.

Chapter 9 by Rannikko, Tornikoski, Isaksson, Löfsten and Rydehell focuses on firm growth in order to answer two research questions: 1) what happens to new technology-based firms (NTBFs) in their first seven years; 2) how the surviving firms grow when different measures of growth are applied. The chapter suggests that much existing growth research is on larger firms and thus leaves out its links with entrepreneurial activity. Second, the chapter highlights the persistent confusion around growth measures and argues for the need for multiple indicators, to allow for comparisons between studies, enabling knowledge accumulation in this area. The authors aim to add new knowledge to the field by adopting a cohort approach, allowing a focus on new and small firms and to study why and when firms exit the population and which firms remain in it. They adopt various different measures of growth in studying NTBFs. Methodologically the chapter is based on the entire population of NTBFs founded in Sweden in 2006 (N=1,525). The findings suggest first that surprisingly many firms from the 2006 cohort still operate in the end of year 2014 (1,072 firms equalling to a survival rate of 70 per cent). Second, independent on the growth measure applied, only a small minority of firms represent high-growth firms (between 0,6–3 per cent of all firms). The number of high-growth firms is highly dependent on the definition. The findings corroborate the idea that few NTBFs account for the main economic benefits in terms of sales and employment growth. However, job generation exceeds job destruction for every year in the 2006 cohort. Sales and employment growth among high-growth firms were correlated, which counters some existing research. Finally, the authors suggest the potential usefulness of the 'kink-point approach' to capture much of the growth excluded in other measures.

TAKING STOCK OF EUROPEAN ENTREPRENEURSHIP RESEARCH

Contextual Embeddedness in European Entrepreneurship Research

Welter and Lasch (2008) highlighted that the focus on European entrepreneurship research underlines the importance of grounding research in its national context. This idea is further corroborated in a recent book (Welter et al., 2016). Schmude et al. (2008) speculated that the trend of the younger generation of researchers towards publishing in international arenas might level out this distinctiveness. However, in particular after Welter's (2011) article, our attention to context has been raised to new levels and it has become increasingly difficult to theorize about entrepreneurship without paying attention to the context. The implications of the need for contextual research was something acknowledged also by Blackburn et al. (2015a) suggesting that, rather than understanding the role of context to be linked to the need to generate research from new, perhaps even exotic geographic regions, there is a need to generate new understandings on how contexts, and the continuous changes in the environments, are also giving birth to new forms of entrepreneurship that need to be contextually investigated.

Through the chapters in this volume, it is clear that the European entrepreneurship scholars are sensitive to contextualizing their research. An excellent illustration is possible through migrant entrepreneurship and the various forms within. The institutional differences and, for example, the very divergent historical roots in migration within the European Union, offer a great environment for researching how diverse institutions and policies impact on migrant entrepreneurship (Jones et al., Chapter 2). By narrowing the focus to the Nordic countries, it is also possible to see that the two neighbouring countries of Sweden and Finland share very different historical trajectories when it comes to the immigration policies and therefore the number of immigrants to these countries over the years. Aaltonen and Akola (Chapter 3) pick up on this matter by suggesting that, due to the relatively recent migration to Finland, it is interesting to study the role of trust and social capital between the immigrant entrepreneurs and the surrounding environment in this context. Furthermore, certain national contexts with certain practices allow the study of certain topics. For example, Yar Hamidi (Chapter 7) suggests that research on SME

boards makes sense in Norway since the Norwegian SME boards are traditionally active. Indeed, one can easily envision how research into SME
boards might be completely hypothetical in many country contexts as they
do not exist or exist in paper only. Yar Hamidi also acknowledges the differences and similarities in the Norwegian corporate governance system to
establish the boundaries and limitations of how the results from the study
may be applicable to other contexts. Similarly, Rannikko et al. (Chapter
9) ground their decision to study growth of new technology-based firms
in the Swedish context, since Sweden is known for its advanced registration system, enabling their ambitious cohort study of following all new
technology-based firms established in the year 2006, with the study carried
out between 2007 and 2013.

While contributions from the UK-based researchers into entrepreneurship are well known (for example, Blackburn and Smallbone, 2008) and
exemplified by Shaw et al. (2017), European entrepreneurship research can
advance by developing research into the various new and emerging contexts. As Welter et al. (2016) suggest, much of our context thinking stems
from the 'other contexts'. For example Pospíšilová (Chapter 5) investigates
co-preneurship in the Slovakian contexts in order to highlight how the
Communist past and also present are reflected in the values, norms and
attitudes in the cultural repertoires when co-preneurs talk about their roles
in work and home spheres. Context was also present in the study through
the family embeddedness perspective. Thus, Pospíšilová contributes to the
emerging awareness within European entrepreneurship research that the
traditional focus on the individual, or the firm, needs to move towards a
much greater appreciation of the need to understand the role of the family
and household in which the entrepreneur is embedded and from which the
firm emerges (Alsos et al., 2014).

Pittaway and Cope (2007) noted in their review article that entrepreneurship education research has been effective in examining different forms of
pedagogy and their value within entrepreneurship education, but there also
seems to be a need for more contextual research in entrepreneurship education. In other words, there needs to be a recognition that context influences
what is meant by 'entrepreneurship' or 'enterprise education' within the
context studied. Axelsson et al. (Chapter 4) contribute to addressing this
omission by contextualizing entrepreneurship in a wider context of political and programmatic discourses in a school context. The authors suggest
that broadening the scope and meaning of entrepreneurship from the
narrow economic understanding may evoke the core of the neo-liberalistic
ideal of entrepreneurship.

Methodological Diversity

Previous reviews of European entrepreneurship research have been uniform in that its distinctiveness lies in the openness to methodological diversity, both when Europe is understood as a whole (Welter and Lasch, 2008), or in specific country contexts (Hjorth, 2008; Blackburn and Smallbone, 2008; Schmude et al. 2008). This openness to diversity is also reflected in the Frontiers in European Entrepreneurship Research series (Hytti et al., 2016; Blackburn et al., 2014; Blackburn et al., 2015b; Welter et al., 2012; Welter et al., 2013). The series is also indicative of the strong European tradition of qualitative research. A majority of chapters in the series use various qualitative methodologies (from different types of case study approaches to discourse analyses, ethnographies to name a few), to apply different research materials (such as interviews, media texts, diaries, secondary sources and so forth). However, a significant amount of quantitative research, relying on primary survey or secondary data, or registry-based data, is also evident in the series. This methodological richness, with an emphasis on qualitative perspectives, is also clear in this volume with research contributions spanning conceptual reviews, to (multiple) case studies involving interview data, as well as additional sources to discourse, analyses of policy texts adopting both realist and interpretivist perspectives. Yet, the volume also includes chapters based on survey- and registry-based data.

European research has also a tradition of questioning taken-for-granted assumptions of entrepreneurship and escaping overemphasizing the so dominant individual agency approach in entrepreneurship research. But this also links to the appreciation of the context (Welter et al., 2016) and a number of points can be made here.

First, entrepreneurship research has contributed to adding and extending these 'celebratory discourses' whether in the form of 'uncritical admiration of the small firm' (Jones et al., Chapter 2), or advocating the single heroic entrepreneur and their agency in entrepreneurship (Ogbor, 2000). In this volume, Jones et al. warn against this when investigating migrant entrepreneurship. Cesaroni and Sentuti (Chapter 6) participate in this discussion by understanding that the individual agency may be bounded by the family (business), and thus it is not sufficient to understand, for example, daughters' access to family business leadership solely from the perspective of their willingness but in connection with their actual role achieved. Lepistö et al. (Chapter 8), for their part, suggest that the individual micro firm as an omnipotent agentic power in strategizing may be an illusion and emphasize the need to understand the strategies in a network context. On the other hand, Yar Hamidi (Chapter 7) noted a lack of focus on the individual in research on company boards that has relied on archival data and assumed boards 'as collectives' to be investigated from the external perspective. Therefore, the study focuses on the chairperson of the board.

Second, much entrepreneurship research has an underpinning assumption of entrepreneurship as a predominantly positive phenomenon, despite some evidence of its dark side and limitations. One example is in the entrepreneurship education research that either explicitly or implicitly seems to be advocating that more entrepreneurship education is better and where axiological questions are largely missing: do we want to? should we? and how should we do it? (Kyrö, 2015). Axelsson et al. (Chapter 4) embrace this view and discuss how, by trying to move away from the neo-liberal ideal of entrepreneurship and broadening the scope, we are actually evoking the core of the economic and market-oriented ideal.

Third, Rannikko et al. (Chapter 9) highlight that, even in areas with an important body of research and one of the established core fields in entrepreneurship research, as with firm growth, research may not have actually been able to address the actual entrepreneurial activity because of methodological challenges. Thus, it is necessary at times to challenge the type of research approaches that we employ in order to actually move towards the direction we wish to go.

Distinctive Clusters of European Entrepreneurship Research

In light of the above discussion – contextualized research and methodological diversity together with heterogeneity of the field in terms of theoretical approaches and paradigmatic lenses – it is not surprising that the Frontiers of European Entrepreneurship Research series continues as a playground for contributions that are embedded within various 'academic disciplines rather than the generation of a new all-embracing small business or entrepreneurship paradigm' (Blackburn and Smallbone, 2008, p.282). Some 20 years ago 'the lack of theory in entrepreneurship' was often identified as a problem in international, particularly US-based, journals (see for example Bull and Willard, 1993; Ripsas, 1998) with the implication (and sometimes exhortation) that entrepreneurship research should strive at it. Perhaps the call for this uniform direction was less prevalent in Europe. Rather the assessment of Blackburn and Smallbone (2008) in terms of the entrepreneurship research in the UK consisting of a number of distinctive clusters is applicable to Europe as a whole. This can be seen by revisiting the Frontiers in European Entrepreneurship Research series in the previous five years (Welter et al., 2012; Welter et al., 2013; Blackburn et al., 2014; Blackburn et al., 2015b; Hytti et al., 2016).

The various facets of *venture growth* have been discussed in many volumes. The contributions have ranged from looking at the role of the entrepreneur (O'Gorman, 2012) to studying the effects of the local environment (Sleutjes et al., 2012) on growth. O'Gorman's (2012) findings suggest that growth may be intrinsic to the founder's decision to found the firm. In addition, the study highlighted the need for longitudinal research in growth studies. Sleutjes et al. (2012) demonstrate how neighbourhood liveliness and cohesiveness are related to firm success and growth. García-Villaverde et al. (2012) on their part aim to understand the relationship between pioneering and new product performance and suggest that pioneering may be a risky strategy for firms. Courault et al. (2014) added a new twist to researching growth and investigated the failure of high-growth SMEs. Their findings suggest that failures resulted due to challenges in addressing pace of development and inadequate profitability (and not from poor market opportunities).

Another important cluster of research links to the *resources and capabilities*. A review article investigating how knowledge is understood in entrepreneurship research, and advocating a need for theory to explain the knowledge construction process of entrepreneurs, is published by Campos and Hormiga in 2012. Brand et al. (2012) challenge the assumptions with regard to codified knowledge for franchising companies and suggest that franchisees also need local knowledge. Wright (2012) discusses how economic conditions may offer opportunities for entrepreneurial mobility but they also pose challenges for assembling the resources required for firm creation and development. Grande (2013) studies resources and capabilities required for successful entrepreneurship in agriculture, and Yavuz et al. (2016) investigate how resources – and resource flexibility – can impact on internationalization in start-ups. Salamonsen (2016) addresses alliances between large and small firms and suggests that the non-spatial proximity (personal relationships, shared experience and industry, mutual dependence) can help small firms succeed in collaborating with large firms. Guerrero and Peña-Legazkue (2014) investigated the relationship between human capital and firm creation, and Gabrielsson et al. (2014) examined how innovation speed in technology start-ups is influenced by technologies and markets, and contribute to the knowledge of how different types of uncertainty influence the commercialization of technologies. Finance is identified as an important resource, and the use of financial bootstrapping on venture growth was examined by Laveren et al. (2012). Crowdfunding and, in particular, equity crowdfunding as a new source of finance for new ventures was studied by Huynh (2016). While funding is important, research by Nevalainen and Eriksson (2016) highlighted the role of non-financial contributions from business angels and the dynamic nature of these contributions.

Close connection between *entrepreneurship and SME research to policy making* was identified as something distinctive to the UK research (Blackburn and Smallbone, 2008). In a UK-based study, Kitching et al. (2013) investigated the administrative burdens in relation to small firms and whether regulations influence – and if so how they influence – small-business performance. But interest into policies is not limited to the UK. Örge (2013) analysed how power relations impact upon entrepreneurship policies, and he demonstrates how policy discourses contribute to legitimizing certain specific policies in Turkey. In addition, he demonstrates how by describing the target as weak the policy maker's heroic role can be emphasized. Bertoni et al. (2013) investigated the effectiveness of public-venture financing in supporting young high-tech companies in Italy.

Another distinctive cluster is related to the *academic entrepreneurship and role of universities in knowledge transfer*. Bianchi et al. (2013) studied the role of technology transfer offices for entrepreneurial universities, and Horner and Giordano (2016) discuss how university–industry partnerships can enhance open innovation at the regional level, and suggest that the universities can have an impact on the region beyond the formal knowledge transfer. But research in this area is also done at the firm and individual level: openness and innovativeness within science-based firms was investigated by Rasmussen and Clausen (2012), and differing characteristics of technology entrepreneurs to networking were studied by Billström et al. (2014); Karhunen and Olimpieva (2016) investigated role identities of science-based entrepreneurs and suggested an emergence of a hybrid role identity.

The development of *entrepreneurial intentions in particular in the educational context* is also an established area of study. Mauer et al. (2013) studied the factors that play a role in the formation of self-efficacy and entrepreneurial intentions of students, and measured all main antecedents to self-efficacy. Guerrero and Urbano (2015) on their part confirmed that the university and the social context plays a role: a favourable perception of the university environment and the social environment, mediated by cognitive factors, had a positive effect on entrepreneurial intentions. Finally, Varamäki et al. (2016) examined the realization of entrepreneurial intentions of students in entrepreneurial behaviour after graduation. They confirmed that intentions measured during education explain behaviour. It may be considered somewhat surprising that entrepreneurship education research beyond the study of intentions is missing from this series, given that it is a field where European entrepreneurship researchers have been very active. This can be seen in the number of highly cited publications from different authors (such as Gibb, 1993; Gibb, 2002; Pittaway and Cope, 2007; Fayolle et al., 2006; Hytti and O'Gorman, 2004), in edited books (for example, Fayolle, 2007; Fayolle and Kyrö, 2008) and the inauguration of the new European research conference (3E) in entrepreneurship education since 2013.

In recent years, a more focused emphasis on *gender issues in entrepreneurship*, understood both as focusing female entrepreneurship and also gendering as a process, can be identified in the series. Marlow (2015) provided a critique of entrepreneurship research projecting women entrepreneurs as underperforming. Tegtmeier and Mitra (2015) demonstrated that human capital accumulation has an impact on entrepreneurial self-efficacy of female entrepreneurs. Thus, women's entrepreneurship, for example, is influenced by education but also the quality of their careers. Göğüş et al. (2015) investigated the gendered consequences of entrepreneurship competitions and suggested that, instead of empowering women, the competitions may in fact produce the contrary results by reaffirming the dominant male and masculine entrepreneurship ideals. Byrne and Fattoum (2015) investigated gender in family business successions and illustrate the gendered nature of successor selection beyond the binary categorization of women and men.

While the bulk of research in the area of small business research focuses on entrepreneurs at the individual level, it is possible to find two exceptions from this Frontiers series in the past five years. First, Schlosser (2014) investigated profiles of SME owners and employees and their differences in relation to firm age and entrepreneurial orientation. The study suggested that SME owners' preference to recruit similar or different employees is connected to the firm. Second, Aaltonen and Hytti (2015) investigated practices hindering employee innovative behaviour in SMEs and suggested two sets of practices, first dealing with the firm size and second with the management style of the chief executive officer (CEO).

By aiming at carving a broader playing field for entrepreneurship, entrepreneurship research has witnessed the emergence of *different forms of entrepreneurship*. Corporate entrepreneurship has been investigated in a large-firm context (Belousova and Gailly, 2012), and Heinonen et al. (2013) on their behalf shifted attention to public health care and intrapreneurship, and identified five boundaries for intrapreneurship in public health-care organizations. Bosma et al. (2014) analysed the prevalence of intrapreneurship across 11 countries, establishing that intrapreneurs were more prevalent in high-income economies. Social entrepreneurship is a fast-growing topic internationally, and Aggestam (2014) and Johannisson et al. (2016) have contributed to this topic. Aggestam (2014) focused on the individual characteristics of social entrepreneurs and their contribution to extreme poverty, and demonstrated that the significance of human activity can shape positive outcomes. In their contribution, Johannisson et al. (2016) investigated practices of social entrepreneurship to identify their structural and processual features. The chapter highlighted the importance of collective effort and local adaption but also financial resources for social enterprises. Institutional entrepreneurship can be seen a paradox, as explained by Hermes and Mainela (2015), as individuals are needed to change the institutions they are part of. Zahra et al. (2013) suggested that understanding the value of entrepreneurship necessitates a better understanding of counterproductive entrepreneurship.

Finally, compared with the international interest in entrepreneurial opportunity research (Ardichvili et al., 2003, Léger-Jarniou and Tegtmeier, 2017) and entrepreneurial orientation (Lumpkin and Dess, 1996, 2001; Wiklund and Shepherd, 2005), it is surprising that only a few chapters in the past years have contributed to research in these two areas. Hurmerinta and Paavilainen-Mäntymäki (2013) study how entrepreneurs identify, evaluate and capitalize on opportunities by investigating diaries. They suggest that the opportunity process is bounded by context and time. Randerson et al. (2014) addressed the relationship between entrepreneurial orientation and firm performance. Their goal is to understand the links between the personality of the manager, the characteristics of the organization and the environment and organizational performance. Hence, we might offer a suggestion that the European entrepreneurship research is more interested in the 'other' topics than in the mainstream, and that even when these mainstream topics are of interest, the angle is very much focused on understanding the contexts.

OUTLOOK FOR FUTURE EUROPEAN ENTREPRENEURSHIP RESEARCH

The emphasis in this chapter has been to give more room for recognizing differences in entrepreneurship research and therefore being sensitive to context. This implies that there is more room than ever for European entrepreneurship research to give priority to the local and particular (Hjorth, 2008), and thus enable research questions that are resonant with this focus – and have gone unnoticed, ignored or bypassed – to be addressed. Hence, we align with Welter et al.'s (2016) suggestion that future research should endeavour to understand the differences but also similarities, and possibly even the configurations of contexts.

Second, a focus on contexts and for questioning the taken-for-granted seems to point towards support for critical entrepreneurship research approaches but hopefully not in isolation/separated from the mainstream. To advance our thinking and our research, it is necessary to assume a critical stance and to invite critical analyses of entrepreneurship, but in ways that are not satisfied with the negative critique of entrepreneurship but ones that aim at (collective) reflection on when, what kind and if entrepreneurship is appropriate (Alvesson and Spicer, 2012). Thus, for example, the suggestion put forward by Zahra et al. (2013) to increase our understanding of counterproductive entrepreneurship deserves attention. This means opening up our analyses to the potential unwanted consequences of entrepreneurship policy making (Örge, 2013) or entrepreneurship education (Axelsson et al., Chapter 4). It is with these thoughts that we conclude by seeing a bright future for the European entrepreneurship research.

REFERENCES

Aaltonen, S. and U. Hytti (2015), 'Practices hindering employee innovative behaviour in manufacturing SMEs', in R. Blackburn, U. Hytti and F. Welter (eds), *Context, Process and Gender in Entrepreneurship: Frontiers in European Entrepreneurship Research*, Cheltenham, UK: Edward Elgar Publishing, pp.153–72.

Aggestam, M. (2014), 'Social entrepreneuring: the case of Swedish philanthrocapitalism', in R. Blackburn, F. Delmar, A. Fayolle and F. Welter (eds) *Entrepreneurship, People and Organisations: Frontiers in European Entrepreneurship Research*, Cheltenham, UK: Edward Elgar Publishing, pp.7–26.

Alsos, G.A., S. Carter and E. Ljunggren (2014), 'Entrepreneurial families and households', in T. Baker and F. Welter, *Routledge Companion to Entrepreneurship*, Routledge Companions in Business, Management and Accounting, Abingdon: Routledge, pp.165–78.

Alvesson, M. and A. Spicer (2012), 'Critical leadership studies: the case for critical performativity', *Human Relations*, **65** (3), 367–90.

Ardichvili, A., R. Cardozo and S. Ray (2003), 'A theory of entrepreneurial opportunity identification and development', *Journal of Business Venturing*, **18** (1), 105–23.

Belousova, O. and B. Gailly (2012), 'Promoting corporate entrepreneurship within a large company: an in-depth case study', in F. Welter, D. Smallbone and A. Van Gils (eds), *Entrepreneurial Processes in a Changing Economy: Frontiers in European Entrepreneurship Research*, Cheltenham, UK: Edward Elgar Publishing, pp.159–76.

Bertoni, F., A. Croce and M. Guerini (2013), 'The effectiveness of public venture capital in supporting the investments of European young high-tech companies', in F. Welter, R. Blackburn, E. Ljunggren and B. Willy (eds), *Entrepreneurial Business and Society: Frontiers in European Entrepreneurship Research*, Cheltenham, UK: Edward Elgar Publishing, pp.79–100.

Bianchi, M., D. Chiaroni, F. Frattini and T. Minola (2013), 'A dynamic capability view on the determinants of superior performance in university technology transfer offices', in F. Welter, R. Blackburn, E. Ljunggren and B. Willy (eds), *Entrepreneurial Business and Society: Frontiers in European Entrepreneurship Research*, Cheltenham, UK: Edward Elgar Publishing, pp.101–23.

Billström, A., D. Politis and J. Gabrielsson (2014), 'Entrepreneurial networks in university spin-offs – an analysis of the external entrepreneur model', in R.

Blackburn, F. Delmar, A. Fayolle and F. Welter (eds), *Entrepreneurship, People and Organisations: Frontiers in European Entrepreneurship Research*, Cheltenham, UK: Edward Elgar Publishing, pp.136–54.

Blackburn, R.A. and D. Smallbone (2008), 'Researching small firms and entrepreneurship in the UK: developments and distinctiveness', *Entrepreneurship Theory and Practice*, **32** (2), 267–88.

Blackburn, R., F. Delmar, A. Fayolle and F. Welter (eds), (2014), *Entrepreneurship, People and Organisations: Frontiers in European Entrepreneurship Research*, Cheltenham, UK: Edward Elgar Publishing.

Blackburn, R., U. Hytti and F. Welter (2015a), 'Introduction: entrepreneurship, contextual, process and gender differentiations', in R. Blackburn, U. Hytti and F. Welter (eds), *Context, Process and Gender in Entrepreneurship, Frontiers in European Entrepreneurship Research*, Cheltenham, UK: Edward Elgar Publishing, pp.1–5.

Blackburn, R., U. Hytti and F. Welter (eds), (2015b), *Context, Process and Gender in Entrepreneurship: Frontiers in European Entrepreneurship Research*, Cheltenham, UK: Edward Elgar Publishing.

Bosma, N., E. Stam and S. Wennekers (2014), 'Intrapreneurship versus entrepreneurship in high and low income countries', in R. Blackburn, F. Delmar, A. Fayolle and F. Welter (eds), *Entrepreneurship, People and Organisations: Frontiers in European Entrepreneurship Research*, Cheltenham, UK: Edward Elgar Publishing, pp.94–115.

Brand, M., E. Croonen and R. Leenders (2012), 'Knowledge acquisition through strategic networks: the case of franchising', in F. Welter, D. Smallbone and A. Van Gils (eds), *Entrepreneurial Processes in a Changing Economy: Frontiers in European Entrepreneurship Research*, Cheltenham, UK: Edward Elgar Publishing, pp.110–38.

Bull, I. and G.E. Willard (1993), 'Towards a theory of entrepreneurship', *Journal of Business Venturing*, **8** (3), 183–95.

Byrne, J. and S. Fattoum (2015), 'The gendered nature of family business succession: case studies from France', in R. Blackburn, U. Hytti and F. Welter (eds), *Context, Process and Gender in Entrepreneurship: Frontiers in European Entrepreneurship Research*, Cheltenham, UK: Edward Elgar Publishing, pp.127–52.

Campos, A. and E. Hormiga (2012), 'The state of the art of knowledge research in entrepreneurship: a ten-year literature review', in F. Welter, D. Smallbone and A. Van Gils (eds), *Entrepreneurial Processes in a Changing Economy: Frontiers in European Entrepreneurship Research*, Cheltenham, UK: Edward Elgar Publishing, pp.177–208.

Courault, J., M. Perez and C. Teyssier (2014), 'The failure of hyper-growth firms: a study of the bankruptcy of French SMEs with high growth potential', in R. Blackburn, F. Delmar, A. Fayolle and F. Welter (eds), (2014), *Entrepreneurship, People and Organisations: Frontiers in European Entrepreneurship Research*, Cheltenham, UK: Edward Elgar Publishing, pp.155–74.

Fayolle, A. (ed.), (2007), *Handbook of Research in Entrepreneurship Education: A General Perspective,* vol. 1, Cheltenham, UK, Edward Elgar Publishing.

Fayolle, A., B. Gailly and N. Lassas-Clerc (2006), 'Assessing the impact of entrepreneurship education programmes: a new methodology', *Journal of European Industrial Training*, **30** (9), 701–20.

Fayolle, A.P. and Kyrö (eds), (2008), *The Dynamics Between Entrepreneurship, Environment and Education*, Cheltenham, UK: Edward Elgar Publishing.

Gabrielsson, J., D. Politis and A. Lindholm Dahlstrand (2014), 'Entrepreneurship and technological innovation: the influence of uncertainty and entrepreneurial ability on innovation speed in new technology start-ups', in R. Blackburn, F. Delmar, A. Fayolle and F. Welter (eds), *Entrepreneurship, People and Organisations: Frontiers in European Entrepreneurship Research*, Cheltenham, UK: Edward Elgar Publishing, pp.116–35.

García-Villaverde, P.M., M.J. Ruiz-Ortega and G. Parra-Requena (2012), 'New moderating factors for the pioneer's success', in F. Welter, D. Smallbone and A. Van Gils (eds), *Entrepreneurial Processes in a Changing Economy: Frontiers in European Entrepreneurship Research*, Cheltenham, UK: Edward Elgar Publishing, pp.68–87.

Gibb, A. (2002), 'In pursuit of a new "enterprise" and "entrepreneurship" paradigm for learning: creative destruction, new values, new ways of doing things and new combinations of knowledge', *International Journal of Management Reviews*, **4** (3), 233–69.

Gibb, A.A. (1993), 'Enterprise culture and education understanding enterprise education and its links with small business, entrepreneurship and wider educational goals', *International Small Business Journal*, **11** (3), 11–34.

Gioia, D.A., K.G. Corley and A.L. Hamilton (2012), 'Seeking qualitative rigor in inductive research: notes on the Gioia methodology', *Organizational Research Methods*, **16** (1), 15–31.

Göğüş, C.I., O. Orge and O. Duygulu (2015), 'Gendering entrepreneurship: a discursive analysis of a woman entrepreneur competition', in R. Blackburn, U. Hytti and F. Welter (eds), *Context, Process and Gender in Entrepreneurship: Frontiers in European Entrepreneurship Research*, Cheltenham, UK: Edward Elgar Publishing, pp.111–26.

Grande, J. (2013), 'Critical resources and capabilities for successful entrepreneurship: the case of agriculture', in F. Welter, R. Blackburn, E. Ljunggren and B. Willy (eds), *Entrepreneurial Business and Society: Frontiers in European Entrepreneurship Research*, Cheltenham, UK: Edward Elgar Publishing, pp.170–93.

Guerrero, M. and I. Peña-Legazkue (2014), 'The effect of human capital on firm creation: evidence from Spain', in R. Blackburn, F. Delmar, A. Fayolle and F. Welter (eds), *Entrepreneurship, People and Organisations: Frontiers in European Entrepreneurship Research*, Cheltenham, UK: Edward Elgar Publishing, pp.27–50.

Guerrero, M. and D. Urbano (2015), 'The effect of university and social environments on graduates' start-up intentions: an exploratory study in Iberoamerica', in R. Blackburn, U. Hytti and F. Welter (eds), *Context, Process and Gender in Entrepreneurship: Frontiers in European Entrepreneurship Research*, Cheltenham, UK: Edward Elgar Publishing, pp.55–86.

Heinonen, J., U. Hytti and E. Vuorinen (2013), 'Intrapreneurial risk-taking in public healthcare: challenging existing boundaries', in F. Welter, R. Blackburn, E. Ljunggren and B. Willy (eds), *Entrepreneurial Business and Society: Frontiers in European Entrepreneurship Research*, Cheltenham, UK: Edward Elgar Publishing, pp.149–69.

Hermes, J. and T. Mainela (2015), 'Institutional entrepreneuring in erratic environments', in R. Blackburn, U. Hytti and F. Welter (eds), *Context, Process and Gender in Entrepreneurship, Frontiers in European Entrepreneurship Research*, Cheltenham, UK: Edward Elgar Publishing, pp.34–54.

Hjorth, D. (2008), 'Nordic entrepreneurship research', *Entrepreneurship Theory and Practice*, **32** (2), 313–38.

Horner, S. and B. Giordano (2016), '"Made in Liverpool": exploring the contribution of a university–industry research partnership to innovation and entrepreneurship', in U. Hytti, R. Blackburn, D. Fletcher and F. Welter (eds), *Entrepreneurship, Universities & Resources: Frontiers in European Entrepreneurship Research*, Cheltenham, UK: Edward Elgar Publishing, pp.168–94.

Hurmerinta, L. and E. Paavilainen-Mäntymäki (2013), 'Grasping the entrepreneurial opportunity process with diaries', in F. Welter, R. Blackburn, E. Ljunggren and B. Willy (eds), *Entrepreneurial Business and Society: Frontiers in European Entrepreneurship Research*, Cheltenham, UK: Edward Elgar Publishing, pp.194–212.

Huynh, T. (2016), 'Entrepreneurship and equity crowdfunding: a research agenda', in U. Hytti, R. Blackburn, D. Fletcher and F. Welter (eds), *Entrepreneurship, Universities & Resources, Frontiers in European Entrepreneurship Research*, Cheltenham, UK: Edward Elgar Publishing, pp.30–48.

Hytti, U., R. Blackburn, D. Fletcher and F. Welter (eds), (2016), *Entrepreneurship, Universities & Resources, Frontiers in European Entrepreneurship Research*, Cheltenham, UK: Edward Elgar Publishing.

Hytti, U. and C. O'Gorman (2004), 'What is "enterprise education"? An analysis of the objectives and methods of enterprise education programmes in four European countries, *Education + Training*, **46** (1), 11–23.

Johannisson, B., J. Alpenberg and P. Strandberg (2016), 'Exploring processes and structures in social entrepreneuring.: a practice-theory approach', in U. Hytti, R. Blackburn, D. Fletcher and F. Welter (eds), *Entrepreneurship, Universities & Resources, Frontiers in European Entrepreneurship Research*, Cheltenham, UK: Edward Elgar Publishing, pp.6–29.

Karhunen, P. and I. Olimpieva (2016), 'Evolution of the scientrepreneur? Role identity construction of science-based entrepreneurs in Finland and in Russia', in U. Hytti, R. Blackburn, D. Fletcher and F. Welter (eds), *Entrepreneurship, Universities & Resources, Frontiers in European Entrepreneurship Research*, Cheltenham, UK: Edward Elgar Publishing, pp.117–45.

Kitching, J., E. Kašperová and J. Collis (2013), 'The bearable lightness of the administrative burden – UK financial reporting regulation and small company performance', in F. Welter, R. Blackburn, E. Ljunggren and B. Willy (eds), *Entrepreneurial Business and Society: Frontiers in European Entrepreneurship Research*, Cheltenham, UK: Edward Elgar Publishing, pp.55–78.

Kyrö, P. (2015), 'The conceptual contribution of education to research on entrepreneurship education', *Entrepreneurship & Regional Development*, **27** (9–10), 599–618.

Laveren, E., D. Helleboogh and N. Lybaert (2012), 'The use of financial bootstrapping in small and medium-sized ventures and the impact on venture growth', in F. Welter, D. Smallbone and A. Van Gils (eds), *Entrepreneurial Processes in a Changing Economy: Frontiers in European Entrepreneurship Research*, Cheltenham, UK: Edward Elgar Publishing Limited, pp.88–109.

Léger-Jarniou, C. and S. Tegtmeier (2017), 'Introduction: reopening the debate – a Delphi panel of the leading scholars in research on entrepreneurial opportunities', in C. Léger-Jarniou and S. Tegtmeier (eds), *Research Handbook on Entrepreneurial Opportunities: Reopening the Debate*, Cheltenham, UK: Edward Elgar Publishing, pp.1–44.

Lumpkin, G.T. and G.G. Dess (1996), 'Clarifying the entrepreneurial orientation construct and linking it to performance', *Academy of Management Review*, **21** (1), 135–72.

Lumpkin, G.T. and G.G. Dess (2001), 'Linking two dimensions of entrepreneurial orientation to firm performance: the moderating role of environment and industry life cycle', *Journal of Business Venturing*, **16** (5), 429–51.

Marlow, S. (2015) *Women, Gender and Entrepreneurship: Why Can't a Woman be More Like a Man?*, in R. Blackburn, U. Hytti and F. Welter (eds), *Context, Process and Gender in Entrepreneurship: Frontiers in European Entrepreneurship Research*, Cheltenham, UK: Edward Elgar Publishing, pp.23–33.

Mauer, R., P. Eckerle and M. Brettel (2013), 'Adding missing parts to the intention puzzle in entrepreneurship education: entrepreneurial self-efficacy, its antecedents and their direct and mediated effects', in F. Welter, R. Blackburn, E. Ljunggren and B. Willy (eds), *Entrepreneurial Business and Society: Frontiers in European Entrepreneurship Research*, Cheltenham, UK: Edward Elgar Publishing, pp.127–48.

Nevalainen, O.M. and P. Eriksson (2016), 'How business angels found a way to contribute non-financially: a processual approach', in U. Hytti, R. Blackburn, D. Fletcher and F. Welter (eds), *Entrepreneurship, Universities & Resources, Frontiers in European Entrepreneurship Research*, Cheltenham, UK: Edward Elgar Publishing, pp.49–69.

Ogbor, J.O. (2000), 'Mythicizing and reification in entrepreneurial discourse: ideology-critique of entrepreneurial studies', *Journal of Management Studies*, **37** (5), pp.605–35.

O'Gorman, C. (2012), 'The role of the entrepreneur in determining growth: a longitudinal analysis of a new venture', in F. Welter, D. Smallbone and A. Van Gils (eds), *Entrepreneurial Processes in a Changing Economy: Frontiers in European Entrepreneurship Research*, Cheltenham, UK: Edward Elgar Publishing, pp.47–67.

Örge, O. (2013), 'Entrepreneurship policy as discourse: appropriation of entrepreneurial agency', in F. Welter, R. Blackburn, E. Ljunggren and B. Willy (eds), *Entrepreneurial Business and Society: Frontiers in European Entrepreneurship Research*, Cheltenham, UK: Edward Elgar Publishing, pp.37–57.

Pittaway, L. and J. Cope (2007), 'Entrepreneurship education: a systematic review of the evidence', *International Small Business Journal*, **25** (5), 479–510.

Randerson, K., C. Bettinelli and A. Fayolle (2014), 'A configurational approach to entrepreneurial orientation', in R. Blackburn, F. Delmar, A. Fayolle and F. Welter (eds), *Entrepreneurship, People and Organisations: Frontiers in European Entrepreneurship Research*, Cheltenham, UK: Edward Elgar Publishing, pp.51–73.

Rasmussen, E. and T.H. Clausen (2012), 'Openness and innovativeness within science-based entrepreneurial firms', in F. Welter, D. Smallbone and A. Van Gils (eds), *Entrepreneurial Processes in a Changing Economy: Frontiers in European Entrepreneurship Research*, Cheltenham, UK: Edward Elgar Publishing, pp.139–58.

Ripsas, S. (1998), 'Towards an interdisciplinary theory of entrepreneurship', *Small Business Economics*, **10** (2), 103–15.

Salamonsen, K. (2016), 'Overcoming the smallness challenge in asymmetrical alliances', in U. Hytti, R. Blackburn, D. Fletcher and F. Welter (eds), *Entrepreneurship, Universities & Resources, Frontiers in European Entrepreneurship Research*, Cheltenham, UK: Edward Elgar Publishing, pp.94–116.

Schlosser, F. (2014), 'Differences in key employees by firm age and entrepreneurial orientation', in R. Blackburn, F. Delmar, A. Fayolle and F. Welter (eds), *Entrepreneurship, People and Organisations: Frontiers in European Entrepreneurship Research*, Cheltenham, UK: Edward Elgar Publishing, pp.74–93.

Schmude, J., F. Welter and S. Heumann (2008), 'Entrepreneurship research in Germany', *Entrepreneurship Theory and Practice*, **32** (2), 289–311.

Shaw, E., Wilson, J. and Pret, T. (2017), 'The process of embedding a small firm in its industrial context', *International Small Business Journal*, **35** (3), 219–43.

Sleutjes, B., F. Van Oort and V. Schutjens (2012), 'Cohesion, liveability and firm success in Dutch neighbourhoods', in F. Welter, D. Smallbone and A. Van Gils (eds), *Entrepreneurial Processes in a Changing Economy: Frontiers in European Entrepreneurship Research*, Cheltenham, UK: Edward Elgar Publishing, pp.24–46.

Tegtmeier, S. and J. Mitra (2015), 'Determinants and measurement of entrepreneurial self-efficacy among women entrepreneurs: empirical evidence from Germany', in R. Blackburn, U. Hytti and F. Welter (eds), *Context, Process and Gender in Entrepreneurship: Frontiers in European Entrepreneurship Research*, Cheltenham, UK: Edward Elgar Publishing, pp.87–110.

Varamäki, E., S. Joensuu-Salo and A. Viljamaa (2016), 'The intention–behaviour link of higher education graduates', in U. Hytti, R. Blackburn, D. Fletcher and F. Welter (eds), *Entrepreneurship, Universities & Resources, Frontiers in European Entrepreneurship Research*, Cheltenham, UK: Edward Elgar Publishing, pp.146–67.

Welter, F. (2011), 'Contextualizing entrepreneurship – conceptual challenges and ways forward', *Entrepreneurship Theory and Practice*, **35** (1), 165–84.

Welter, F., R. Blackburn, E. Ljunggren and B. Willy (eds), (2013), *Entrepreneurial Business and Society: Frontiers in European Entrepreneurship Research*, Cheltenham, UK: Edward Elgar Publishing.

Welter, F., W.B. Gartner and M. Wright (2016), 'The context of contextualizing contexts', in F. Welter, W.B. Gartner and M. Wright (eds), *A Research Agenda for Entrepreneurship and Context*, Cheltenham, UK: Edward Elgar Publishing, pp.1–15.

Welter, F. and F. Lasch (2008), 'Entrepreneurship research in Europe: taking stock and looking forward', *Entrepreneurship Theory and Practice*, **32** (2), 241–8.

Welter, F., D. Smallbone and A. Van Gils (eds), (2012), *Entrepreneurial Processes in a Changing Economy: Frontiers in European Entrepreneurship Research*, Cheltenham, UK: Edward Elgar Publishing.

Wiklund, J. and D. Shepherd (2005), 'Entrepreneurial orientation and small business performance: a configurational approach', *Journal of Business Venturing*, **20** (1), 71–91.

Wright, M. (2012), 'Entrepreneurial mobility, resource orchestration and context', in F. Welter, D. Smallbone and A. Van Gils (eds), *Entrepreneurial Processes in a Changing Economy: Frontiers in European Entrepreneurship Research*, Cheltenham, UK: Edward Elgar Publishing Limited, pp.6–23.

Yavuz, R.S., H. Sapienza and Y. Chu (2016), 'Resource flexibility, early internationalization and performance', in U. Hytti, R. Blackburn, D. Fletcher and F. Welter (eds), *Entrepreneurship, Universities & Resources, Frontiers in European Entrepreneurship Research*, Cheltenham, UK: Edward Elgar Publishing, pp.70–93.

Zahra, S.A., R.K. Pati and L. Zhao (2013), 'How does counterproductive entrepreneurship undermine social wealth creation?', in F. Welter, R. Blackburn, E. Ljunggren and B. Willy (eds), *Entrepreneurial Business and Society: Frontiers in European Entrepreneurship Research*, Cheltenham, UK: Edward Elgar Publishing, pp.11–36.

2. Migrant entrepreneurship: taking stock and moving forward

Trevor Jones, Monder Ram and
María Villares-Varela

INTRODUCTION

Around the turn of the millennium, the expanding field of research on immigrant-origin entrepreneurship became animated by a major change in theoretical direction. Little short of a complete paradigm shift, the emergence and progress of *mixed embeddedness theory* (Kloosterman et al., 1999) demanded a wholesale rethink of a hitherto one-sided discourse. Since its inception more than four decades previously (Light, 1972), the field had been dominated by upbeat accounts of ethnic minorities as surprisingly, indeed counterintuitively, successful as self-employed business protagonists. This was usually attributed to their privileged insider access to the social capital of their co-ethnic communities (Ward, 1987). Attractive though this stress on community solidarity may be, the ethnic resources narrative became progressively exposed as unbalanced, as placing almost its entire emphasis on the supply of minority entrepreneurs with little thought for why there should be a demand for them. Responding to this lack of contextualization, Kloosterman et al. (1999) proposed a much more holistic model of 'mixed embeddedness' (ME) specifically designed to spotlight the interplay between ethnic social capital and the external business environment in which it must seek its pay-off. Essentially ME seeks to show that firms are simultaneously embedded in two interconnected dimensions.

Drawing on research done in the UK in the last decade, this chapter traces this shift from a largely ideologically driven approach to one of critical realism. We shall also expand upon those aspects of mixed embeddedness we judge most fruitful for future research in the field. Among these, we have identified (1) the importance of cross-border research; (2) entrepreneurship and racism; (3) household-firm nexus and an intersectional stand; and (4) researching the social contribution of migrant firms.

CHANGING TIMES FOR MIGRANT ENTREPRENEURSHIP

Very much in tune with ME's preoccupation with context, we feel bound to present the evolving research agenda as an expression of the march of Economic History itself. Most observers of twentieth-century history would agree with the designation of 1980 as a watershed year in which the 'Golden Age of Capitalism' (Chang, 2014, p.79) gave way to a new era of neo-liberalism (see also Hobsbawm, 1984). According to these authors, the high growth rates and rising living standards of the earlier period were enabled by a mixed economy coupled with a welfare state in which capitalist wealth creation was both maximized and regulated by the state to ensure its fair distribution. As Chang (2014, p.96) himself points out, however, this equilibrium had been toppled by the 1980s and 'By the mid-1990s, neo-liberalism had spread throughout the world.' At the outset key neo-liberal policies – such as privatization of state-owned enterprises, reduced taxation of the wealthy and advocacy of enterprise – had been spearheaded in the UK and the USA under the Thatcher and Reagan administrations. In 1980s Britain, a key policy theme was the 'enterprise culture' (Keats and Abercrombie, 1991) with small independent firms presented as the new drivers of economic development and with an 'implied assumption of policy . . . that if constraints upon the small firms were lifted, this would lead to job creation' (Atkinson and Storey, 1994, p.3). Whatever the exact mechanism, there was indeed a spectacular upsurge of both employment and self-employment during the decade (Campbell and Daly, 1991) and immigrant-origin entrepreneurs were widely celebrated for their starring role in this remarkable business rejuvenation (Rafiq, 1985; Ward, 1985, 1986). Continuing the overarching theme of ethnic resources, a spate of studies singled out Britain's heavily self-employed South Asian communities as the very embodiment of the communal solidarity and cultural values appropriate for the promotion and support of entrepreneurship (Ballard and Ballard, 1977; Helweg, 1986; Metcalf et al., 1996; Werbner, 1984).

Beyond the 1980s, Asians have continued to be presented as a business success story, with additional glitz and glamour thrown into the mix for good measure. Representative here is McEwan et al.'s (2005) work on Birmingham, where both South Asian and Chinese firms are presented as key to the penetration of emerging global markets by the local West Midlands economy. As Chang (2014, pp.97–8) rather sardonically reminds us, neo-liberalism promoted 'globalization' as 'the defining concept of the time . . . those who resisted this inevitability were derided as the "modern Luddites"'. Doubtless our own riposte to McEwan et al. (2005), which demonstrated that the rank and file of minority firms do not remotely benefit from transnational connectivity (Jones et al., 2010), consigns us inescapably to Luddite outer darkness.

As we suggested earlier, there is a sense in which this ethnic resources logic – and the neo-liberal narrative within which it nests – might be described as 'ideological' rather than evidence-based. Even before the entrepreneurial 1980s had drawn to a close, numerous sceptics were in varying degrees echoing Storey and Johnson's (1987) theme 'Small Is Ugly', in a growing sense of unease at the uncritical admiration of the small firm (Curran, 1986; Scase and Goffee, 1982). Most compellingly, Rainnie (1989) argued that the new free-market era was one of acutely uneven development, a happy hunting ground for corporate capital but decidedly less so for the small entrepreneur increasingly subordinated for the benefit of the former. Increasingly the neo-liberal enterprise culture came to resemble a faith-based mythology rather than an objectively supported rationale (Dannreuther and Perren, 2013).

Narrowing this down to immigrant-origin firms, we find a similar widening gulf between proclamation and actuality. In particular the proliferating swarms of Asian firms whose sheer numbers were assumed to denote entrepreneurial success were, on deeper examination, found to be mostly plying their trade in barely profitable labour-intensive activities, sustainable only by murderously long hours of work (Jones et al., 1989, 1994; Ram and Jones, 2008). This glaring contradiction between vast quantity and low quality could not be resolved even by case studies of breathtakingly profitable Asian firms (Dhaliwhal and Amin, 1995), since these proved to be completely unrepresentative of the rank-and-file Asian business community.

MIXED EMBEDDEDNESS: THE IMPORTANCE OF CONTEXT

After some reflection it became increasingly apparent to many researchers that most minority-owned firms, far from leading a triumphal entrepreneurial renaissance, were in reality operating in a kind of business ghetto of leftover markets unwanted by entrepreneurs from the majority population (Jones et al., 1992). It is this process of entrepreneurial exclusion that forms the pivot of mixed embeddedness theory, whose initial insight is that ethnic social networks do indeed create the indispensable trust upon which commercial exchange rests; but that this micro sphere (Kloosterman, 2010) of ethnic resources is far too circumscribed to support more than a relative handful of very small-scale entrepreneurs. Development beyond this requires venturing into the mainstream market, where minority entre-preneurs are competitively disadvantaged by lack of capital and skills, an unfamiliar business environment and racist discrimination (Jones et al., 2014). Consequently they must occupy essentially unwanted market space in such sectors as low-order retailing, catering and what Kloosterman (2010, p.31) describes rather scathingly as 'small-scale manufacture of clothing in sweatshops'. Even where these activities are actually expand-ing (restaurants, personal services), their ease of entry ensures a continual influx of new minority firms, with competition ratcheted up to unsustain-able levels (Jones et al., 2000; Jones and Ram, 2007a).

Clearly this switch in perspective has enabled a much more realistic understanding of the immigrant-origin entrepreneur in the advanced economy. Perhaps most striking of all is the way that the most recent wave of ME-inspired research in the UK has revealed the new migrant entrepre-neurs of the twenty-first century to be experiencing the very same problems that plagued their South Asian predecessors (Jones et al., 2014; Sepulveda et al., 2011; Ram et al., 2015). In this way, ethnic-minority entrepreneurial disadvantage is revealed as an inbuilt structural relationship rather than something contingent upon the nationality, culture, geographical origins or any other inherent trait of the entrepreneurs themselves.

FUTURE DIRECTIONS

Cross-border Research

If the condition of the ethnic-minority firm seems to be constant over time, the same cannot be said about the space dimension, where a con-siderable degree of international variation is almost a defining feature (Kloosterman and Rath, 2003). On this question we note that another of the key contributions of ME is the attention paid to the role of the state and the very substantial influence of legal regulation on market opportu-nities for minority firms; or, as Kloosterman (2010, p.37) has it, 'the size and shape of an opportunity structure are also contingent on the broader institutional framework'. On one level, the market space available for all independent entrepreneurs can be significantly curtailed by the state's eco-nomic role, as for example when the scope of public health provision leaves little room for private enterprise. On another level, the direct regulation of business entry may deny access to specified groups and Kloosterman (2010, p.38) uses the example of Austria and Germany, where 'barriers may even be specifically directed towards immigrants protecting markets against newcomers'.

Relating this to our earlier comments on the neo-liberal shift, we can immediately trace the 1980s rise of immigrant business to the gradual diminution of the old welfare state/mixed economy. Since the creation of market space for small entrepreneurs of all ethnicities depends on privatization, it follows that the spread of minority entrepreneurship follows the global diffusion of neo-liberalism as charted by Harvey (2005). Yet this diffusion process is extremely uneven, with leaders and laggards, some nation-states eagerly adopting and others highly resistant, with the advanced nations of the world depicted by Zizek (2016, p.12) as roughly split between 'the so-called Anglo-Saxon model' and the 'French-German model, which is to preserve as much as possible of the "old European" post-war welfare state'. Amplifying this, Judt (2015, p.229) notes: 'European hesitation over unregulated markets and the dismantling of the public sector and local resistance to the American model'.

Broadly speaking, then, the world divides into a neo-liberal Anglo world (as in the USA and the UK); and a continental Europe where the full flowering of neo-liberalism has been held somewhat at bay, 'circumscribed neo-liberalism' as Harvey (2005) calls it. While holding to the general truth that deregulated neo-liberal economies are more favourable to minority enterprise, Kloosterman (2010) is not entirely dogmatic on this point, understandably since there is a serious dearth of the kind of empirical cross-border research that would be necessary to thoroughly validate the hypothesis. As Kloosterman and Rath (2003, p.3) observe: 'Notwithstanding the institutionalization of research on immigrant entrepreneurship in many countries, cross-border comparisons have been scarce.' They attribute this mainly to wildly varying statistical and categorical definitions from one country to another but, whatever the reason, the absence of comparative research designed to measure any given ethnic community's entrepreneurial performance in two or more countries presents a truly tempting and urgently needed research opportunity.

Apart from the sheer innovative satisfaction of venturing into uncharted territory, there is a need to challenge the blandness of unqualified assumptions about the entrepreneurial benefits of deregulation. As apparent from Chang's (2014) section on 'managed capitalism', the state can be as much a positive contributor to entrepreneurial development as a drag upon it, a reality certainly supported by the very rare instances of cross-border study to date. For example, Yasin's (2014) study of Pakistani entrepreneurs in three European countries suggests that those in the deregulated UK economy did considerably less well than those in Norway and Denmark, mainly because those operating in the latter received superior business and educational support from the public sector. Similarly Jones and McEvoy (1992) discovered that South Asian entrepreneurs in Canada outperformed their co-ethnics in the UK, partly because of a state-created multicultural social environment in which they felt more secure.

It seems that a true understanding of the political-economic forces shaping immigrant entrepreneurship can only be reached by a major expansion of this international dimension. Judging from Kloosterman and Rath's (2003) justified caution about non-comparable official statistics, we would imagine that any truly penetrative research would need to bypass such sources and to devise original and independent interview samples. UK research experience would cast an optimistic light on this, given the minimal use of any official sources before the present century (Ram and Jones, 2008).

Racist Exclusion and Disadvantage

Strongly implied in much of the early optimistic literature on ethnic community business resources was the feeling that business ownership provided a kind of antidote to, a buffer against or even an escape from the kind of racist discrimination commonly experienced by racialized minorities. Against this, however, a steady stream of evidence accumulating over the past three decades or more in Britain reveals widespread distress amongst business owners at what they perceive as prejudicial treatment by banks and indeed the entire range of business gatekeepers (see summaries in Ram and Jones, 2008). Evidently the business realm faithfully reflects the racial disadvantage built in to the world at large, an unpalatable truth that was expressly foregrounded in Jones and McEvoy's (1992) survey of South Asian, African-Caribbean and white firms in 15 localities across England.

Somewhat surprisingly, however, while the exposure of these iniquities seemed likely to spark a wave of similar revelatory investigations, the research community appears to have fallen largely silent on the question of racist malpractices in business. The possibility that entrepreneurs might struggle against ideological obstacles over and above the normal commercial hazards of entrepreneurship has certainly lost any analytical centrality it might once fleetingly have attained. Yet even though the spotlight has moved away, the problem itself certainly has not.

Among the few continuing attempts to trace the direct links between racism and entrepreneurship, perhaps the most helpful have been Virdee's recent examinations of South Asians in the post-war British labour market (Virdee, 2010, 2014). Central to Virdee's thrust is the realization that racism performs much of its most destructive work even before business entry. In the case of the post-war South Asian migrant stream to Britain, 'a significant proportion, including those with high educational qualifications, were proletarianised due to the widespread operation of a colour-coded racism and reduced to working in semi-skilled and unskilled manual work' (Virdee, 2010, p.86). Piling on further disadvantage, the deindustrialization of the 1970s/1980s left many of them 'unemployed or forced them into self-employment' (Virdee, 2010, p.86). This author stresses that post-Fordist restructuring was not a race-neutral process but 'in actual fact deeply racialized' (Virdee, 2014, p.148).

Needless to say, entry into business with only modest savings scraped together from years of low wage earning is a prime cause of the acute undercapitalization that bedevilled the first wave of Asian entrepreneurs in the UK. Throughout this author's work, there is an uncompromising view of UK labour market changes as profoundly discriminatory, with any social mobility achieved by Asians mainly driven by collective anti-racist pressure at the political level rather than by the individual agency of workers and entrepreneurs (Virdee, 2010). In itself, this pinpoints the very thorny issue of entrepreneurial agency. Much as we ourselves have been struck by the strategic ingenuity of Asian business owners (Ram and Jones, 2016) we would warn against the kind of overemphasis on their agential capabilities that might play down the power of external disabling forces (Jones and Ram, 2007b).

Once again, the ME rationale would suggest that the latest wave of EU migrant and refugee entrepreneurs will inevitably be confronted by similar structural disadvantage. Notwithstanding their 'whiteness', post-Soviet economic migrants 'have found themselves at the receiving end of growing hostility to immigration, some of it racially inflected' (Fox, 2013, p.1871). Such antipathy has been sharpened by a recent UK political agenda dominated by the question of EU membership and in this context it is hardly surprising that Cook et al. (2010) find many of their interviewed East European workers in Britain complaining of an enormous gap between their qualifications and their low-quality jobs. Here the closeness of the replication of the earlier Asian experience is almost uncanny.

If all this built-in bias and oppression appears as morally outrageous, then it palls into relative insignificance when set against the horrors faced by refugees and asylum seekers, propelled by 'the desire to leave behind their devastated habitat and re-join the promised land of the developed West' (Zizek, 2016, p.85), only to find themselves unwanted. This plight is graphically summarized by Kundnani (2007, p.3), who relates that, when those expelled 'as a result of warfare, ethnic conflict or political repression' struggle to Europe, 'they are then demonised as a threat'. Speaking of a 'new racism' emerging in the 1990s, this author describes how the wretched of the Earth appealing for humanitarian sanctuary are transformed by 'stigmatising discourses' into scrounging interlopers.

Yet despite a life-threatening context, where the expression 'hostile environment' morphs from metaphor to concrete reality, surprising numbers of virtually penniless refugees somehow manage to set up businesses (Jones et al., 2014). Against what extraordinary odds this is achieved is set out by Sepulveda et al. (2006). It is evident that, whether refugees or economic migrants, racialized minority entrepreneurs can no longer be presented as confronted solely by the neutral forces of the market. We would argue that as part of a renewed determination to confront the unwarranted stigmatization of these communities, researchers might devote more attention to highlighting the positive socio-economic benefits bestowed upon the receiving society by their entrepreneurs. Hitherto, where the economic benefits of diversity have been examined they have been focused mainly upon a high-flying transnational elite (Nathan, 2015), but it is high time that similar celebration be showered on the struggling rank and file (Ram and Jones, 2016).

Household-firm Nexus and an Intersectional Stand

Similarly to the omission of racisms and social exclusion from the analysis of migrant entrepreneurship, gendered disadvantage has also been marginalized in this area of work. In fact, evaluating gender and ethnicity simultaneously has not been common, and the field has been labelled as 'gender-blind' by feminist scholars. The spaces left in the market to start up business for migrant groups are also conditioned by specific gendered positions in the labour market, but also by the ways in which productive and reproductive work are organized. A framework of Total Social Organization of Labour (Glucksmann, 1995) is useful to unpack the ways in which labour is organized in a given society in relation to individuals, institutions (such as family and/or firms), and the different activities available in the market. In relation to migrant entrepreneurship, this framework would help us to understand how, for example, setting up a business by migrant entrepreneurs relates to the different resources the individual has, but also to the ways in which the household is structured and how formal, informal, paid and unpaid work are organized. These arrangements are underpinned by particular understandings of gender identity and relations.

Hence, research in the area of migrant entrepreneurship ought to be sensitive to gendered positions within the countries of origin, destination and within families and local communities. These aspects have been researched in the area of migrant family firms and race and organizations: for example, working in a migrant family firm can reflect resistance and/ or compliance with family norms, expectations and gender identification (Katila, 2008; Essers et al., 2010). However, gender cannot be understood in isolation from other axes of social difference (Anthias and Yuval Davis,

1989), given that its interactions with class, ethnicity and/or disability also shape the way enterprises emerge and the way in which work is organized. Hence, an intersectional stand (Crenshaw, 1995; Acker, 2000) allows us to capture the interaction of different variables and its effects on work and employment This has been explored by authors such as Essers and Benshop (2009) by, for example, looking at the interaction with Islam for women entrepreneurs implementing an intersectional approach.

Social Contribution of Migrant Entrepreneurs

Whilst the emergence of migrant small firms run as well as the nature of work and employment within the ethnic economy have been significantly researched, accounts looking at the social contribution of migrant businesses have been limited (Zhou and Cho, 2010). Over a decade ago, Zhou (2004) reflected upon the ways in which migrant entrepreneurship literature has been focused on the economic achievements of the group, their financial contributions and the ways in which this type of economic incorporation compares to paid employment, without paying much attention to their non-economic effects. Despite this omission, the overall precarity of migrant entrepreneurship (Jones and Ram, 2011, Ram and Jones, 2008; Jones and Ram, 2007b) contrasts with the important social contribution that migrant firms make to local economies.

Recent research on migrant entrepreneurship in the UK (Ram et al., 2015) shows that migrants not only provide employment for themselves and their workers. These firms also have an impact on other migrant workers, since they provide training, skills and mentoring for other co-ethnics. At a local community level, migrant entrepreneurship revitalizes neglected urban spaces; caters for their local communities at very competitive prices; demands public services; may act as safe havens for neighbours; constitutes hubs for information exchange for newcomers; and facilitates social integration. These aspects related to the social value of the firms should be researched in an interdisciplinary and comparative setting.

CONCLUSION

This chapter has discussed the evolution of the field of ethnic/migrant entrepreneurship in the last decades, with a particular focus on the British experience. Perspectives that have celebrated the upsurge of ethnic minority businesses have predominantly dominated this field. The celebratory narratives show migrant entrepreneurs as an example of integration success, and as a win-win outcome for the migrants and the societies where they have settled. In these accounts, migrant entrepreneurs mobilize their specific ethnic resources to generate employment for themselves, their families and their communities, while not becoming a burden for the state. However, contextualized accounts have nuanced the importance of social capital for migrant entrepreneurs by reflecting on the role of the state regulations and the spaces left available in the market for migrant entrepreneurs. Mixed embeddedness has brought the impact of structures back to the analysis of migrant entrepreneurship, and their interplay with personal networks.

Despite these major advances in the field, there is still major scope for moving forward the study of migrant entrepreneurship. The lack of comparative accounts opens crucial research questions in order to understand the role and impact of welfare provision, migration policies, and business regulations on migrant entrepreneurs. We have also argued that the celebratory discourses on migrant entrepreneurship should be balanced by a deeper reflection on racism and social exclusion. Further research is needed in relation to how the emergence of migrant entrepreneurship is preceded by racialized exclusion from the labour market and broader social processes. Similarly, migrant entrepreneurship is conditioned by gendered structures of paid and unpaid work. Accounts looking at gender and migrant entrepreneurship should be further developed to grasp the ways in which the organization of productive and reproductive work leaves spaces available in the market for the emergence of migrant entrepreneurship. Moreover, the sustainability of the firms is also conditioned by gendered arrangements in the household and in the firm. We propose an intersectional stand to capture the ways in which ethnic, gender and class positions impact on migrant entrepreneurship. Finally, the contribution of migrant firms beyond an economic dividend should also be explored, in order to grasp the social value of these companies, from providing employment and skills, to social integration.

REFERENCES

Acker, J. (2000), 'Revisiting class: thinking from gender, race, and organizations', *Social Politics: International Studies in Gender, State & Society*, 7 (2), 192–214.
Anthias, F. and N. Yuval Davis (1989), *Woman-nation-state*, New York, USA: St. Martin's Press.
Atkinson, J. and D. Storey (eds) (1994), *Employment, the Small Firm, and the Labour Market*, London, UK: Routledge.
Ballard, R. and C. Ballard (1977), 'The Sikhs: the development of South Asian settlement in Britain', in J. Watson (ed.), *Between Two Cultures*, Oxford, UK: Blackwell, pp.21–56.

Campbell, M. and M. Daly (1991), 'Self-employment into the 1990s', *Employment Gazette*, June, 269–92.

Chang, H-J. (2014), *Economics: the User's Guide*, London, UK: Pelican.

Cook, J., P. Dwyer and L. Waite (2010), 'The experiences of accession 8 migrants in England: motivations, work and agency', *International Migration*, **49** (2), 54–79.

Cook, J, P. Dwyer and L. Watts (2011), 'The experiences of Accession 8 migrants in England: motivations, work and agency', *International Migration*, **49** (2), 54–78.

Crenshaw, K. (1995), *Critical Race Theory: The Key Writings that Formed the Movement*, New York, USA: The New Press.

Curran, J. (1986), 'The survival of the petit bourgeoisie: production and reproduction', in J. Curran, J. Stanworth and D. Watkins (eds), *The Survival of the Small Firm*, vol. 2, Aldershot, UK: Gower, pp.204–27.

Dannreuther, C. and L. Perren (2013), 'Uncertain states: the political construction of the small firm, the individualisation of risk and the financial crisis', *Capital & Class*, **37** (1), 37–64.

Dhaliwal, S. and V. Amin (1995), *Profiles of Five Asian Entrepreneurs*, London, UK: Asian Business Institute.

Essers, C. and Y. Benschop (2009), 'Muslim businesswomen doing boundary work: the negotiation of Islam, gender and ethnicity within entrepreneurial contexts, *Human Relations*, **62** (3), 403–23.

Essers, C., Y. Benschop and H. Doorewaard (2010), 'Female ethnicity: understanding Muslim migrant businesswomen in the Netherlands', *Gender, Work and Organization*, **17** (3), 320–40.

Fox, J.E. (2013), 'The uses of racism: whitewashing new Europeans in the UK', *Ethnic and Racial Studies*, **36**, 1871–89.

Glucksmann, M. (1995), 'Why work? Gender and the total social organisation of labour', in J. Harding (2012), *Border Vigils: Keeping Migrants Out of the Rich World*, London, UK and New York, USA: Verso.

Harvey, D. (2005), *A Brief History of Neoliberalism*, Oxford, UK: Oxford University Press.

Helweg, A. (1986), *Sikhs in England*, London, UK: Oxford University Press.

Hobsbawm, E. (1984), *Workers: Worlds of Labor*, London, UK: Pantheon.

Jones, T., G. Barrett and D. McEvoy (2000), 'Market potential as a decisive influence on the performance of ethnic minority business', in J. Rath (ed), *Immigrant Businesses*, Basingstoke, UK: Macmillan.

Jones, T., J. Cater, P. De Silva and D. McEvoy (1989), 'Ethnic business and community needs, report to the Commission for Racial Equality', Liverpool, UK: Liverpool Polytechnic.

Jones, T. and D. McEvoy (1992), 'Resources ethniques et égalités des chances: les entreprises indo-Pakistanaises en Grande-Bretagne et au Canada', *Revue Européene des Migrations Internationales*, **8**, 107–26.

Jones, T., D. McEvoy and G. Barrett (1992), *Small Business Initiative: Ethnic Minority Business Component*, Swindon, UK: ESRC.

Jones, T., D. McEvoy and G. Barrett (1994), 'Raising capital for the ethnic minority small firm', in A. Hughes and D. Storey D (eds), *Finance and the Small Firm*, London, UK: Routledge.

Jones, T. and M. Ram (2007a), 'Urban boosterism, tourism and ethnic minority enterprise in Birmingham', in J. Rath (ed), *Tourism, Ethnic Diversity and the City*, London, UK: Routledge, pp.50–66.

Jones, T. and M. Ram (2007b), 'Re-embedding the ethnic business agenda', *Work, Employment and Society*, **21** (3), 439–58.

Jones, T. and Ram, M. (2011) 'Ethnic entrepreneurs and urban regeneration', in A. Southern (ed.), *Enterprise, Deprivation and Social Exclusion: the Role of Small business in Addressing Social and Economic Inequalities*, London, UK: Edward Elgar.

Jones, T., M. Ram and N. Theodorakopoulos (2010), 'Transnationalism as a force for ethnic minority enterprise', *International Journal of Urban and Regional Research*, **34**, 3, 565–85

Jones, T., M. Ram, P. Edwards, A. Kiselinchev and L. Muchenje (2014), 'Mixed embeddedness and new migrant enterprise in the UK', *Entrepreneurship and Regional Development*, **26** (5–6), 500–520.

Judt, T. (2015), *When the Facts Change: Essays 1995–2010*, London, UK: Vintage.

Katila, S. (2008), 'Negotiating moral orders in Chinese business families in Finland: constructing family, gender and ethnicity in a research situation', *Gender, Work and Organization*, **17** (3), 298–310.

Keats, R. and N. Abercrombie (1991), *Enterprise Culture*, London, UK: Routledge.

Kloosterman, R.C. (2010), 'Matching opportunities with resources: a framework for analysing (migrant) entrepreneurship from a mixed embeddedness perspective', *Entrepreneurship and Regional Development*, **22** (1), 25–45.

Kloosterman, R. and J. Rath (2003), *Immigrant Entrepreneurs: Venturing Abroad in the Age of Globalization*, Oxford, UK: Oxford University Press.

Kloosterman, R., J. van Leun and J. Rath (1999), 'Mixed embeddedness: (in)formal activities and immigrant businesses in the Netherlands', *International Journal of Urban and Regional Research*, **23** (2), 252–66.

Kundnani, A. (2007), *The End of Tolerance: Racism in the 21st Century*, London, UK: Institute of Race Relations.

Light, I. (1972), *Ethnic Enterprise in America*, Berkeley, CA, USA: University of California Press.

McEwan, C., J. Pollard and N. Henry (2005), 'The "global" in the city economy: multicultural economic development in Birmingham', *International Journal of Urban and Regional Research*, **29** (4), 916–33.

Metcalf, H., T. Modood and S. Virdee (1996), *Asian Self-employment: the Interaction of Culture and Economics in England*, London, UK: Policy Studies Institute.

Nathan, M. (2015), 'After Florida: towards an economics of diversity', *European Urban and Regional Studies*, **22** (1), 3–19.

Rafiq, M. (1985), 'Asian businesses in Bradford: profile and prospect', Bradford: Bradford Metropolitan Council.

Rainnie, A. (1989), *Industrial Relations in Small Firms*, London, UK: Routledge.

Ram, M. (1994), *Managing to Survive: Working Lives in Small Firms*, Oxford, UK, Blackwell.

Ram, M., P. Edwards, T. Jones, A. Kiselinchev and L. Muchenje (2015), 'Getting your hands dirty: critical research in a state agency', *Work, Employment and Society*, **29** (3), 462–78.

Ram, M. and T. Jones (2008), *Ethnic Minorities in Business in Britain*, Milton Keynes, UK: Small Business Research Trust.

Ram, M. and T. Jones (2016), 'The two faces of migrant entrepreneurship in the UK', *e-Organizations and People*, **22** (3), 25–33.

Scase, R. and R. Goffee (1982), *The Entrepreneurial Middle Class*, London, UK: Croom Helm.

Sepulveda, L., F. Lyon, A. Botero and S. Syrett (2006), *Refugees, New Arrivals and Enterprise: Their Contributions and Constraints*, London, UK: Small Business Service and Equal II.

Sepulveda, L., S. Syrett and F. Lyon (2011), 'Population super-diversity and new migrant enterprise: the case of London', *Entrepreneurship and Regional Development*, **23** (7/8), 469–97.

Storey, D., and S. Johnson (1987), 'Small is ugly', *New Society*, **81** (July), 21–2.

Virdee, S. (2010), 'The continuing significance of "race": racism, anti-racist politics and labour markets', in A. Bloch and J. Solomos (eds), *Race and Ethnicity in the 21st Century*, London, UK: Palgrave Macmillan.

Virdee, S. (2014), *Racism, Class and the Racialised Outsider*, Basingstoke, UK: Palgrave Macmillan.

Ward, R. (1985), 'Minority settlement and the local economy', in B. Roberts, R. Finnegan and D. Gallie (eds) *New Approaches to Economic Life*, Manchester, UK: Manchester University Press pp.198–211.

Ward, R. (1986), 'Ethnic business and economic change: an overview', *International Small Business Journal*, **4** (3), pp.10–12.

Ward, R. (1987), 'Ethnic entrepreneurs in Britain and Europe', in R. Goffee and R. Scase (eds) *Entrepreneurship in Europe*, London, UK: Croom Helm.

Werbner, P. (1984), 'Business on trust: Pakistani entrepreneurship in the Manchester garment trade', in R. Ward and F. Reeves (eds), *Ethnic Communities in Business*, Cambridge, UK: Cambridge University Press.

Yasin, N. (2014), 'A cross-national comparative study of immigrant entrepreneurship in the United Kingdom, Denmark and Norway: a qualitative investigation of business start-up experiences', PhD thesis, University of Huddersfield.

Zhou, M., (2004), 'Revisiting ethnic entrepreneurship: convergencies, controversies, and conceptual Advancements', *International Migration Review*, **38** (3), 1040–74.

Zhou, M. and M. Cho (2010), 'Noneconomic effects of ethnic entrepreneurship: a focused look at the Chinese and Korean enclave economies in Los Angeles', *Thunderbird International Business Review*, **52** (2), 83–96.

Zizek, S. (2016), *Against the Double Blackmail: Refugees, Terror and Other Troubles with the Neighbours*, London, UK: Allen Lane.

3. The role of trust and bridging social capital in immigrant business owners' start-up process

Satu Aaltonen and Elisa Akola

INTRODUCTION

Finland today offers an intriguing arena for immigrant entrepreneurship studies, and one far removed from the traditional context of the old colonial states, big metropolises or multicultural regions (Aliaga-Isla and Rialp, 2013). Significant immigration is a relatively recent phenomenon in Finland with the total stock of first- and second-generation immigrants tripling from 113,000 in the year 2000 to 340,000 in 2015. Consequently, Finland's first-generation immigrants constitute the majority of the stock (85 per cent in 2015). The number of self-employed entrepreneurs with an immigrant background (foreign by nationality or native language) has more than tripled over the past decade, increasing the representation of immigrant entrepreneurs among the whole entrepreneur group in Finland (Statistics Finland, 2016). Although immigration has increased, first- and second-generation immigrants still constitute only 6 per cent of the Finnish population.

The short history of immigration together with the relatively small number of immigrants creates an environment lacking ethnic enclaves (Wilson and Portes, 1980), apart from in a few of the largest urban areas. Therefore, immigrant entrepreneurs do not generally serve only their own ethnic community (Joronen, 2012). Hence, even if ethnic (see Portes, 1998; Kloosterman et al., 1998; Ram et al., 2008) or family-based (Sanders and Nee, 1996) social capital (SC) helps to overcome the liabilities connected to the start-up process such as the liability of newness (Stinchcombe and March, 1965; Aldrich and Fiol, 1994; Abatecola et al., 2012), the liability of foreignness (Zaheer, 1995), and the liability of outsidership (Johanson and Vahlne, 2009), it cannot be used in Finnish cases to the same extent as in states with established ethnic communities. The importance of bridging

SC (Putnam, 2000; Li, 2004; Aldrich and Kim, 2007; Light and Dana, 2013) and trust building between the immigrant business owner and the surrounding society is accordingly more apparent in the Finnish context.

It has been claimed that the benefit gained from an ethnic group's internal SC has been overstated, and that has distracted from viewing ethnic entrepreneurs as part of the wider environment constituted by the local, regional and national institutions, political, and socio-economic systems (Kloosterman et al., 1999; Ram et al., 2008). Similarly, the fact that most empirical studies have focused on bonding SC has led to calls for more analytical studies of the role of *bridging SC* in immigrant entrepreneurship (Kanas et al., 2009; Davis and Bartkus, 2010; Light and Dana, 2013). The current study aims to answer both calls.

The use of the concept of SC has been criticized on the grounds of vagueness (Li, 2004), and the relationship between trust and SC is controversial too (Davis and Bartkus, 2010). Trust building has been recognized as essential in all start-up processes (Turkina and Thai, 2013;Welter and Kautonen, 2005), yet research on trust building as it affects immigrant start-ups remains very rare. The current study is part of a larger research project focused on empirically examining the forms and interconnectedness of bridging SC and trust in immigrant businesses' start-up processes in Finland. This chapter scrutinizes four cases to answer the call to 'explore the emergence of trust-based relationships as well as circumstances in which trust may be lost' (Welter and Smallbone, 2006, p.469).

The chapter applies a novel synthesis of Nahapiet and Ghoshal's (1998) three-dimensional model of SC and Höhmann and Malieva's (2005) categorization of the forms of trust to case studies chosen from an original data set of 64 interviews. Both occasions of trusting and distrusting were recognized, and processes contributing to building or damaging trust were identified. These occasions were positioned in an analytical framework of trust and SC to validate the framework.

The chapter is structured as follows. A literature review briefly describes the core concepts of the chapter: mixed embeddedness, SC and trust. In the following section, case selection, data gathering and the principles of analysis are presented. The cases are then presented, followed by the results and discussion.

LITERATURE

The forms and practices of entrepreneurship are shaped by local social practices, bonds and ties, shared values, within-group trust and bounded solidarity (Aldrich and Waldinger, 1990; Anderson and Miller, 2003;

Kalantaridis and Bika, 2006; McKeever et al., 2015) instead of some abstract idealized market or social forces beyond the actors themselves (Granovetter, 1985; Ram et al., 2008). Kloosterman et al. (1999) introduced the concept of *mixed embeddedness* to emphasize the constant interplay and layers of contexts between the immigrants themselves, their own social networks and the wider socio-economic and politico-institutional environment of the surrounding society (see also Jones et al., 2014). The role and importance of SC and trust in the immigrant business start-up process are therefore always context dependent and can be understood only by understanding the ways in which they are embedded in the social environment.

Social Capital

Social capital became a popular term at the turn of the twenty-first century (Portes, 1998; Putnam, 2000; Adler and Kwon, 2002). Immigrant entrepreneurship studies have mainly used SC to describe the resources that immigrant entrepreneurs gain from *bonding SC* (Putnam, 2000) within their own ethnic community, either in the new country or transnationally (Oliveira, 2007; Ram et al., 2008), or the limitations to entrepreneurial activity caused by high levels of bonding SC (Granovetter, 1985; Portes, 1998; Woolcock, 1998; Li, 2004; Light and Dana, 2013).

The focus of this chapter is on how *bridging SC* (Putnam, 2000; Li, 2004; Light and Dana, 2013) is increased by stocking up the reservoirs of trust in the immigrant business start-up process (Lewicki and Brinsfield, 2010). Bridging SC comprises the contacts outside the immigrant's own ethnic and socio-economic group and comes into play in dealings with potential clients, authorities and other stakeholders relevant to the start-up process (Davidsson and Honig, 2003; Katila and Wahlbeck, 2012).

Bridging SC has proven beneficial to immigrant entrepreneurs (Kanas et al., 2009; Light and Dana, 2013), but it does have limits. First, connecting with the members of the dominant group requires acceptance. In order for that to happen several racial, cultural and class barriers must be broken (Li, 2004; Jones et al., 2014). In this respect, different ethnic groups are in different positions depending on their status in the host country (Jones et al., 2014; re. social exclusion in Finland see Jasinskaja-Lahti et al., 2006; Mannila and Reuter, 2009). Business owners' ability to benefit from increased SC is also dependent on other forms of capital they possess and their class status (Ram et al., 2008).

This chapter will apply the three dimensions of SC: the *structural*, the *relational* and the *cognitive* (Nahapiet and Ghoshal, 1998) that are applicable both to the bonding and bridging forms of SC. The structural dimension refers to the structures of the social system and the relations of social networks as a whole. The linkages between people and units in those systems are impersonal. By the relational dimension of SC, we mean the personal relationships between people that influence their behaviour. Through those relations people fulfil their social motives. The resources providing shared representations and systems of meaning (including shared narratives) create the cognitive dimension of SC. Those systems of meaning are embedded in cultures and communities of practice. These dimensions reflect the different layers of context (Kloosterman et al., 1999; Jones et al., 2014), as well as providing a proxy of cultural capital included in its cognitive dimension (for a critique of this interpretation, see Light and Dana, 2013).

The dimensions of SC are interrelated. They can be mutually reinforcing, though are not always so. SC resides in relationships (Bourdieu, 1986) and, therefore, it has qualities that other forms of capital do not have: it is not transferable from one context to another and it does not decrease in use – on the contrary it most probably increases (Nahapiet and Ghoshal, 1998). Although there has been debate over whether SC is really a form of capital (see for example Adler and Kwon, 2002) there seems to be a general consensus that it is transferable into other forms of capital, which is also an essential aspect of its definition (Anthias, 2007; Bourdieu, 1986; Nahapiet and Ghoshal, 1998).

Trust

Trust has been defined in many ways. We use Misztal's (1996, pp.9–10) definition of trust as a belief that the 'results of somebody's intended action will be appropriate from our point of view'. A common feature in many definitions is the emphasis on the trustor's belief that the other(s) (trustees) are benevolent. Research literature on trust and entrepreneurship is extensive but somewhat unstructured, probably because of its multidimensional nature. The concept of trust has 'recursive links between different levels, forms and sources' (Welter, 2012, p.196). Therefore, some studies concentrate on the sources of trust, some on its objects, some on its effects and some on the processes of trust building, to name a few (Welter, 2012).

If there are several strands to the study of trust, similarly there are also quite diverse opinions on the relationship between trust and SC (Lewicki and Brinsfield, 2010). It is commonly agreed that trust and SC are closely interrelated. However, opinions on the form of the relationship differ (Adler and Kwon, 2002). The concepts can be treated as synonyms; trust can be seen as a form or as a source of SC, or trust can be seen as a collective asset resulting from SC. Building on Putnam's definition (2000),

Stickel et al. (2010) state that *values, networks* and *trust* are in a constant three-way interaction with each other and constitute the antecedents of SC.

The current research categorizes the levels of trust as the *personal, collective* and *institutional* (see for example Höhmann and Malieva, 2005; Welter and Kautonen, 2005; Welter, 2012). Personal trust is trust between persons or towards a person. Sources of personal trust are, among other things, a person's characteristics, experiences, emotions or knowledge. Collective trust, on the other hand, is based on actual or perceived characteristics of groups, recommendations or professional standards. The objects of collective trust are meso-level entities like communities and organizations. On the firm level, collective trust can refer to things like reputation and image. Institutional trust is trust of infrastructure, laws, government and authorities, and the informal rules of society. Collective trust and institutional trust enable an organization to do business with previously unknown people (Welter, 2012).

Within these categories, trust can be either general or particular (Patulny and Svendsen, 2007), and a trustor's trust or distrust of some particular person, group of people, or a societal institution can grow into generalized *trust* or *distrust* or vice versa. Similarly, trust or distrust of objects on a certain level affects the development of trust on other levels. Trust and distrust are seen as separate but linked dimensions (Lewicki et al., 1998), rather than the opposite ends of the same continuum. For example, the same entity can be trusted on one issue and distrusted on another. Figure 3.1 demonstrates the focus of our study in the trust and SC framework.

Although reciprocity is widely seen as a common element of most definitions of personal and collective trust (Welter, 2012), trust relationships between entities are not symmetrical. Both trust and distrust are dyadic and bidirectional phenomena (Koorsgaard et al., 2014). Trust can be reciprocal (one party's trust affects the other party's trust), mutual (the level of trust is shared among the parties) or asymmetric (the level of trust is different between parties). While empirical evidence for the causes for asymmetric trust is limited, there are indications that diversity within the dyad may cause asymmetric trust, and asymmetry can be disruptive to the dyad (Koorsgaard et al., 2014).

The trust an immigrant has in the dominant ethnic group and its members, and also the trust of the members of the dominant group towards the immigrant, does not begin at a zero level. Initial trust is based on the values and personal traits of the trustor; perceptions of the trustee based on appearance, race, behaviour; and institutional arrangements that raise the level of SC and increase the likelihood of trusting judgements

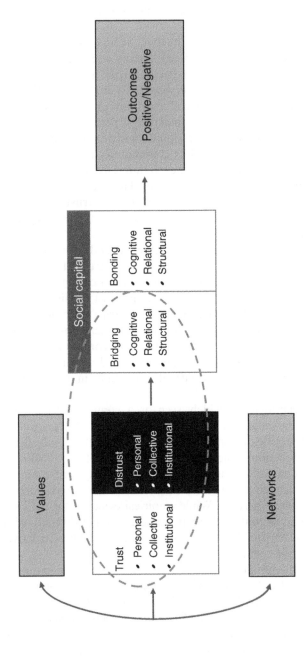

Figure 3.1   The theoretical framework of the study

(Lewicki and Brinsfield, 2010). Social stratification, forms of exclusion and racism have a bearing on the initial level of trust in each immigrant entrepreneur (Jones et al., 2014). All the above are context sensitive and vary across cultures (Gill and Butler, 2003).

METHODOLOGY

The current study follows Eisenhardt's (1989) process of building theory from case study research. The data informing this study is based on 64 interviews with immigrant business owners in Finland. As there is no single register for immigrant entrepreneurs in Finland, we used convenience and snowball sampling methods in our selection of interviewees (Heinonen, 2010). The final set of 64 interviews consists of two sets of semi-structured interviews originally collected separately. In both cases an immigrant entrepreneur is defined as a person who has immigrated to a new country and started a business there. In both studies the interviewees were asked to relate the story of their business start-up. Themes of trust and networks occurred frequently in their stories. Therefore, we returned to the theoretical basis to look for previous research on trust and SC.

Most interviews were conducted face to face, but some were conducted by telephone owing to time constraints. The interviews lasted between 30 and 90 minutes, and all were recorded. The four interviews that are used in this chapter were conducted by two interviewers, so as to permit one researcher to observe, take notes and fill any gaps in questioning (Eisenhardt, 1989). The researchers closely investigated 14 cases of the 64. Those cases were selected based on the thickness of the description and the theoretical relevance of the narratives. As our focus shifted from the general prerequisites for a successful immigrant business start-up to the role of SC and trust in these processes, we narrowed down the cases further, finally selecting only four cases so as to achieve a context-sensitive understanding of the topic (Kloosterman et al., 1999; Welter, 2012).

The selection of the final four cases is based on their potential to reveal different aspects of the role of trust and SC in the immigrant start-up process, and hence to make the process of interest transparently observable and useful in extending the emergent theory (Eisenhardt, 1989; Pettigrew, 1990). We also wanted to choose cases from different business sectors, since we supposed the role of trust to be quite different in different business sectors due to different kinds of customer–vendor relationships. We also chose entrepreneurs from different ethnic backgrounds and of both genders, since those characteristics have a bearing on the attitudes of the host society towards an individual (Jasinskaja-Lahti et al., 2006;

Mannila and Reuter, 2009). The selection of cases was both instrumental (Stake, 1995) and exploratory (Yin, 2003; Bassey, 1999). Two researchers conducted both within-case and cross-case analysis to test and modify the theoretical framework (Hsieh and Shannon, 2005). Having two people working on the analysis prompted complementary insights and increased the confidence in the coding.

RESULTS

In order to illustrate the role of trust in the start-up process and the ways in which trust is built we offer short vignettes based on the selected four cases. Following Van Maanen (1995) and Eriksson et al. (2008), we use vignettes as impressionistic stories that we have dramatized. In our study, the vignettes are not direct extracts from the interview recordings and our notes, but have been constructed from that material to clarify key points. The aim is not to offer a thick description (Geertz, 1973), but rather to show specific episodes (Eriksson et al., 2008) of the start-up process that exemplify the forms of trust in their socially embedded context. We will first introduce the selected four cases and then present and analyse short vignettes focusing on the role of trust and trust building in them.

Laticia – a Business Consultant from the Netherlands Antilles

Laticia is a 32-year-old female from the Netherlands Antilles. She has a university degree from the Netherlands. She has been living in Finland with her Finnish husband since 2005. Laticia experienced some difficulties in finding a job in Finland, mostly because she could not speak Finnish. However, she took a language course that helped her to get a position as a trainee in a local school. Gradually she got new jobs but always with fixed-term contracts and not completely appropriate to her education. In 2008, she established a business offering consultancy in intercultural communication, team building and presentation skills in order to be able to work in the field in which she was trained. At the time of the interview, Laticia's business was three years old.

Laticia's vignette (Vignette 1) illustrates how building trust and SC are active processes and can take many forms. Laticia operates in the service sector where the offering is intangible and thus creating trust and credibility for the business is even more important and challenging compared to selling goods. Being a professional in intercultural communication and having lived in foreign countries, Laticia understood the importance of adapting to a new culture. However, she also felt she did not fit the stereo-

---

VIGNETTE 1:   NETWORK, NETWORK, NETWORK!

When the idea of starting a business occurred to Laticia, she began systematically to prepare for it. She joined a business start-up course for foreigners in order to get help in designing her business. The course provided a Finnish mentor, who was highly significant in encouraging her into entrepreneurship. The mentor helped her to devise and test her business plan and also organized business premises for her. Although Laticia could have operated her consultancy from home, she thought that as an immigrant it was necessary to rent premises in order to make her business appear more credible and easily approachable. She invested in office decoration, a website, brochures and business cards, and ensured they were all professional, coherent and visually appealing.

Laticia visited the local business service centre, applied for a start-up grant and received one. The service in the business service centre was friendly and helpful. She thought it was partly because she had a Finnish surname and partly because the business adviser already knew she was on the entrepreneurship course. Laticia also networked diligently and promoted her business at every opportunity. She also sought to make friends outside work through pursuing hobbies; as she points out, 'you never know which contacts will turn out to be valuable in the long run'. For example, she kept in touch with a person who had once interviewed her for a position she did not get. This connection eventually led her to the Junior Chamber of Commerce and an invitation to speak at a big entrepreneurs' event, which in turn led to an article about her business in the local entrepreneur magazine.

---

type of an immigrant entrepreneur – with no degree, owning a kebab shop or pizzeria. She felt she must fight against the stereotype to acquire credibility as a trustworthy immigrant consultant, hence her decision to invest in having a business premises (a relational dimension of SC).

Laticia saw all forms of networking as effective means to build SC. She took part in various events with business in mind, but saw them also as an opportunity to learn of Finnish culture. Even though Laticia had not faced racial prejudice, her comment on having a Finnish family name guaranteeing her friendly service at the business service centre reflects the prejudices that immigrants expect to encounter.

Inga – a Craft Shop Owner from Estonia

In 2000, 30-year-old Inga had a good job as a middle manager in a factory in Estonia. The salary was quite good, but she came to Finland in the summer to pick strawberries to supplement it. During her stay she met a Finn and the following year moved to Finland. At that time, migrants required a contract of employment to obtain a work permit. Her first jobs in Finland were on foodstuff production lines, something quite different

---

VIGNETTE 2:   PLEASE COME IN, I WON'T BITE

The day Inga opened her craft shop, she was confident that enthusiastic customers would rush in to see what was new in the town, as they might in her home town in Estonia. But the reality was somewhat different. During the first half-year, people would peek suspiciously and shyly into the shop window, but did not enter. Inga was confused but the business owners next door assured her that this was typical in Finland and eventually the customers would venture in. Inga worked hard to persuade people to come in and see what she had to offer. 'Looking does not cost anything', she said. The next half-year passed and, little by little, people started to come in. Some locals even dared to use her services, were satisfied and recommended Inga to friends. It took more than one year after opening before actual sales started to pick up.

After three years of operation, the craft shop is a personification of Inga such that her customers want to do business only with her, not with her employees. Inga has actually found it difficult to find trustworthy, enthusiastic employees with a similar entrepreneurial mindset as her own. It is challenging both for Inga and her customers to trust that someone else could provide the same level of service.

---

from her previous job. Inga could hardly speak any Finnish and there were no language courses available for Estonians at that time. She was quite shocked by the reduction in her social status, but as her language skills improved, she was able to get better jobs.

In 2008, Inga opened a craft shop in a small, rural town in southern Finland. In doing so, she realized a long-held ambition to start a business. She had a clear vision for offering clothing repairs, needlework and handicrafts, based on sewing and doing needlework all her life and on vocational training in the field acquired in Estonia. The company was three years old at the time of the interview. Most of her clients are Finns.

Vignette 2 illustrates how building trust requires time. Although Finland and Estonia are neighbouring countries with similar languages, Inga feels that cultural differences play a part. Those differences are most notable in mentality and pace of life. Inga explains that Estonians are more outgoing, impatient and enterprising than Finns. Most of Inga's customers are older, rural ladies who she relates to, since she considers them hard working and enterprising due to their experiences of harder times. Her trust in youth was not high and she felt that a good workforce is really hard to find.

Inga feels that learning Finnish has been very important to acquiring the trust of her clientele. Selling sewing supplies while offering a clothing repair service has lowered the threshold to enter the shop, since less trust is required in the retail trade than in selling services that entail some aspect of intimacy. Inga used her own initiative to build trust within the local entrepreneurship community. The more Inga and her contacts trusted each other, the more they communicated and co-operated and, accordingly, more SC was accumulated.

Mikhail – a Café Owner from Russia

Mikhail is a 30-year-old male entrepreneur from Russia with a university degree from Russia, and ten years' work experience in large information and communications technology (ICT) corporations. Mikhail visited a university town in Finland regularly for a few years and became friends with many young immigrant students there. These contacts proposed jointly opening a café in Finland and, tired of the corporate environment, Mikhail decided to move there with his new wife. He found Finland a good place to do business and to raise children, since there is little corruption and the public services are of a high standard.

At the time of the interview, the café had been running for one year. After spending most of their own savings on the start-up costs of the company, the young friends got the idea to try crowdfunding. They believed in the firm and were able to convince their satisfied customers of its viability too. The crowdfunding opportunity was advertised on social media and with some pop-up presentations in a local square. The company ended up having over 30 shareholders.

VIGNETTE 3: THEY JUST GIVE TRIVIAL PIECES OF ADVICE!

After running the café for weeks by himself from 10 a.m. to 10 p.m., Mikhail decided to investigate employing an assistant as cheaply as possible. He sought advice at the local employment office. His expectations were high, since the reputation of the Finnish public sector is good, and therefore he trusts it. The meeting proved frustrating. The public business adviser sat behind his desk and turned to his computer when Mikhail asked how to find a good but cheap employee for the café. The adviser read the advice from the internet and repeated it to Mikhail. 'That I could have done myself! Why would I go to get some advice if all that was available online?', Mikhail huffs. 'I would have expected him to familiarize himself with our business and tailor a solution that best suits our needs.' After that visit Mikhail no longer thought very highly of public business services.

His next idea was to visit a neighbouring café and ask its owner how he organized staff for his business. The girl behind the counter smiled at him when he entered the café. He asked for the owner and they started chatting. Everything went smoothly until Mikhail asked for concrete advice, and the owner seemed reluctant to give him any. Mikhail was confused. He states that entrepreneurs are unwilling to share information or co-operate to develop their business sector due to envy and distrust – even if co-operation would benefit the whole sector.

In the business pre-start-up phase, Mikhail placed a lot of trust in the fairness of the Finnish authorities and business environment (Vignette 3). Mikhail's story illustrates how a strong institutional trust can be shaken by one adverse experience. The visit to the business adviser did not meet Mikhail's expectations and dented his trust in the skills of the staff at the employment centre. Another trust relationship that had effect on Mikhail's post-start-up process was the low level of collective trust among café owners in the town. The atmosphere of distrust among this community prevented him from acquiring SC from networking with local colleagues.

On the other hand, the start-up process was clearly advanced by Mikhail having a close circle of friends, which provided both relational and cognitive forms of bonding SC. The friends had strong ties and they shared the same cognitive world, an immigrant and university background and being young, urban nomads. The same criteria applied to the main segment of the café's clientele.

Rahim – an Ethnic Grocery Store Owner from Iraq

Rahim is a 25-year-old male running an ethnic grocery store. His family came to Finland as refugees from Iraq when Rahim was seven years old. Despite initial language problems, Rahim succeeded in obtaining a vocational qualification in business. Rahim thinks that entrepreneurship is in his blood. He is an extrovert who gets along with people easily. His uncle is also self-employed, so has been a kind of role model for Rahim. Rahim tells us how satisfied he has been with the way the bank, accountant and business service authorities have treated him, which partly signals that he had expected something else.

The ethnic-food grocery store is already his third company. It had run for a year at the time of the interview. It is located in a suburb of 9,000 inhabitants, of whom one-third are immigrants. Almost 60 different languages are spoken there and over 40 nationalities represented. In addition to the grocery business Rahim also sublets premises to other immigrant entrepreneurs. Gradually Rahim has become a figurehead for local immigrant entrepreneurs, which together with his excellent language skills and vocational qualifications lends him credibility in the Finnish-speaking business community too. The shop sells food from all over the world and the clientele is very mixed. While Rahim's Arab background gives him credibility in selling products from the Middle East, his ethnic background is hardly a resource when selling food stuffs from Eastern Europe or the Far East.

Despite living most of his life in Finland and speaking fluent Finnish, Rahim felt that he was treated unequally by the public authorities owing to

---

VIGNETTE 4:   WHY AM I MISTREATED?

Rahim is involved in many things such as associations, politics and charity, which have contributed positive publicity for his business in the media. But the best advert is when customers publicize their good experiences by word of mouth. However, now he has run the business for a year but the fresh-meat section that should be the heart of his grocery store remains empty, which influences the number of customers. Rahim says he has done everything by the book, but the food safety authorities have denied permission to open a meat section. Rahim thinks that the law has been misinterpreted in his case. He is frustrated and feels that the authorities have not treated him fairly: 'I am put under the microscope. My treatment is not equal. Nothing like this is required from the (Finnish) entrepreneurs upstairs.'

---

his immigrant background (Vignette 4). However, by the time of the interview he had started to fight back. His general trust towards Finnish society was so strong that he felt that injustices could be addressed. Hence, he had contacted local media and his friends in politics to publicize his case, which he could not have done without a high level of SC within the community. That capital was established during his 18-year residence in Finland, active participation in associations, charity and politics, where he had gained both cognitive and relational SC, even if his structural SC was low due to his immigrant and refugee background.

Summary of Results

The current research identifies trust relationships between the business owner and the clientele, the business owner and the entrepreneurship community, the business owner and the authorities, and the business owner and employees. We recognized occasions of both trusting and distrusting, and identified factors used to build trust or destroy it. During the analysis, separate maps for outward/inward trust and distrust were used; in Table 3.1 each occasion is positioned in a 3x3 map of the dimensions of trust and SC.

Positioning the units of analysis into the framework revealed the overlapping and interdependence of the dimensions of SC. For instance, if we look at the distrust of the clientele towards Inga and her business, the same occasion of distrust affected both cognitive and relational SC. Furthermore, the trust was dependent on the point of view taken – the categorization was different if the object of the customers' trust was the entrepreneur (personal trust) or his/her firm (collective trust).

Although trust building is viewed as a process, our cases show that it is

Table 3.1 Forms of trust and dimensions of social capital in the cases

		Trust		
		personal trust/distrust	collective trust/distrust	institutional trust/distrust
Social capital	cognitive	(1) Inga: distrust in customer relations (2) Inga: distrust of employees (3) Inga: trust among entrepreneur community (5) Laticia: distrust in customer relations	(1) Inga: distrust in customer relations	
	relational	(1) Inga: distrust in customer relations (2) Inga: distrust of employees (3) Inga: trust among entrepreneur community (4) Laticia: distrust in customer relations (9) Rahim: trust among entrepreneur community	(1) Inga: distrust in customer relations (2) Inga: distrust of employees (7) Mikhail: distrust among entrepreneurial community (9) Rahim: trust among entrepreneur community	(8) Mikhail: distrust to public authorities (10) trust/distrust in public authorities
	structural	(6) Laticia: trust among entrepreneur community (7) Mikhail: distrust among entrepreneurial community		

48

by no means a linear one. The cases revealed some specific occasions that either halted the process or reversed it. Distrust of the skills (Mikhail) or fairness (Rahim) of the authorities was based on the behaviour of one individual. Moreover, occasions boosting trust building were evident, such as meetings with a bank teller, an accountant or business adviser (Inga and Laticia). The cases illustrate how betraying someone's trust happens more easily than building trust.

Limitations

Trust building is a process in time and therefore studying it ideally demands longitudinal research methods. Although our interviews allowed the entrepreneurs to tell their stories freely and we encouraged them to recall the early days of their business start-up, there is a legitimate danger of deliberately or subconsciously relating false memories or introducing ex post facto reasoning.

Another limitation of our study is simultaneously a strength; that is, it being based on four case studies. Case studies are always context depend-ent and not generalizable as such, but they can reveal interdependences and mechanisms that quantitative methods cannot. The cases have now tested our conceptual framework. The next step will be to return to the data and analyse all 64 interviews with this framework. This will then allow us to offer some generalizations.

DISCUSSION AND CONCLUSIONS

What is the role of trust and bridging SC in immigrant business owners' start-up processes in the Finnish context? Our results shed some light on this complex question by supporting the finding of Welter and Kautonen (2005) that personal trust becomes important between the start-up company and its customers in contexts where there is a lack of collect-ive and institutional trust.

The stories of our interviewees seem to back up the intuitively appeal-ing connection that shared codes and language will strengthen the trust between actors. Among the practical means used to stock the reservoirs of trust and to create bridging SC (cognitive, relational and structural) were learning the Finnish language and building an understanding of the culture and its narratives, joining entrepreneurship courses and mentoring, having a Finnish spouse and a Finnish family name, actively networking and courting media publicity. These findings reveal the interconnectedness of SC to other forms of capital (cultural, human, financial and symbolic) with which it is transferrable by definition (Anthias, 2007; Bourdieu, 1986;

Nahapiet and Ghoshal, 1998). However, a person's relative position in the community affects the opportunities available to exploit these different forms of capital in business (Ram et al., 2008).

The role of trust in different fields of business seems to differ too. The amount of SC required seems to differ if products or services are offered to private consumers or to business-to-business customers. However, that is hardly straightforward. The valuations and level of conservatism of the clientele (for example, Inga's elderly rural lady customers versus Mikhail's young, multicultural and urban customers) affect the trust-building process, as does the nationality of the immigrant. The time required for the trust-building process came as something of a surprise to our immigrant entrepreneurs.

When the business idea is based on ethnic resources, the ethnic background of the entrepreneur can lend much-needed credibility and prompt an even higher initial level of trust among the clientele than local business owners would have. Obvious examples can be found in the field of ethnic restaurants, language services, cross-border trade and so on. Rahim is an excellent example of this.

ACKNOWLEDGEMENTS

The authors gratefully acknowledge the financial support of the European Commission (ELIE-project no. 2010-3477/001-001), the Finnish Ministry of Economic Affairs and Employment (Maahanmuuttajayrittäjien palvelutarpeet-project no. TEM/687/13.01.01/2014), and the Strategic Research Council at the Academy of Finland (SWiPE-project no 303667).

REFERENCES

Abatecola, G., R. Cafferata and S. Poggesi (2012), 'Arthur Stinchcombe's "liability of newness": contribution and impact of the construct', *Journal of Management History*, **18** (4), 402–18.

Adler, P.S. and S.W. Kwon (2002), 'Social capital: prospects for a new concept', *Academy of Management Review*, **27** (1), 17–40.

Aldrich, H.E. and C.M. Fiol (1994), 'Fools rush in? The institutional context of industry creation', *Academy of Management Review*, **19** (4), 645–70.

Aldrich, H.E. and P.H. Kim (2007), 'Small worlds, infinite possibilities? How social networks affect entrepreneurial team formation and search', *Strategic Entrepreneurship Journal*, **1** (1–2), 147–65.

Aldrich, H.E. and R. Waldinger (1990), 'Ethnicity and entrepreneurship', *Annual Review of Sociology*, **16**, 111–35.

Aliaga-Isla, R. and A. Rialp (2013), 'Systematic review of immigrant entrepreneurship literature: previous findings and ways forward', *Entrepreneurship & Regional Development*, **25** (9–10), 819–44.

Anderson, A.R. and C.J. Miller (2003), 'Class matters: human and social capital in the entrepreneurial process', *The Journal of Socio-Economics*, **32** (1), 17–36.

Anthias, F. (2007), 'Ethnic ties: social capital and the question of mobilisability', *The Sociological Review*, **55** (4), 788–805.

Bassey, M. (1999), *Case Study Research in Educational Settings*, Milton Keynes, UK: Open University Press.

Bourdieu, P. (1986), 'The forms of capital', in J. Richardson (ed.), *Handbook of Theory and Research for the Sociology of Education*, New York, USA: Greenwood, pp.241–58.

Davis, V.O. and V.O. Bartkus (2010), 'Organizational trust and social capital', in V.O. Davis and J.H. Bartkus (eds), *Social Capital: Reaching Out, Reaching In*, Cheltenham, UK and Northampton, MA, USA: Edward Elgar Publishing, pp.319–38.

Davidsson, P. and B. Honig (2003), 'The role of social and human capital among nascent entrepreneurs', *Journal of Business Venturing*, **18** (3), 301–31.

Eisenhardt, K.M. (1989), 'Building theories from case study research', *Academy of Management Review*, **14** (4), 532–50.

Eriksson, P., E. Henttonen and S. Meriläinen (2008), 'Managerial work and gender – ethnography of cooperative relationships in small software companies', *Scandinavian Journal of Management*, **24** (4), 354–63.

Geertz, C. (1973), *The Interpretation of Cultures: Selected Essays*, New York, USA: Basic Books.

Gill J. and R.J. Butler (2003), 'Managing instability in cross-cultural alliances', *Long Range Planning*, **36** (6), 543–63.

Granovetter, M. (1985), 'Economic action and social structure: the problem of embeddedness', *American Journal of Sociology*, **91** (3), 481–510.

Heinonen, J. (2010), 'Maahanmuuttajayrittäjät ja vastuullinen liiketoiminta. Kokemuksia, käsityksiä ja käytäntöjä', Web reports 65, Siirtolaisuusinstituutti, accessed 26 September 2015 at www.migrationinstitute.fi/files/pdf/webreport/webreport_065.pdf.

Höhmann, H.-H. and E. Malieva (2005), 'The concept of trust: some notes on definitions, forms and sources', in H.-H. Höhmann and F. Welter (eds), *Trust and Entrepreneurship: A West–East Perspective*, Cheltenham, UK and Northampton, MA, USA: Edward Elgar Publishing, pp.7–23.

Hsieh, H.-F. and S.E. Shannon (2005), 'Three approaches to qualitative content analysis', *Qualitative Health Research*, **15** (9), 1277–88.

Jasinskaja-Lahti, I., K. Liebkind and R. Perhoniemi (2006), 'Perceived discrimination and well-being: a victim study of different immigrant groups', *Journal of Community & Applied Social Psychology*, **16** (4), 267–84.

Johanson, J. and J.E. Vahlne (2009), 'The Uppsala internationalization process model revisited: from liability of foreignness to liability of outsidership', *Journal of International Business Studies*, **40** (9), 1411–31.

Jones, T., M. Ram, P. Edwards, A. Kiselinchev and L. Muchenje (2014), 'Mixed embeddedness and new migrant enterprise in the UK', *Entrepreneurship & Regional Development*, **26** (5–6), 500–520.

Joronen, T. (2012), *Maahanmuuttajien yrittäjyys Suomessa*, Helsingin kaupunki, Tietokeskus, Tutkimuksia 2/2012, Helsinki: Edita Prima.

Kalantaridis, C. and Z. Bika (2006), 'In-migrant entrepreneurship in rural England: beyond local embeddedness', *Entrepreneurship and Regional Development*, **18** (2), 109–31.

Kanas, A., F. Van Tubergen and T. Van der Lippe (2009), 'Immigrant self-employment testing hypotheses about the role of origin and host-country human capital and bonding and bridging social capital', *Work and Occupations*, **36** (3), 181–208.

Katila, S. and O. Wahlbeck (2012), 'The role of (transnational) social capital in the start-up processes of immigrant businesses: the case of Chinese and Turkish restaurant businesses in Finland', *International Small Business Journal*, **30** (3), 294–309.

Kloosterman, R., J. van der Leun and J. Rath (1998), 'Across the border: immigrants' economic opportunities, social capital and informal business activities', *Journal of Ethnic and Migration Studies*, **24** (2), 249–68.

Kloosterman, R., J. Van Der Leun and J. Rath (1999), 'Mixed embeddedness: (in) formal economic activities and immigrant businesses in the Netherlands', *International Journal of Urban and Regional Research*, **23** (2), 252–66.

Koorsgaard, M.A., H.H. Brower and S.W. Lester (2014), 'It isn't always mutual: a critical review of dyadic trust', *Journal of Management*, **41** (1), 47–70.

Lewicki, R.J. and C.T. Brinsfield (2010), 'Trust, distrust and building social capital', in V.O. Davis and J.H. Bartkus (eds), *Social Capital. Reaching Out, Reaching In*, Cheltenham, UK and Northampton, MA, USA: Edward Elgar Publishing, pp.275–303.

Lewicki, R.J., D.J. McAllister and R.J. Bies (1998), 'Trust and distrust: new relationships and realities', *Academy of Management Review*, **23** (3), 438–58.

Li, P.S. (2004), 'Social capital and economic outcomes for immigrants and ethnic minorities', *Journal of International Migration and Integration/Revue de l'Integration et de la Migration Internationale*, **5** (2), 171–90.

Light, I. and L.-P. Dana (2013), 'Boundaries of social capital in entrepreneurship', *Entrepreneurship Theory and Practice*, **37** (3), 603–24.

Mannila, S. and A. Reuter (2009), 'Social exclusion risks and their accumulation among Russian-speaking, ethnically Finnish and Estonian immigrants to Finland', *Journal of Ethnic and Migration Studies*, **35** (6), 939–56.

McKeever, E., S. Jack and A. Anderson (2015), 'Embedded entrepreneurship in the creative re-construction of place', *Journal of Business Venturing*, **30** (1), 50–65.

Misztal, B.A. (1996), *Trust in Modern Societies*, Cambridge, UK: Polity Press.

Nahapiet, J. and S. Ghoshal (1998), 'Social capital, intellectual capital, and the organizational advantage', *Academy of Management Review*, **23** (2), 242–66.

Oliveira, C.R. (2007), 'Understanding the diversity of immigrant entrepreneurial strategies', in L-P. Dana (ed.), *Handbook of Research on Ethnic Minority Entrepreneurship*, Cheltenham, UK and Northampton, MA, USA: Edward Elgar, pp.61–82.

Patulny, R.V. and G.L.H. Svendsen (2007), 'Exploring the social capital grid: bonding, bridging, qualitative, quantitative', *International Journal of Sociology and Social Policy*, **27** (1–2), 32–51.

Pettigrew, A.M. (1990), 'Longitudinal field research on change: theory and practice', *Organization Science*, **1** (3), 267–92.

Portes, A. (1998), 'Social capital: its origins and applications in modern sociology', *Annual Review of Sociology*, **24**, 1–24.

Putnam, R.D. (2000), *Bowling Alone: The Collapse and Revival of American Community*, New York, USA: Simon & Schuster.

Ram, M., N. Theodorakopoulos and T. Jones (2008), 'Forms of capital, mixed embeddedness and Somali enterprise', *Work, Employment & Society*, **22** (3), 427–46.

Sanders, J.M. and V. Nee (1996), 'Immigrant self-employment: the family as social capital and the value of human capital', *American Sociological Review*, 231–49.

Stake, R.E. (1995), *The Art of Case Study Research*, Thousand Oaks, CA, USA: Sage.

Statistics Finland (2016), StatFin database [Finnish version], accessed 15 September 2016 at http://pxnet2.stat.fi/PXWeb/pxweb/fi/StatFin/.

Stickel, D., R.C. Mayer and S.B. Sitkin (2010), 'Understanding social capital: in whom we trust?', in V.O. Davis and J.H. Bartkus (eds), *Social Capital. Reaching Out, Reaching In*, Cheltenham, UK and Northampton, MA, USA: Edward Elgar Publishing, pp.304–18.

Stinchcombe, A.L. and J.G. March (1965), 'Social structure and organizations', *Advances in Strategic Management*, **17**, 229–59.

Turkina, E. and M. Thi Thanh Thai (2013), 'Social capital, networks, trust and immigrant entrepreneurship: a cross-country analysis', *Journal of Enterprising Communities: People and Places in the Global Economy*, **7** (2), 108–24.

Van Maanen, J. (ed.) (1995), *Representation of Ethnography*, London, UK: Sage.

Welter, F. (2012), 'All you need is trust? A critical review of the trust and entrepreneurship literature', *International Small Business Journal*, **30** (3), 193–212.

Welter, F. and T. Kautonen (2005), 'Trust, social networks and enterprise development: exploring evidence from East and West Germany', *International Entrepreneurship and Management Journal*, **1** (3), 367–79.

Welter, F. and D. Smallbone (2006), 'Exploring the role of trust in entrepreneurial activity', *Entrepreneurship Theory and Practice*, **30** (4), 465–75.

Wilson, K.L. and A. Portes (1980), 'Immigrant enclaves: an analysis of the labor market experiences of Cubans in Miami', *American Journal of Sociology*, **86** (2), 295–319.

Woolcock, M. (1998), 'Social capital and economic development: toward a theoretical synthesis and policy framework', *Theory and Society*, **27** (2), 151–208.

Yin, R.K. (2003), *Case Study Research: Design and Method*, 3rd ed., Thousand Oaks, CA, USA: Sage.

Zaheer, S. (1995), 'Overcoming the liability of foreignness', *Academy of Management Journal*, **38** (2), 341–63.

4. Is what's good for business good for society? Entrepreneurship in a school setting

Karin Axelsson, Linda Höglund and Maria Mårtensson

INTRODUCTION

Entrepreneurship was recently introduced, via political aspirations, in the school environment in hopes of securing future economic growth by stimulating children's and adolescents' interest in, and attitudes towards, entrepreneurship. Energized by the common view that entrepreneurship can be taught (Cope, 2005; Landström and Benner, 2010; Rae and Carswell, 2000), there are currently numerous educational initiatives worldwide seeking to encourage its application (Klapper and Refai, 2015; Komulainen et al., 2011) albeit with varying content and results (Leffler, 2009). According to Fayolle (2013), this worldwide development will affect the field of education in theory and in practice.

Entrepreneurship has its roots in economics and therefore the traditional image of the entrepreneur is linked to business activities (Gibb, 2002) where the entrepreneur is sometimes described as super(hu)man (Berglund, 2013; Smith, 2010). However, even though the economic discourse of entrepreneurship still prevails in many parts of society, there are also researchers (for example Hjorth and Steyaert, 2004; Höglund, 2015) suggesting the existence of other discourses reframing entrepreneurship into a more societal phenomenon affecting our everyday lives. In this context, there is a small but growing research field highlighting the importance of studying entrepreneurship in its wider context of political and programmatic discourse (for example Dahlstedt and Hertzberg, 2012; Gill, 2014; Korhonen et al., 2012; Leffler, 2009). With the aim of contributing to this research agenda, we take a discourse approach, drawing upon Miller and Rose's (1990) view on governmentality and the concepts of programme and technology.

A programme can be understood as a certain rationale – a certain framework for action – outlining how ideal ends are to be achieved (Miller and Rose, 1990; Rose and Miller, 1992). Technology is the tool used to make programmes operable in practice (Miller, 2001). So far, previous research has tended to concentrate on the programmatic level, thus neglecting the technologies used in practice (Bührmann, 2005). However, programmatic ideas must be practical; they need to be translated and implemented in local organizational contexts to make them work in 'real life' in the daily activities of organizations (Miller and Rose, 1990).

In Sweden, such a programmatic initiative was the introduction of the Strategy for Entrepreneurship in Education in 2009 (Government Offices of Sweden, 2009). However, as argued in this chapter, to make entrepreneurship operable within the school setting it has to be interpreted into its specific context using different technologies. Nevertheless, the understanding of how entrepreneurship initiatives are interpreted in the school setting is so far limited (Axelsson et al., 2015; Axelsson and Mårtensson, 2015). Therefore, this study is motivated by the lack of studies investigating how programmatic initiatives are made operable in practice. In relation to this, we state the following research question: how is the programmatic initiative, the Strategy for Entrepreneurship in Education, made operable in practice by means of the technology, a competence development initiative?

The chapter is structured as follows: after the introduction, we present the theoretical perspective on our analysis. Thereafter, we address our approach and methods. In the subsequent section, we present how entrepreneurship has been translated into the school setting. Finally, we discuss our results in relation to the theoretical concepts of programme and technology and present our conclusions.

THEORETICAL PERSPECTIVE

We work with the theoretical perspective of governmentality and the concepts of programme and technology, as a way of understanding how the Strategy for Entrepreneurship in Education is made operable in practice. We also address research from entrepreneurship in a school setting.

Governmentality

The term governmentality was first coined by Foucault in the late 1970s and, as Bragg (2007) noticed, it has received a huge amount of attention ever since. Foucault (1991) sometimes used the 'art of government' as a way to broadly define governmentality, and he argued that governing does not originate from, or belong to, the state apparatuses. Rather, governing is made up of a broad repertoire of technologies of governance, operating throughout the entire social field, crossing boundaries, for example between public and private, state, market and civil society, political and commercial and citizen and consumer (Dahlstedt and Hertzberg, 2012). It is hence related to both government and state politics, but not solely; it also includes a wide range of different tools for control, one of which is the control of self. Governmentality thus becomes a way for governments to try to produce the citizens best suited to fulfil their own policies. In other words, governmentality could be described as a method of governing that encourages action of the self, by the self, rather than through formal institutions of the state (Bragg, 2007).

Government programmes are systematic discursive frameworks and, within those frameworks, policies are defined and government objectives specified (Rose and Miller, 1992). Programmes are described as being prescriptive as well as analytic, and they seek to link everyday work (in schools, for instance) with broader political objectives and rationalities. A programme can be understood as a certain rationale – a certain framework for action – outlining how ideal ends are to be achieved (Miller and Rose, 1990; Rose and Miller, 1992). Whereas programmes are essentially 'aspirational performance ideas' (Miller and Power, 2013, p.5), technologies form the grounded basis for the realization of these ideas. In other words, technology is the tool used to make programmes operable in practice (Miller, 2001). The concept of technology refers to a particular method to analysing the activity of governing through governmentality; one that pays great attention to the actual tool required by various authorities to achieve what they think is desirable (Miller and Rose, 1990). In this chapter, the focus is on the government's desire to introduce entrepreneurship in schools through the technology of a competence initiative as a way to make the entrepreneurship strategy operable in practice.

Enterprising self
As stated above, governing is not solely done by the state. It is also done by individuals. Rose (1996) labels this as 'the enterprising self'. The idea of an enterprising self builds on a (political) belief in a need to create the entrepreneurial citizens (Dean, 1999) necessary to shape future society (Berglund, 2013). The literature on enterprising self has links to what kind of society we aim for and how the individual's responsibility is stated in relation to the government. The enterprising self could be described as someone who will make an enterprise out of her life (du Gay, 1991). Prior research (for example Brunila and Siivonen, 2014) argues that it is only through being an enterprising self that we are able to become lifelong learners who actively contribute to the market economy. Therefore, in this

setting, governmentality involves the reconstruction of a wide range of institutions, activities, relationships and staff along the lines of the market. As du Gay (1991, p.46) states, this played a pivotal role in encouraging 'market penetration' into all areas of social and cultural life, including schools (Berglund, 2013), for the purpose of cultivating enterprising subjects. In other words, autonomous, self-regulating, productive individuals who take responsibility for their own future through their own efforts.

Similarly, Bührmann (2005) argues that the enterprising self is defined by the steering of action, feeling, thinking and willingness based on an orientation towards such criteria as economic efficiency and entrepreneurial calculation. As such, the subject of enterprise is a repetition of the traditional economic man (du Gay et al., 1996/2005). According to du Gay (1994), enterprise is deployed as a critique of bureaucratic organizational governance (and as a solution to the problems posed by globalization), by delineating the principles of a novel approach of governing organizational and personal conduct. Thus, it embraces the importance of individuals acquiring and exhibiting more market-oriented, proactive, empowered and entrepreneurial attitudes, behaviours and capacities.

Entrepreneurship in a School Setting

In a school setting, the discourses of entrepreneurship and enterprise that have so far prevailed are an *entrepreneurship discourse* and an *enterprising discourse* (Leffler, 2014) and their respective relationships and tensions. Within the entrepreneurship discourse, the focus is on business activities such as starting new ventures, management of small and medium-sized companies, making business plans, opportunity- and advantage-seeking, intrapreneurship and innovation (Höglund, 2015). Within the broader enterprise discourse, the aim is rather to promote personal development and enhance entrepreneurial skills, for example, a pupil's ability to become self-responsible, flexible, active (Brunila and Siivonen, 2014), initiating, participative, self-confident and creative (Johannisson, 2010; Leffler, 2014).

There is no clear-cut division between the two discourses, and within them there are several ways of defining and describing entrepreneurship (Gibb, 2002). They are partially overlapping and partially complementary. This creates confusion, since similar concepts sometimes are used simultaneously. For example, Komulainen et al. (2011) identify internal and external entrepreneurship education; external aligning with the entrepreneurship discourse and internal aligning with an enterprising discourse. At the same time, researchers such as Falk Lundqvist et al. (2014), and Axelsson and Mårtensson (2015), have a broader definition of entrepreneurship, labelling entrepreneurial learning as an empirical concept developed by teachers in a practical setting. According to them, entrepreneurial learning relates to the enterprising discourse.

The discourses on entrepreneurship and enterprising thus raise different tensions (Axelsson and Mårtensson, 2015). One is the discursive battle for the school arena regarding the many faces of entrepreneurship (Leffler, 2009). Another is that teachers are ambiguous in teaching external (or entrepreneurship) education with a business focus. They generally prefer the internal (or enterprising) approach, which is addressed by Korhonen et al. (2012). Komulainen et al. (2011) reinforce this idea, stating that teachers see the promotion of external entrepreneurship as being in conflict with the basic values of education, and it is therefore substantially rejected as the aim of schooling. A strong business emphasis and a view of the entrepreneur as a superhuman (Smith, 2010), or an individualist greedily taking advantage of other people, may obstruct the implementation of entrepreneurship in schools (Berglund, 2013). The teachers' approach is important since teachers, according to Korhonen et al. (2012), play the most important role in the process of transforming entrepreneurship education into teaching practices and learning outcomes. They have the most important influence on students' interests at school (Hattie, 2009) and they strongly affect how, and to what extent, the curriculum is implemented (Sharma and Anderson, 2007). Therefore, teachers' views on, and attitudes towards, entrepreneurship affect both its implementation and its legitimacy.

METHODOLOGY

The starting point of our study is a programme called the Strategy for Entrepreneurship in Education, launched by the Government Offices of Sweden in 2009. Based on this, the Swedish National Agency for Education undertook different entrepreneurship initiatives to implement the strategy. The study investigates one of the agency's chosen technologies for implementing its task, namely an activity concerning calls for funding for competence development. Drawing upon Rose and Miller's (1992) concepts of programme and technology means adopting a discourse approach. This is addressed later in this section, through the study of discursive practices.

The Programme

The programme – the Strategy for Entrepreneurship in Education – is influenced by European initiatives such as the Organisation for Economic Co-operation and Development reports (OECD, 1989) and the European Community's (2007) framework concerning key competencies for lifelong learning, drawing attention to entrepreneurship and employability. The strategy focuses on three main ideas: (1) self-employment must become as natural as becoming an employee; (2) the importance of practising entrepreneurial skills; and (3) entrepreneurship should run like a common thread throughout the education system. The system's role is to help pupils develop and exercise the necessary knowledge, competencies and approaches. This is exemplified by the Government Offices of Sweden (2009, p.2):

> Education that inspires entrepreneurship can provide young people with the skills and enthusiasm to set up and run a business [. . .] Many young people are positive to the idea of starting up a business, but are hesitant because they do not know how to, or do not dare to invest in an idea of their own [. . .] Entrepreneurial skills increase the individual's chances of starting and running a company.

The entrepreneurial competencies are chosen with the entrepreneur as a role model. The preface and introductory text states the following (Government Offices of Sweden, 2009, pp.1–2):

> Being self-employed must be as natural a choice as being an employee [. . .] Many of the distinctive features of a good entrepreneur – the ability to solve problems, think innovatively, plan one's work, take responsibility and coop- erate with others – are also qualities that students at different levels need to develop to complete their studies and to be successful in their adult lives [. . .] Entrepreneurship education may include the specific knowledge required to start and run a business, such as business administration and planning. Entrepreneurship education can also develop more general skills that are equally useful outside the business world, such as project management and risk management. Educating entrepreneurs also means inspiring people to be cre- ative and take own responsibility for achieving a goal.

The Technology

The technology in focus is the competence initiative of the National Agency for Education. The purpose for using the technology was to stimulate the implementation of the strategy for entrepreneurship in edu- cation (the programme) by offering possibilities for the schools to develop knowledge and understanding. This study covers educational organizers that received funding for competence activities for school personnel for the years 2009, 2011, 2012 and 2013 (2010 is not included, as the National Agency for Education did not fund any activities that year).[1] For more information, see Axelsson (2015).

During the studied period, 457 educational organizers applied for funding, amounting to approximately EUR 20 million. However, due to the agency's budget constraints, funding was only granted for approximately EUR 3.1 million. Our study includes 42 of the 232 applications accepted, chosen by a representative of the National Agency for Education through random selection. After the first selection of ten cases per year, five more were added to adjust and ensure geographic spread, as well as size and representation of both private and public schools. Three cases were eliminated due to incomplete reports or activities. Ultimately, 39 public and three private educational organizers participated in the study. The selected schools represent the entire chain in the Swedish school system: from preschool, preschool class, compulsory school, upper secondary school, adult education, special school and after-school centre. The investment that funded these competence initiatives lasted from 2009 to 2014. Table 4.1 provides an overview of the empirical material for this study and delineates the empirical data by: a coded number, educational organizer (private or public), year of application as well as included school forms. The educational organizer submits the evaluation reports the year after the application. To contextualize and anchor the quotes they connect to the table by the coded number (1–42). Further, it is visible if the quotations are from the application (appl.) or evaluation report (eval.).

We analysed both the applications and the evaluation reports, 84 texts in all, focusing on how they were described and accounted for. This enabled us to study both the initial ambitions of what entrepreneurship in a school setting was planned to look like, and what it developed into. Funding is received for, and used within, a specific budgetary year. The texts in the applications and evaluation reports followed a template laid down by the National Agency for Education. The template consists of a number of headings under which the educational organizer could freely narrate and reflect. These are the narratives we analysed.

The Study of Discursive Practices

Consistent with Burr (2003), we argue that a discourse could be understood as a way of talking about and understanding the world through text and language. As argued in the introduction, there has been a lack of studies focusing on the process of how entrepreneurship programmes are made operable in the school setting. Monitoring a process by means of a discourse approach is an ideal way of gaining knowledge and insights into human phenomena, because it attempts to see society through the ways people make sense of the world in their contexts. The linguistic turn in organization studies has been credited with shifting the focus of entrepreneurial studies towards social constructionist views (Hjorth and Steyaert, 2004). Drawing upon these ideas, our starting point is that we as people

Table 4.1   *An overview of the empirical material*

no.	Educational organizer	Year of application	School forms
1.	Public	2009	Compulsory school
2.	Public	2009	Compulsory school
3.	Public	2009	Compulsory school
4.	Public	2009	Compulsory school
5.	Public	2009	Compulsory school
6.	Public	2009	Compulsory school
7.	Private	2009	Preschool, compulsory school
8.	Public	2009	Compulsory school
9.	Public	2009	Compulsory school
10.	Public	2009	Compulsory school
11.	Public	2011	Upper secondary school
12.	Public	2011	Upper secondary school
13.	Public	2011	Preschool, compulsory school, special school
14.	Public	2011	Upper secondary school
15.	Public	2011	Preschool, preschool class, compulsory school
16.	Public	2011	Preschool class, compulsory school, special school
17.	Public	2011	Preschool, preschool class, compulsory school
18.	Public	2011	Upper secondary school, adult education, special school
19.	Public	2011	Upper secondary school
20.	Public	2011	Compulsory school
21.	Public	2011	Compulsory school, upper secondary school
22.	Public	2011	Upper secondary school
23.	Private	2012	Compulsory school
24.	Public	2012	Preschool, compulsory school, after school center
25.	Public	2012	Preschool, preschool class, compulsory school, special school, after school center
26.	Public	2012	Preschool
27.	Public	2012	Preschool class, compulsory school, special school, after school center
28.	Public	2012	Upper secondary school
29.	Public	2012	Upper secondary school
30.	Public	2012	Compulsory school, upper secondary school
31.	Public	2012	Compulsory school
32.	Public	2012	Preschool, preschool class, compulsory school, upper secondary school, special school, adult education, after school center
33.	Public	2013	Compulsory school, upper secondary school
34.	Public	2013	Compulsory school, after school center

Table 4.1   (continued)

no.	Educational organizer	Year of application	School forms
35.	Public	2013	Preschool, preschool class, compulsory school, upper secondary school, special school, adult education, after school center
36.	Public	2013	Preschool, preschool class, compulsory school
37.	Public	2013	After school center
38.	Public	2013	Preschool, preschool class, compulsory school, after school center
39.	Public	2013	Compulsory school
40.	Public	2013	Preschool, preschool class, compulsory school, upper secondary school, special school, adult education, after school center
41.	Private	2013	Preschool, preschool class, compulsory school, after school center
42.	Public	2013	Preschool

operate within an active language; a language that, when it is represented, produces a discourse that creates its object of concern, in this chapter entrepreneurship in a school setting.

Though there is a commonality in discourse analysis in focusing upon language and language usage, there is also a broad spectrum of views on discourse. A large number of researchers in this field (for example Alvesson and Kärreman, 2000; Burr, 2003) observe that there is no clear consensus on what discourses are and how to analyse them. In this chapter, we use the concepts of programme and technology, based on the discursive ideas of Rose and Miller (1992). These, in turn, draw upon Foucauldian traditions. However, although Foucauldian traditions are theoretically strong, they tend to be weak regarding what methods to use in analysing discourse (Alvesson and Kärreman, 2000). With that in mind, we were inspired by discursive psychology and its view of doing discourse analysis on a meso level, where the study of discursive practices is central (Alvesson and Kärreman, 2000; Potter and Wetherell, 1987). Such an analysis focuses on what people are doing with discourses (as in the discursive practice) and not what discourses are doing to people, as in the Foucauldian approach. How different aspects of entrepreneurship are consumed and produced by people in text and talk then becomes the focus (Potter and Wetherell, 1987). An important part of our analysis of the discursive practices has been not only to understand the constitutive parts of discourse (how people consume discourses), but also the constructive parts (how people produce discourses). Another important element of this context is power. From this perspective power focuses on what ideas and practices are taken for granted and seen as truth, and what ideas and practices are marginalized.

FINDINGS – INTERPRETATIONS OF ENTREPRENEURSHIP IN PRACTICE

In this chapter we take an interest in studying the discursive practice of making the Strategy for Entrepreneurship in Education (the programme) operable in practice through the competence initiative (the technology). In doing so, we could interpret that the schools initially privileged (or consumed) the entrepreneurship discourse, but later moved towards letting the enterprising discourse prevail. These two discourses have been addressed in past literature (see the theoretical section in this chapter). However, by the time we were able to also interpret that, a new discourse emerged (was produced), one that had not been addressed in the literature: the entrepreneurial approach. This process is described in this section.

The Entrepreneurship and Enterprising Discourses Prevail

At the beginning of 2009, most of the schools said they were applying for funding to learn more about entrepreneurship. At this time, entrepreneurship was described in a narrower economic sense (cf. Gibb, 2002). This meant that the texts in the applications and evaluation reports tended to draw on the *entrepreneurship discourse* and the language of creation, development and growth of companies, with an economic value. One of the main reasons put forward by the educational organizers for learning more about entrepreneurship was based on a societal need for more people to start their own businesses and become self-employed, which is one of the main objectives of the strategy. At the same time, it also aims at making students more employable in local industry. As noted in one of the applications: '[The] companies [in the municipality] seek co-workers with "entrepreneurial skills." For increased competitiveness, societal growth and reduced unemployment, more enterprising individuals are required' (no.1, appl.). The expectations the students face is that they attain a more: 'positive attitude towards starting a business and dare to be more enterprising' (no.3, appl.).

However, already as early as 2009 some were drawing on the enterprising discourse in their applications and evaluation reports. Consistent with previous research (Axelsson and Mårtensson, 2015; Korhonen et al., 2012), we noticed a confusion between how they used the entrepreneurship and the enterprising discourses and what language they attached to each discourse. For example, the title and/or aims of the applications could be based on an entrepreneurship discourse, while descriptions of the planned competence initiative were based on the enterprising discourse. It is also noticeable that although a majority of the applications initially described entrepreneurship and devoted themselves to it, this changed once the competence initiative was completed. Essentially, the evaluation reports followed a rather more enterprising discourse. The following quote by an applicant exemplifies this shift and ambiguity:

> [The school] will continuously transmit knowledge on entrepreneurship and self-employment [. . .] and enhance knowledge and understanding of the import-ance of industry; both in the local and wider perspectives. Ultimately, this can inspire youth to give more consideration to opportunities for self-employment. (no.6, appl.)

This application seems to place more emphasis on entrepreneurship and industrial knowledge. Later in the evaluation report, however, the same applicant instead promoted and highlighted their wish for 'entrepreneurial learning to permeate both teaching and learning', as in using an enterprising discourse. Moreover, one of the participating teachers cited in this evaluation report clearly stated that: 'My mission as a teacher is not to make the children become entrepreneurs [. . .] On the contrary, I want to help them become enterprising; daring to help themselves and highlighting their own strengths' (no.6, eval.).

From 2011, there was a clear shift in the way competence activities were presented. The aim and goal was opened up and transformed into more of an enterprising discourse. This discourse entertains a broader view of entrepreneurship, but is still based on the assumptions of an economic and business logic (Leffler, 2009, 2014) and has similarities with the ideas related to the enterprising self (Berglund, 2013). First, the focus lies more on internal skills and competencies, sometimes referred to as 'entrepreneurial competencies.' Second, these are to be developed by the individual, in his or her personal development process of becoming enterprising. The competencies expressed in the analysed documents include such things as the pupils being encouraged to become flexible, creative, independent, good at problem solving and taking initiatives – much consistent with findings from previous research (for example Johannisson, 2010; Leffler, 2014). Furthermore, the empirical material showed that co-operation skills, strong motivation and drive were also promoted as important. Third, these competencies are considered relevant for future working life in most parts of society and no longer exclusively related to business. When describing the competence activities, in both the applications and evaluation reports, the idea was articulated that the teachers' goal should be to help pupils become entrepreneurial. As said, not necessarily to become business entrepreneurs but, more importantly, to become useful and employable within the municipality, in public organizations as well as in private companies. The expectations of the pupils as presented are to: 'reach success during their studies and in their future working lives' (no.19, appl.). They will also develop: 'self-confidence and self-esteem, in combination with great self-awareness' (no.28, appl.).

The enterprising ingredient is presented as positive for the students. As the quote from the evaluation states: 'All children and adolescents are given the opportunity to develop their best self for the future' (no.1, eval.). The teachers are expected to change their tutorial and working methods to create an enterprising practice. Education has to be based on the pupils' life world, on their questions and queries, as well as being participative and instilling a desire to learn.

The Entrepreneurial Approach

During the latter years of the studied technology (2012–14) another, even broader, third discourse emerged: the *entrepreneurial approach*. To summarize: this approach develops entrepreneurship in scope and in space; from an initial, isolated competence initiative within a school to encompassing the whole school and the entire educational system. It further expands to include the surrounding society and become woven into the individual's everyday life. Within this new discourse, the educational organizers emphasized entrepreneurship as a learning approach, describing it as something accessible and necessary for all pupils and all teachers. It should become a natural ingredient in the everyday school milieu and be regarded as positive for everyone in society. We will now elaborate on some aspects of the approach a bit more.

First, this widening of entrepreneurship is detectable in the scope of its operations. The initial competence initiative was considered an isolated activity and executed within a limited project and/or a specific part of the school. Following the introduction of the entrepreneurial approach, it was instead described as something being introduced and applied in *all* educational activities; in every subject and every programme, as well as embedded in interdisciplinary projects. To quote: 'Entrepreneurial learning permeates all the operations at the X school' (no.35, appl.).

Consequently, the approach concerns *all* pupils. On the one hand, this was described as an opportunity for individuals to build their self-esteem and confidence; as an instrument helping them to fulfil their own paths and dreams, maximizing opportunities and to create a life of their choice.

There were many descriptions of this, both in the applications and the evaluation reports. For example: 'In the long run, we want entrepreneurial learning to encompass all pupils' everyday lives, from preschool to adult education' (no.34, appl.).

The teachers will: 'Support the students' personal development through stimulating their creativity, curiosity, self-confidence and will to create solutions to their own ideas, with the purpose of becoming competent and responsible individuals' (no.13, eval.). Students will learn to: 'become entrepreneurs in their own lives and be the driving force in their own learning process' (no.5, appl.).

On the other hand, there are hardly any reflections or considerations in the analysed empirical material on whether this approach will fit all pupils. This approach put the individual pupil's interests at the centre of attention and transferred the responsibility to him or her (Berglund, 2013). There were frequent statements that pupils were to be fostered by an entrepreneurial approach and take greater personal responsibility for their own learning, such as: 'With entrepreneurial pedagogy enhance the pupils' participation in the development of education in that the pupils take a bigger responsibility for their own learning' (no.30, eval.).

This means that *all* the teachers are included as well. The activities were described as involving the whole teaching team and/or every teacher at the school. A few examples of this: 'Every teacher develops and uses an entrepreneurial approach when it comes to [all] working methods, pupils' assignments and assessment procedures' (no.18, appl.).

Interestingly, the entrepreneurial approach also expanded the scope of the individual school. The competence initiative seemed to involve more and more levels of the educational system. There were several descriptions like this: 'All levels of the [educational] system have to define their assignment regarding entrepreneurial learning and anchor it within the organization' (no.34, appl.); '[Entrepreneurship and entrepreneurial learning] will profile the entire school organization in all its areas' (no.41, eval.).

Some of the analysed texts also refer to the importance of a common thread for entrepreneurial learning from preschool to upper secondary school, thereby addressing the need to accomplish a progression and link the developmental steps: 'There is a visible red thread of entrepreneurial learning throughout the entire educational organization and there is cooperation regarding this [development] between the school forms' (no.38, appl.); '[this thread must be] possible both to describe, see, and experience' (no.32, appl.).

However, the spread of entrepreneurship did not end with the school or the municipal educational system. Consistent with what Leffler (2009) and Axelsson and Mårtensson (2015) noted in previous research, the widening also tended to include interactions and co-operation with surrounding society. This increased substantially from 2013. The educational organizers began to link entrepreneurship in the school setting to the school's study and vocational guidance, thereby strengthening the view that entrepreneurial learning and external co-operation between schools and working life are linked. In the reports from 2013, industry was described as playing a more active part and was portrayed as being important to school development and students' learning processes, including through companies' involvement in reference groups or study visits. For example, some educational organizers argued that co-operation with the surrounding society helps the school to be up to date and adjusted to reality. Involvement of external actors in the learning situation was meant to bring meaning and enhance the pupils' motivation through the involvement of the world outside school. This was because industry could bring genuine and tangible tasks through which pupils could be challenged.

Nevertheless, the expectations and spread of the entrepreneurial approach did not stop there. Some educational organizers also wanted to expand the scope of entrepreneurial learning by integrating the whole municipality. One educational organizer wrote: 'Ongoing work to further develop entrepreneurial learning will be realized within the entire municipality' (no.27, eval.).

Further, the entrepreneurial approach affects *all* aspects of the individual's everyday life. It is considered useful in managing education, during spare time, in future working life, i.e. practically 24/7. For instance, one educational organizer stated that: 'An entrepreneurial approach must permeate what we do in our everyday lives; it cannot be something that is handled in parallel' (no.23, appl.).

In other words, the entrepreneurial approach encompasses everyone, everywhere, all the time. Moreover, it related entrepreneurial learning to higher goals and values for both society and the individual. For example, the approach was intended to help develop democratic values in society at large: 'The aim of [the project] is to develop entrepreneurial learning [. . .] to reduce unemployment and develop democracy, in order to give pupils the necessary skills for today's society in their lives after school' (no.35, appl.).

According to the applications and the evaluation reports, the entrepreneurial approach also brought a number of additional benefits such as: 'Children/pupils get a sense of meaning and motivation to go to preschool/ school, which in the long run will lead to a safer, more sustainable environment, as well as ultimately promoting the attainment of higher goals' (no.36, appl.).

DISCUSSION

In the introduction, we stated the following research question: how is the programmatic initiative, the Strategy for Entrepreneurship in Education, made operable in practice by means of technology, a competence development initiative? We did this by analysing the discursive practices that took place when making the programme operable through technology. The findings of this analysis showed how the entrepreneurship and enterprising discourses prevailed in the beginning, but subsequently competed with the emergence of a new discourse, the entrepreneurial approach. In this part of the chapter, we give a summarized discussion of the findings in relation to the programme, as well as addressing possible consequences of the new entrepreneurial approach.

Technology Stretching the Interpretations of the Programme

Different parts of the programme tend to be emphasized depending on which period we study during the programme implementation. To recall: the programme focuses on three main ideas – self-employment becoming as natural as being employed; practising entrepreneurial skills mainly with a businessperson as the role model; and that entrepreneurship should run like a common thread throughout the education system. For example, at the beginning of 2009, the studied programme, with its main clauses focusing on entrepreneurship in a business and economic sense, were consistent with technology. This means that within technology at this time, the language used and the interpretations made by the educational organizers followed the entrepreneurship discourse. A great coherence between programme and technology was thus exemplified.

From 2011, the educational organizers shifted their focus towards an enterprising discourse. During this period, they also started to stretch the interpretations of the programme. This is noticeable, for instance, in relation to the entrepreneurial skills. Here, there is a shift in both the skills to focus on and for what purpose. In the programme, the main clauses strongly link the entrepreneurial skills to the business entrepreneur as a role model. Pupils are made to practise competencies so that they can start and run a company – risk assessment and project planning, for example. Other, broader, generic skills related to personal development are not so much highlighted. When they are mentioned in the programme, they appear as subordinate clauses. However, turning to technology, the educational organizers switched their emphasis as to which skills to focus on in practice. When practising entrepreneurial skills, they tend to favour and upgrade the skills mentioned in the subordinate clauses, stating that they are useful for broader purposes, including employability.

With the emergence of an entrepreneurial approach that takes on an even broader perspective with its spread from the defined school setting to everyday life (including such things as life-long learning, co-operation with society and democratic values) the technology is stretching the programme. This expansion from entrepreneurship being a subject or an ingredient related to business within the school, to an entrepreneurial approach where the acquired entrepreneurial skills are to be used everywhere – in everyday life and around the clock, is not to be found in the programme but frequently in the technology. As such, it would be possible to state that the educational organizers in this study, with their broader entrepreneurial approach, seem to take the strategy a step further, both stretching and surpassing the initial ideas and content of the programme. In this way, educational organizers chose to highlight subordinated clauses and marginal parts of the programme. Thus, they no longer draw upon the main statements of the programme; instead the subordinate clauses became the main clauses.

It would be possible to state that the educational organizers in this study, with their broader entrepreneurial approach, seem to take the strategy a step further, surpassing and stretching the initial ideas and content of the programme. In this sense, it would also be possible to argue that the schools have become entrepreneurial themselves, widening the discourse to better fit their own view of their assignment based on the national curricula. It therefore does exceed the scope of the programme. However, it could also be argued that it moves closer to one of the schools' important goals of educating good democratic citizens. The teachers achieve this by constructing an entrepreneurial approach discourse, highlighting the language of democracy and values in society. Further, consistent with what researchers such as Korhonen et al. (2012), Komulainen et al. (2011) and Axelsson and Mårtensson (2015) have indicated, teachers seem reluctant to work with entrepreneurship in the narrower economic sense. This might also explain why, rather than drawing upon the entrepreneurship discourse, the schools are expanding their interpretations of the programme.

Possible Consequences of the New Broader Entrepreneurial Approach

We identified three tensions between more traditional interpretations of entrepreneurship and the emerging entrepreneurial approach. First, a tension between political and societal needs and the freedom of the individual; second, a tension between entrepreneurship as a tool for democracy and exclusion; and third, a tension between the idea that everyone is invited (inclusion) and the norms of entrepreneurship. We thus aim to shed light on aspects often forgotten when it comes to entrepreneurship in general, but more importantly in school settings.

First, the idea of the entrepreneurial approach is, on the one hand, marketed and portrayed as a great opportunity for the pupils, offering them the possibility of reaching their full potential and maximizing their opportunities to follow their own paths and dreams. On the other hand, what if the individual's dreams and wishes are not consistent with the neo-liberal-inspired political and societal needs? One might question whether it is possible to combine the talent hunt and the fostering of useful citizens with personal development, 'free' dreams, and self-fulfilment. What if they do not match? Which of the two views – the individual's dreams or the societal needs of enterprising people – are actually the overriding concern? This tension is related to the ideas of the enterprising self (Rose, 1996), or political needs of entrepreneurial citizens (Dean, 1999), where this duality is visible. For instance, there are similarities with the view of enterprising selves as self-responsible and accepting the responsibility for oneself and one's actions (du Gay et al., 1996/2005). People are supposed to make an enterprise of themselves, while at the same time they are expected to help fulfil the political and societal goals as enterprising selves and entrepreneurial citizens.

Second, the entrepreneurial approach could be viewed as a tool for democracy or as a tool for exclusion. The entrepreneurial approach should contribute to active participation of all pupils, with a possibility for them to influence their work and their learning environment. This can be seen as a tool for democracy, which is visualized in the empirical material. However, at the same time this means that an increased responsibility is transferred to the pupil as per the theories of the enterprising self (Berglund, 2013; Brunila and Siivonen, 2014; Korhonen et al., 2012). With the entrepreneurial approach, the use of words such as 'responsibility' and 'foster' in relation to pupils becomes more frequent.

It has been suggested that working according to enterprising principles will make students 'become competent and responsible individuals'. In previous research literature, becoming an entrepreneurial self is often presented as obtainable for everyone (Ainsworth and Hardy, 2008), but du Gay (1995) points out the risks of marginalization and exclusion of those who are unable, or reluctant, to behave in the expected entrepreneurial way. In our empirical material, there are no reflections on, or considerations of, whether this approach really fits all pupils. In other words, what will happen to those who do not fit the requirements?

The entrepreneurial approach builds on a belief that everyone is invited (inclusion). It comprises everyone, all pupils and all teachers. This specifically addresses the third tension connected to the traditional norms of entrepreneurship. The end client of entrepreneurship education is the society in which it is embedded. This means that entrepreneurship outcomes should adequately meet the social and economic needs of all stakeholders: pupils, teachers, families, organizations, regions and countries (Fayolle, 2013). From prior research, we learned that a more traditional view of entrepreneurship could lead to a number of consequences. For instance, the norms of entrepreneurship are largely inspired by ideals connected to the white middle class and in particular to middle-aged men (Berglund, 2013; Gill, 2014). Consistent with this, Leffler (2012, p.37) argues that 'entrepreneurship is an extremely gender-impregnated construction'. Similarly, Korhonen et al. (2012) argue that previous research in entrepreneurship showed that the ideal individual qualities and abilities of an entrepreneur (for example being active, competitive, independent and willing to take risks) have surreptitiously set an invisible norm that has justified masculine and middle-class values as bases for entrepreneurship, with the consequence that other values and classes are excluded. Moreover, what is regarded as gender specific affects how entrepreneurship is exercised in practice. We do not yet know how such things as gender, ethnicity or age will be handled or developed within the entrepreneurial approach in the future. The risk may be that this new discourse either excludes or marginalizes the same groups as the traditional entrepreneurship discourse, or it might marginalize new groups of people. On the other hand, the new entrepreneurial approach might lead to a development where rather additional groups are included, which in the long run might change the traditional images. However, it is too early to tell, and more research on the subject is needed.

CONCLUSIONS

With this chapter we contribute to the small but growing research field that highlights the importance of studying entrepreneurship in its wider context of political and programmatic discourse (see for example Dahlstedt and Hertzberg, 2012; Gill, 2014; Korhonen et al., 2012; Leffler, 2009) by addressing how programmatic initiatives are made operable in practice. We enhance this understanding by analysing the interpretations of entrepreneurship in the school setting from a perspective of governmentality and the concepts of programme and technology. In so doing, we highlighted some of the assumptions made when it comes to entrepreneurship, such as 'what is good for business is also good for society'. As our study shows, this is not necessarily the case. Instead, we demonstrated that the programme, with its initial business focus and entrepreneurship discourse, was challenged and developed into a new entrepreneurial approach that expanded in both scope and space. We argue that the schools did not fully accept the intentions of the programme; rather they challenged them and transformed subordinate clauses into main clauses, thereby stretching the purpose of the programme.

In our study, it became obvious that the teachers became entrepreneurial themselves, widening the discourse to better fit their own perception of their assignment and beliefs, and perhaps to avoid working with entrepreneurship in the narrower economic sense, as suggested by for example Komulainen et al. (2011) and Korhonen et al. (2012). Therefore, teachers and staff recast and changed both the language and interpretations of what entrepreneurship is and could be. That is, they altered entrepreneurship into an entrepreneurial approach. However, we all need to be careful with, and observant of, what new images of the 'new entrepreneurial citizen' and its norms this might bring forth. When adopting this broader approach, there is a risk that the teachers will 'become victims of their own pursuit'. This is because the education system encourages young people to become entrepreneurial individuals, managing themselves in every aspect of their lives with the focus on becoming citizens who are masters of their own dreams and productive and useful to their countries. As such, society might produce a generation of self-conducting managers (du Gay et al., 1996/2005), subjects capable of acting in an advanced liberal western democracy. Therefore, in their ambition to avoid entrepreneurship with business connotations by widening the discourse, they simultaneously further strengthen and acknowledge the idea, in Dean's (1999) or Rose's (1996) words, of the enterprising self. Thus, teachers in the schools come full circle and once again end up at the core of an economic and market-oriented neo-liberalistic entrepreneurship.

NOTE

1. The term educational organizer should be understood as the entity within the Swedish system that organizes and is legally responsible for education. It can be private as well as public and, in practice, an educational organizer might be, say, a municipality, a company, an association or foundation (Ministry of Education, 2010).

REFERENCES

Ainsworth, S. and C. Hardy (2008), 'The enterprising self: an unsuitable job for an older worker', *Organization*, **15** (3), 389–405.

Alvesson, M. and D. Kärreman (2000), 'Varieties of discourse: on the study of organizations through discourse analysis', *Human Relations*, **53** (9), 1125–49.

Axelsson, K. (2015), En analys av Skolverkets satsning på utvecklingsmedel för entreprenörskap i skolan [An analysis of the the Swedish National Agency for Education's investment in development funds of entrepreneurship in education], Mälardalen University.

Axelsson, K., S. Hägglund and A. Sandberg (2015), 'Entrepreneurial learning in education preschool as a take-off for the entrepreneurial self', *Journal of Education and Training*, **2** (2), 40–58.

Axelsson, K. and M. Mårtensson (2015), 'Introducing entrepreneurship in a school setting – entrepreneurial learning as the entrance ticket', paper presented at the ICEIRD Conference, Sheffield 18–19 June.

Berglund, K. (2013), 'Fighting against all odds: entrepreneurship education as employability training', *Ephemera: Theory & Politics in Organization*, **13** (4), 717–35.

Bragg, S. (2007), '"Student voice" and governmentality: the production of enterprising subjects?', *Discourse: Studies in the Cultural Politics of Education*, **28** (3), 343–58.

Brunila, K. and P. Siivonen (2014), 'Preoccupied with the self: towards self-responsible, enterprising, flexible, and self-centred subjectivity in education', *Discourse: Studies in the Cultural Politics of Education*, **26** (1), 1–4.

Bührmann, A.D. (2005), 'The emerging of the entrepreneurial self and its current hegemony: some basic reflections on how to analyze the formation and transformation of modern forms of subjectivity', *Qualitative Social Research*, **6** (1), Art. 16.

Burr, V. (2003), *Social Constructionism*, 2nd edn, London, UK and New York, USA: Routledge.

Cope, J. (2005), 'Toward a dynamic learning perspective of entrepreneurship', *Entrepreneurship Theory and Practice*, **29** (4), 373–97.

Dahlstedt, M. and F. Hertzberg (2012), 'Schooling entrepreneurs: entrepreneurship, governmentality and education policy in Sweden at the turn of the millennium', *Journal of Pedagogy*, **3** (2), 242–62.

Dean, M. (1999), 'Risks, calculable and incalculable', in D. Lupton (ed.), *Risk and Sociocultural Theory: New Directions and Perspectives*, Cambridge, USA: Cambridge University Press, pp.131–59.

du Gay, P. (1991), 'Enterprise culture and the ideology of excellence', *New Formations*, **13** (1), 45–61.

du Gay, P. (1994), 'Making up managers: bureaucracy, enterprise and the liberal art of separation', *The British Journal of Sociology*, **45** (4), 655–74.

du Gay, P. (1995), *Consumption and Identity at Work*, London, UK: Sage Publications Ltd.

du Gay, P., G. Salaman and B. Rees (1996/2005), 'The conduct of management and the management of conduct: contemporary managerial discourse and the constitution of the "competent" manager', *Journal of Management Studies*, **33** (3), 263–82; edited version (2005), 40–57.

European Community (2007), 'Key competences for lifelong learning: European reference framework', Education and Culture DG, Lifelong Learning Programme Luxembourg: Office for Official Publications of the European Communities.

Falk Lundqvist, A., P-G. Hallberg, E. Leffler and G. Svedberg (2014), *Entreprenöriellt lärande: i praktik och teori* [Entrepreneurial Learning: In Practice and Theory], Stockholm, Sweden: Liber AB.

Fayolle, A. (2013), 'Personal views on the future of entrepreneurship education', *Entrepreneurship and Regional Development*, **25** (7–8), 692–701.

Foucault, M. (1991), 'On governmentality', in G. Burchell, C. Gordon and P. Miller (eds), *The Foucault Effect*, Brighton, UK: Harvester, pp.87–104.

Gibb, A. (2002), 'In pursuit of a new "enterprise" and "entrepreneurship" paradigm for learning: creative destruction, new values, new ways of doing things and new combinations of knowledge', *International Journal of Management Reviews*, **4** (3), 233–69.

Gill, R. (2014), '"If you're struggling to survive day-to-day": class optimism and contradiction in entrepreneurial discourse', *Organization*, **21** (1), 50–67.

Government Offices of Sweden (2009), *Strategy for Entrepreneurship in the Field of Education*, Västerås, Sweden: Edita.

Hattie, J. (2009), *Visible Learning: A Synthesis of Over 800 Meta-analyses Relating to Achievement*, London, UK: Routledge.

Hjorth, D. and C. Steyaert (2004), *Narrative and Discursive Approaches in Entrepreneurship*, Cheltenham, UK: Edward Elgar.

Höglund, L. (2015), *Strategic Entrepreneurship: Organizing Renewal in Established Organizations*, Lund, Sweden: Studentlitteratur.

Johannisson, B. (2010), 'The agony of the Swedish school when confronted by entrepreneurship', in K. Skogen and J. Sjovoll (eds), *Creativity and Innovation: Preconditions for Entrepreneurial Education*, Trondheim, Norway: Tapir Academic Press, pp.91–105.

Klapper, R. and Refai, D. (2015), 'A Gestalt model of entrepreneurial learning', in D. Rae and C. Wang (eds), *Entrepreneurial Learning: New Perspectives in Research, Education and Practice*, London, UK: Routledge, pp.156–77.

Komulainen, K., P. Naskali, M. Korhonen and S. Keskitalo-Foley (2011), 'Internal entrepreneurship – a Trojan horse of the neoliberal governance of education? Finnish pre- and in-service teachers' implementation of and resistance towards entrepreneurship education', *Journal for Critical Education Policy Studies*, **9** (1), 341–74.

Korhonen, M., K. Komulainen and H. Räty (2012), 'Not everyone is cut out to be the entrepreneur type: how Finnish school teachers construct the meaning of entrepreneurship education and the related abilities of the pupils', *Scandinavian Journal of Educational Research*, **56** (1), 1–19.

Landström, H. and M. Benner (2010), 'Entrepreneurship research: a history of scholarly migration', in H. Landström and F. Lohrke (eds), *Historical Foundations of Entrepreneurship Research,* Cheltenham, UK: Edward Elgar, pp.15–45.

Leffler, E. (2009), 'The many faces of entrepreneurship: a discursive battle for the school arena', *European Educational Research Journal*, **8** (1), 104–16.

Leffler, E. (2012), 'Entrepreneurship in schools and the invisible of gender: a Swedish context', in T. Burger-Helmchen (ed.), *Entrepreneurship – Gender, Geographies and Social Context*, Rikeja: InTech, pp.31–52.

Leffler, E. (2014), 'Enterprise learning and school subjects – a subject didactic issue?' *Journal of Education and Training*, **1** (2), 15–30.

Miller, P. (2001), 'Governing by numbers: why calculative practices matter', *Social Research*, **68** (2), 379–96.

Miller, P. and M. Power (2013), 'Accounting, organizing, and economizing: connecting accounting research and organization theory', *The Academy of Management Annals*, **7**, 555–603.

Miller, P. and N. Rose (1990), 'Governing economic life', *Economy and Society*, **19** (1), 1–31.

Ministry of Education (2010), 'Skollag' [Education Act], (2010:800)/SFS 2010:800, Issued: 2010-06-23.

OECD (1989), *Towards an 'Enterprising' Culture: Challenges for Education and Training*, Paris: OECD/CERI.

Potter, J. and M. Wetherell (1987), *Discourse and Social Psychology: Beyond Attitudes and Behavior*, London, UK: Sage Publications Ltd.

Rae, D. and M. Carswell (2000), 'Using a life-story approach in researching entrepreneurial learning: the development of a conceptual model and its implications in the design of learning experiences', *Education and Training*, **42** (4/5), 220–27.

Rose, N. (1996), *Inventing Our Selves*, Cambridge, UK: Cambridge University Press.

Rose, N. and P. Miller (1992), 'Political power beyond the state: problematics of government', *The British Journal of Sociology*, **43** (2), 173–205.

Sharma, A.C. and W. Anderson (2007), 'Recontextualization of science from lab to school: implications for science literacy', *Science and Education*, **18** (9), 1253–75.

Smith, R. (2010), 'Masculinity, doxa and institutionalisation of entrepreneurial identity in the novel *Cityboy*', *International Journal of Gender and Entrepreneurship*, **2** (1), 27–48.

5. Cultural repertoires of the division of labour market and family responsibilities between Slovak entrepreneurial couples and their gendered nature

Marie Pospíšilová

INTRODUCTION

Contemporary research in the area of entrepreneurship highlights the contextual embeddedness of entrepreneurship. The emphasis on context is based notably on criticism of the conventional entrepreneurial research, which mostly applied an individual perspective and disregarded structural influences, which both restrict and enable entrepreneurship (Welter, 2011). As pointed out by some authors, gender may even be understood as a central category influencing, and influenced by, all other contexts (Welter, 2011). Family embeddedness is understood as one of those contexts influencing entrepreneurship (Aldrich and Cliff, 2003; Brush et al., 2014; Dyer, 2003; Heck and Trent, 1999; Welter, 2011), studying the influence of this environment also upsets the conventional idea of entrepreneurship as a gender-neutral concept (Garcia and Welter, 2011).

Although there is no absolute agreement on the term copreneurs (Fitzgerald and Muske, 2002), general papers concur that they are partners (married couples or 'romantic partners') who share their responsibilities in both business and family, work and intimate spheres. Copreneurs are different from other family businesses in that they have a close relationship between the partners: they function as a whole or as a system (Marshack, 1994, p.52). Blenkinsopp and Owens (2010, p.359) mention that the union is realized through the 'romantic element' of partnership, which makes this unit specific and convenient for studying family and entrepreneurial dynamics. We challenge the romantic nature of this element – not all copreneurial couples need have a romantic component. We assume that the partnership element is similar to other partnerships in business – as Kamm and Nurick (1993) noted – work with other people who you admire, know and trust is one of the most important elements for joining a new firm. The specificity of the partnership element in entrepreneurial couples is that it could work in the process of dividing up work and household roles, which are interconnected in those couples. This characteristic helps us to face the critique of the usual definition of copreneurship as a gendered concept – the thing is that traditional definitions are based on ownership, commitment, the condition of shared risk, or joint establishment of the business and so on (Fitzgerald and Muske 2002, p.4), ignoring the family sphere.

From this point of view, copreneurship appears to be a convenient setting where – due to the tight linkage between the home and work spheres – we can study the family embeddedness of entrepreneurship and the gendered nature of this embeddedness (Blenkinsopp and Owens, 2010). In this research we specifically study discursive practices about division of tasks at home and at work, paying close attention to how those practices are gendered and embedded in cultural settings. We approach this topic through the concept of cultural repertoires in an attempt to uncover the apparent automaticity of this division. Through revealing the gendered nature of the arguments used, we can reveal arguments that are used to justify inequalities in this area.

Focus on this area is particularly important because we can study the specificity of copreneurial couples to other entrepreneurship partners, focusing on the role of the partnership element in combination with sharing responsibilities at home and at work. Studies on specific aspects of copreneurship are very rare. We can also approach how the seemingly unquestioned reasoning of division of household and work tasks is embedded in culture (through studying cultural repertoires) and how this is gendered. This can reveal reasons for some conflicts in understanding the role of the entrepreneur and their partner, either at home or at work. Understanding those conflicts can help copreneurs to gain balance in the division of roles in both spheres. A focus on the specific context – Slovakia as a post-Communist country – could enrich contemporary research in two ways. First, not much research has been done on the social aspects of entrepreneurship in post-Communist countries in comparison to western countries, so we can give heightened attention to this context. Second, it can show how specific features coming from the Communist past and now are embedded in norms, values and attitudes (looking at it through cultural repertoires) and how those influence the form of copreneurship.

LITERATURE REVIEW

In the literature review we will first describe the current trends in research into copreneurship and how our research fits in this. We will then describe in more detail the concept of cultural repertoires, which is our theoretical framework. As we would like to study the gendered nature of talking about the division of roles at home and at work, we will continue with an explanation of our approach to gender, and finally we will show more in detail the Slovak context, which influences the arguments used for division of roles in couples.

Research into Copreneurship

Research into copreneurs has already studied the division of roles between partners. Since it did not deal with the domestic sphere in the early stages, it produced the notion that shared responsibilities in the business imply sharing responsibilities in the home sphere as well (Bowman, 2009, p.10). Kathy Marshack (1994, 1998) has taken a critical stand against this notion and found that the actual division of roles between the home and work spheres is rather traditional – men have the main leading role in the business (McAdam and Marlow, 2012; Smith, 2000). This is due to not only the gendered nature of roles in society but also the greater effort of women to avoid conflict and thus conform to socially recognized roles rather than oppose them (Larsen, 2006). Moreover, the division of traditional roles between the work and home spheres leads to a heroization of men's roles in the work sphere (Connell, 2005; Williams, 2001), women's increasing invisibility in business (McAdam and Marlow, 2012) and belittling of domestic work. The rather traditional division of roles attributed to copreneurship therefore attributes different values to each of the spheres. The notion of equal division of roles in copreneurship has also been criticized by Maura McAdam and Susan Marlow. They decided to study the less frequent configurations where a woman is in the leading position of an enterprise (McAdam and Marlow, 2012). The neglected 'invisible' role of women has also been criticized. For example, Sharon M. Danes and Patricia D. Olson focused their research on companies where an invisible role of women is expected (companies owned by their male partners). In reality, however, their results indicated that the range of women's roles is broad, often highly visible (Danes and Olson, 2003).

However, none of the papers deals with various types of arrangements in a single research project, which is what we attempt here. This focus enables us to assess the universal or specific nature of arguments used for division of roles in various arrangements. We follow up on our previous research where we also studied a post-Communist environment, specifically the Czech Republic. Our research showed that formal and informal institutions influence the division of roles in both family and household and thus it is highly gendered in the Czech Republic (Dlouhá et al., 2014; Jurik et al., 2016; Křížková et al., 2014). Research in a Slovak setting as presented in this chapter looks deeper into the specificity of copreneurial couples – a combination of partnership elements and interconnectedness between the home and work spheres.

Cultural Repertoires

We have chosen the theoretical framework of cultural repertoires for our research. It is based on an understanding of culture as a 'toolkit' (Lamont, 1992, 1995, 1999; Swidler, 1986, 2001). According to Ann Swidler, we cannot understand the influence of culture on action as defining goals and values, but as providing tools from which individuals choose and based on which they construct more long-term action strategies (Silber, 2003, p.431; Swidler, 1986, p.273; Weber, 2005, p.228). In this understanding, culture (or cultural repertoires) represents a store of available tools – rituals, symbols, customs, stories, abilities, worldviews and acting styles that can be used in various configurations to solve various types of problems (Swidler, 1986). Both individuals and groups choose among them based on the situation and which of them are available, and they mobilize them at both the discursive and interactive levels in their actions. Cultural repertoires describe both the enabling and limiting effects of culture on actions – they are limiting, limited, flexible and relatively stable, but never absolutely static and closed (Silber, 2003, p.431). They exist independently of actors and are available to them, but they are also grasped, used and practically reshaped by them (Lamont and Thèvenot, 2000, pp.5–6; Silber, 2003, p.438). An individual's freedom consists of the fact that he or she can choose and construct strategies, which permit a great variability of action. The fact that an individual utilizes a certain repertoire does not mean that he or she has no alternatives in the form of other repertoires (Grznár et al., 2014). That said, repertoires are often internally heterogeneous – they contain diverse, even contradictory elements and tools. Neither action nor repertoires have to be internally coherent or systematic; the contrary is true: the concept permits improvisation, dissonance and even logical contradiction between components. Following on this theoretical approach, we formulate our research question – how copreneurs in our research utilize specific cultural repertoires in talking about the division of labour in the home or work spheres, and what repertoires, components and tools they choose and what positions the individuals hold in the business and the family based on these repertoires.

Gender as Doing Structures

We understand entrepreneurial and gender roles not as something stable but rather as something negotiated, socially constructed. We thus build on social constructivism (Berger and Luckmann, 1966; West and Zimmerman, 1987). In agreement with West and Zimmerman (1987, p.145), we see gender as constantly done in social interactions. Through doing gender people sustain, reproduce and render legitimate the institutional arrangements that are based on sex categories (West and Zimmerman, 1987, p.146).

The concept of cultural repertoire provides space to study the gendered nature of talking about roles in entrepreneurial couples. Entrepreneurs use cultural repertoires as narrative resources or sets of discursive practices that are used for each other's role at home and in entrepreneurship. We see gender relations as being produced in talking about the division of roles through rational sorting and optimal matching of tasks to household members and alignment with the roles of husband, wife, man or woman (Berk, 1985). They negotiate their own identities and roles in relation to their vision of masculinities and femininities (similarly to Redman, 2001). In our research we focus on doing gender as doing structures (Nentwich and Kelan, 2014). We see assumptions about work and family roles as gendered, and through cultural repertoires we would like to reveal how those structures are augmented as natural. Women and men in our research talked about their and their partner's roles at home and at work and through this they reveal their assumptions about women's and men's role in those spheres. So we study how structures become gendered through talking about roles at home and work and how those structures shape entrepreneur's expressions.

Slovak Setting

Since we are interested in the gendered nature of talking about division of roles between the home and work spheres in the Slovak setting, we focus on the values, norms and attitudes corresponding to it, specifically those connected to the roles of men and women in the family and household. Based on the approach of Aidis et al. (2007), who focuses on the nature of gender relationships in transition countries, we have defined our principal spheres of interest: traditional attitudes to the position of women and men on the labour market, religious values, the view of entrepreneurship (as a male activity), family values and values originating from the Socialist past (Aidis et al., 2007; Welter et al., 2003).

The Slovak setting is influenced by the country's Socialist past. The tradition of private ownership and entrepreneurship was interrupted until the Velvet Revolution of 1989, when the centrally planned economy slowly began to transform into a market economy. In the Socialist period, there was a pressure for full employment both for women and men, but there was quite strong vertical and horizontal segregation of the labour market (Čermáková, 1995). Due to traditional division of roles at home, women were expected to do unpaid housework in addition to their paid jobs (known as double burden) (True, 2003, p.39), which is still common today. The situation is supported by the strong Roman Catholic tradition: 68.9 per cent of the population professed Catholicism in 2002 (Výrost, 2011, p.10). Nowadays there is a predominant notion (among both men and women) that both partners ought to contribute to the family budget (Výrost, 2011), influenced among other things by the low wages in Slovakia and the necessity to secure the family with double incomes. At the same time, there is an enduring opinion that women should care for the family, while men's role is understood as the financial provision of the family (Bútorová, 2008). The conviction of the natural division of roles between the family and the work sphere also leads to men not perceiving women as equally capable in the work sphere with men (Bútorová, 2008). However, the emphasis on the traditional division of roles disrupts the men's sense of identity, particularly in consequence of the economic crisis, which has often jeopardized their breadwinning roles. Care for children under school age is also seen as a woman's primary task (Výrost, 2011). Parents generally prefer home care for preschool children to institutional care (Bodnárová et al., 2005). This depends on multiple factors: the long parental leave, which is three years in Slovakia (Bednárik, 2012); the low availability of childcare services (Bodnárová et al., 2005); and the traditional idea that a preschool child suffers if the mother does not dedicate herself to the child adequately (Výrost, 2011).

As for the entrepreneurial orientations and attitudes, Slovaks consider entrepreneurial opportunities to be extremely low compared to other European Union (EU) countries (Amorós and Bosma, 2014) and women perceived even less opportunities than men (Pilková et al., 2015). In 2014 the same percentage of women as men perceived entrepreneurship as a good career choice, but women felt that they have fewer capabilities than men and they have a much greater fear of failure (Pilková et al., 2015). Generally speaking, the perceived drawbacks of Slovakia's business environment include inadequate state support to small and medium-sized enterprises, a high administrative burden, and a lack of enterprise support schemes (GEM, 2014). Within the EU, Slovakia is a country with one of the highest proportions of necessity-driven business[1] (women and men start an enterprise out of necessity in 36 per cent of the cases) (Kelley et al., 2012).

METHODOLOGY

Since we decided to study micropractices of negotiating and constructing roles at the couple level, we chose a qualitative methodology – in-depth interviews. Qualitative methods are also suitable because they provide a more egalitarian collaborative relationship with participants (McDowell, 2011). We chose to do in-depth interviews because we could catch arguments used in reasoning copreneurial division of household/business tasks. Those arguments are very often undeclared in everyday interaction; through interviews we can challenge this naturalness.[2] Interviews could serve not only for studying the form of cultural repertoires, but also specific ways they are used. Our interview partners were copreneurs and we stressed the importance of the partnership element and sharing of home and work spheres. Hearing both sides was thus important – to see not only their own view of their own roles but also their partner's roles. We decided to do separate interviews because we would like to hear the supressed voices – mostly it is women who are engaged in business in invisible positions (Lewis and Massey, 2011). That is why in our search for copreneurs we apply a definition of copreneurs similar to that mentioned by Fitzgerald and Muske (2002), that is, self-definition by respondents. In our opinion, this definition is best at describing the invisible roles as well, be they held by male or female entrepreneurs.

We concentrated on entrepreneurial couples engaged in the same business in various positions. In connection to previous research, we did not want to study only 'typical' couples – those where the man is in the leading position, or 'extreme' cases, where the woman is the leader. We therefore searched for joint enterprises where partners work in various positions (choice of maximum case variation: Neergaard, 2007, p.262), not from a formal point of view as much as an informal one (based on whom the entrepreneurs regarded as the main person in the business). We thus strove to include in our sample enterprises where the main position is attributed to the woman, the man, where the positions are divided equally and where there is an unequal division but without a leading position. We did not want the results to be affected by the gendered nature of the line of work that the copreneurs follow, so we searched for entrepreneurial couples in sectors that are not regarded as typically male or female. At the same time, due to our focus on negotiating roles within a couple, we chose businesses of a smaller size (up to 20 employees), as we assumed larger companies not to have such frequent contact between the partners and negotiation of roles. Due to these requirements (notably the requirement to identify different variations on the division of roles in the business) and due to the unavailability of official data that would describe entrepreneurial couples as we have defined them, we chose to make our selection in several ways.

We searched for copreneurs through our acquaintances, business clubs and business support organizations, as we expected they would be able to recommend entrepreneurs with the given characteristics. Simultaneously, we searched for entrepreneurial couples via the internet and various popularization articles from which we could learn more about their arrangements. In total, interviews with 11 couples with the given characteristics were conducted. The couples' detailed characteristics are shown in Table 5.1.

The interviews were made with each of the partners separately, thus totalling 21 interviews (one of the male entrepreneurs declined to participate). Since we were interested in what repertoires the different male and female entrepreneurs utilize when talking about dividing their responsibilities in the home and work spheres, we focused on these issues in the interviews: how the communicating partner views their own role, their partner's role, or the shared role (and those of other actors such as the broader family, institutions, and so forth, if any). The interviews took from 45 to 90 minutes, and were carried out in late 2014 and early 2015.

The process of interviewing could be influenced also by the interview situation. The interviews were conducted by female researchers, so the gender could have been done not only by words, in revealed repertoires, but also in the interview situation and influence statements (Deutsch, 2007). It was present in the interviews, for example, when a female interviewer asked a male participant about his role at home. Sometimes they didn't feel comfortable, because they felt that there is an expectation (from the interviewer) that they do those tasks. We noted the details of interview situations into field notes. The method of data production must be taken into account while reading the analysis and results.

ANALYSIS

In the analysis we searched for cultural repertoires used for talking about roles in work and home spheres. Culture was seen as resources and strategies of action, while cultural repertoires were viewed as patterns or common ways to do something (Swidler, 1986). We were looking for the arguments supporting a certain arrangement of dividing tasks between the home and work spheres. We were looking not only to the repertoires but also into the praxis of using them. The aim was to see not only the form of those repertoires, but also the combination of different repertoires used, and possible conflict in the usage. For this reason we used the analytical steps designed by Gioia et al. (2012). In connection to this methodology, we focused in the first phase generally on the reasoning in talking about the speakers' roles in the enterprise and the home sphere and the principles of

Table 5.1 List of interview respondents (pseudonyms only)

Couple	Pseudonyms	Age	Number and age of children	Number of employees	Role in entrepreneurship	Business type	Region
1	Krištof Katarína	18–34	1 (0–5 years old)	Less than 10	Equal	Creative product/sales	Rural
2	Ľubica	50 and up	2 (both 25 and up)	From 10 to 20	Man is head	Service	Urban
3	Paulína Pavol	18–34	1 (0–5 years old)	Less than 10	Woman is head	Sales	Urban
4	Juraj Justína	35–50	3 (15–19, two others 25 and up)	Less than 10	Woman is head	Sales	Urban
5	Zdenko Zlatica	18–34	2 (both 0–5 years old)	Less than 10	Equal	Creative product/sales	Rural
6	Vratko Viera	50 and up	3 (20–24, two others 25 and up)	Less than 10	Man is head	Service	Urban
7	Danica Dušan	50 and up	2 (both 25 and up)	Less than 10	Man is head	Sales	Urban
8	Antónia Andrej	35–50	2 (15–19 and 20–24 years old)	Less than 10	Equal	Sales/Service	Rural
9	Ivo Ivica	50 and up	3 (15–19, two others 25 and up)	Less than 10	Equal	Sales	Urban
10	Belo Bea	18–34	0	Less than 10	Woman is head	Sales	Urban
11	Matúš Mária	50 and up	3 (all three 20–25 years old)	From 10 to 20	Man is head	Service	Urban

their division. This was an open coding phase. This produced several dozen codes. In the second step, we compared them and searched for similarities and differences among them (similarly to the axial coding of Strauss and Corbin, 1998). This produced several dozen first-order concepts – the first level of analysis; examples are mentioned in Table 5.2. In the next step, we followed the methodology of Gioia et al. (2012, p.20) to search for a structure inside these codes. Strauss and Corbin (1998) refer to an analogous step as theoretical sampling. This resulted in second-order themes, shown in Table 5.2. The repertoires were then compiled as the next step, as an aggregated dimension of the themes in the second level. This produced a total of five repertoires, used in the interviews in division of responsibilities and roles in both the work and home spheres. Table 5.2 illustrates the three levels of analysis.

In the final step, we created the structure and relationships among these categories (second-order themes and aggregated dimensions), which establish the structure of arguments and point at the interconnectedness of the repertoires and themes contained in them. This was the phase where we focused on praxis of using repertoires. Those relationships are described in the analysis part. Among other things, it highlights the fact that repertoires used in the work sphere may or may not be related to those used in the domestic sphere. It must also be noted that the different repertoires were not used exactly in this form and on their own. The repertoires used often mingled, or only parts were used, or they were used in slightly different ways. These differences will be indicated in the findings from the analysis.

FINDINGS

As already mentioned, the analysis revealed five repertoires used in talking about dividing roles and responsibilities in the home and work spheres. These were the traditional, function-based, responsibility, collective and competence-based repertoires. Each of the below paragraphs will describe one of the repertoires. First we will introduce the form of the repertoire in the work sphere, followed by the form in the domestic sphere. Afterwards, we will deal with if and how the repertoires were connected between the work and home spheres. Each repertoire description will be coupled with a description of situations in which it was used and in which it is of importance. For each repertoire, we will also point out how they exhibited the 'partnership element' and how it connects the work and home spheres, which is specific for copreneurship. The last two repertoires were less mentioned in the interviews, so we give them less space in the analysis. The analysis outcomes are accompanied by quotes that illustrate

Table 5.2   Data analysis by Gioia (2012) – from concepts to themes to aggregate dimensions

First-order concepts (examples)	Second-order themes	Aggregate dimensions
If a woman worked more in the firm she would be a bad mother	Home as symbolically women's and work as men's domain	Traditional repertoire
Trying to achieve a compromise	'Typical' man's and woman's tasks	
Childcare is the woman's task	Man as breadwinner, woman as caretaker	
Career is more important for men because they are ambitious	Argument of 'natural' division	
Work of partner at home is financial benefit for family	Appreciation of partner's work	
	Importance of consensus	
	Trust, reliance on partner	
...		
Doing housework because of interest in it (mainly women)	Division of tasks based on skills, will and interest	Competence-based repertoire
Men don't do work at home because they don't like it	Delegation of tasks to someone else (in case of lack of interest)	
Orientation of business based on skills of one of the partners	Respect for partner's will in final decision (at work)	
...		
Leading role means responsibility for final decision	Position in family/at work determines responsibility in this domain	Functional repertoire
Partner is a good leader	Admiration of the leader's competences (at work)	
Partner needs his/her space in his/her domain		
...		

		Responsibility repertoire
Entrepreneurship means that you have to do everything on your own	Responsibility based on ownership	
No choice to do/not to do something	Impossibility to delegate some tasks to someone else	
Partner is working hard because she/he does what no one else wants to do	Doing partner's responsibilities in case of necessity	
...	Appreciation of doing hard work (at work)	
		Collective repertoire
Everyone does everything	Collective responsibility for collectively owned (home/firm)	
There are not precisely defined functions	Unspecified tasks, equal division as natural	
Making main decisions exclusively with partner	Partnership as a place of trust and reliance (at work)	
...		

the arguments. Pseudonyms appear in the quotes (see Table 5.1 for more detailed couple characteristics); those of partners in the same couple start with the same letter.

Traditional Repertoire

The first repertoire to be revealed based on the analysis was the traditional repertoire. The underlying logic is the woman's caretaker role and the man's breadwinner role. The primary responsibility of men was seen in securing finances for the family, and its place was seen in the work sphere. The women's primary role was understood in the home sphere. This might not apply only to the division of primary roles in the home and work spheres, but also the division of tasks in the business based on what are 'typically female' and 'typically male' activities. The typically male ones included manual work as well as decision making in the company, while the typically female activities were things such as communication and administration. The division was based on the argument of 'naturalness' or 'obviousness' of differences between male and female actions, determined by the different dispositions of men and women, which are given 'by nature':

> I realize that men are more demanding on themselves, more ambitious, which is probably natural and normal. And we women . . . Well, now that I have a young child, I have this feeling that I should rather care for the family. (Katarína)

The argument of male and female jobs was often not based on abilities; for example, Antónia mentioned the following: 'I can also do those hard jobs, I can manage them, but I don't do them. That's his place, it's divided like that, and it's right.'

The traditional repertoire was not necessarily associated with breadwinning. There were cases of women not applying the traditional repertoire in the work area (they saw themselves as equal partners in business, for example) but also considered their role in the household as primary, with the justification that they are women. At the same time, this repertoire involved greater appreciation for the man's work, that is work that brings economic profit. The female entrepreneurs emphasized that they cannot 'disturb' or 'task' their male partners at work with care for the household: 'My husband's relaxation is more important to me than insisting that he empty the bin' (Maria).

In cases where the male partner also had a conventional employment in addition, the female partner played the main role in the enterprise. However, there was an emphasis on the male partner's breadwinning role (the family was dependent on the male's income in all the cases). An enterprise in which the female partner played the main role was described as her 'distraction'. In such cases, the female partners frequently used different repertoires and did not describe their roles as secondary. The relationship that the repertoire establishes between the family and work sphere is evident at first sight. The partnership element that appeared in this repertoire in some cases was the element of mutual agreement on women's greater involvement at home and men's at work. In one case, the male partner took the traditional division of roles for granted, but also perceived the value of the female partner's contribution in the housework sphere as equal to his economic contribution. In this repertoire, the partnership element manifested itself, for example, when men spoke about their primary role in the enterprise (described as breadwinning) and when they involved their female partner in their enterprise. To them, their female partner stood for more than an ordinary associate – they felt certain that confidential corporate information would 'stay in the family'; they knew that this is a person they can 'rely on' and who in fact cannot leave the company.

Competence-based Repertoire

The second repertoire that we identified based on the analysis was one based on individual competences (competence-based repertoire). In the work sphere, the argumentation behind the division of responsibilities and roles here was based on individual abilities, will and enthusiasm. Within this repertoire, partners mentioned that they hold the roles in the business because they 'like' them, that it is an area that they 'know', are 'good at', and so on. If neither partner liked some activities or found them outside their competencies, they delegated such work to employees or someone else involved in the enterprise. Difficulties appeared where these areas not popular with anyone could not be delegated, mostly due to lack of finance or human resources. Household roles were described in a similar fashion: Andrej mentioned he liked cooking, and Pavol's partner said the same about him. However, the competence-based repertoire was gendered. The women said much more often that they like the everyday household jobs (unlike their male partners) or that (unlike their male partners) they 'do not mind' doing them. On the other hand, men were mostly in favour of more technical and one-off household jobs. There was also a problem in the households with jobs that neither felt like doing or dedicating so much time to (cleaning, childcare). Some then considered external arrangements, whether through family networks (which were preferred) or paid services (childminders, kindergartens). Paid services were generally dismissed for financial reasons or due to a general mistrust in such services or due to their unavailability: 'Of course there's only a kindergarten in the village, he's too young for that, he'd have to go to a nursery. But it's quite difficult with nurseries in Slovakia, I don't think they have enough room' (Katarína).

It was in cases of unavailability of external help that some female entrepreneurs mentioned having 'brought down the standards' – for example, tidiness at home. The competence-based repertoire was admittedly used in both the spheres – home and work – but independently of one another, and it was not typically associated with any of the other repertoires. What was specific, however, was the connection between the traditional and competence-based repertoires among women who had a young child in the family. They understood their role as a caring one and said that they were satisfied with it, but they were also used to applying their talents in the work sphere. The conflict between the repertoires was described by their male partners. Some of the women said that they were satisfied with their role, but their male partners then emphasized their partner's dissatisfaction with being associated only with the carer's role. Competence-based division was not mentioned as a clear and simple division (interests overlapped or there was no one to assume them in certain areas). An element specific for partnership was respect for the other and mutual agreement, which was mentioned in the final division of roles in both spheres. In the case of Zolo and Zlatica, the roles were divided based on competences, but they had to take care that 'neither of us felt humiliated or harmed' (Zlatica).

Functional Repertoire

It follows from the analysis that the communication partners also described their entrepreneurial roles very functionally: they utilized a functional repertoire. This repertoire was based on formal functions, roles held by the entrepreneurs. In some cases, roles in the business were also attributed based on the moral 'ownership' of the founding idea of the enterprise. This was particularly the case of businesses where women held the primary position. Here, the functional repertoire was used by men when describing their own and their female partners' roles in the business. The men understood the female owner's function, their female partner's leading role (idea) in the enterprise as forming their position of 'advisors'. This secondary position meant to them not making decisions in the company. But Pavol, for instance, stated that he directed his female partner in her decisions inconspicuously. The functions in the enterprise based on which roles were attributed did not need to be hierarchical. An example is the repertoire use by Krištof and Katarína. In this case, according to what they said, the division of roles consisted in each having their own specialization in the shared company for which they were responsible. The competence-based repertoire was also applied in the household. The one who made the most decisions in an area was attributed the leading role in that area. Acceptance of a leading role and all decisions became a precondition for the partnership: 'So he knew from the start that if we wanted to be together, he would be forced to move with me' (Bea).

The interlinkage of the functional repertoire could be seen in this example of Bea and Belo, who had the work and family environments very closely interlinked. The female partner's position as one defining the direction and the derivation of other roles from that position was present both at home and in the enterprise. Although, as already mentioned, the female partner's position in the enterprises collided with the man's breadwinning repertoire; her role was not always only underplayed. The value of the leading role was supported by an element originating from the partnership. The males spoke of their female partners with admiration, as did Pavol about Paulína: 'Paulína is able to feel many things with her intuition; 99 per cent of the time she hits what these people need. She just does a great job' (Pavol).

Yet this notion was gendered. Admiration of hard work in the business sphere was connected with less work in the home sphere only for men.

Responsibility Repertoire

Another, fourth repertoire was labelled the responsibility repertoire. In this repertoire, there was a strong sense of responsibility for a partners' own enterprise. The link between the company ownership and the necessity to do a given task was perceived here. For example, some of the entrepreneurs, such as Ivo, mentioned the fact that they do some tasks in the business because: 'I don't want to have anyone else do it because I know it would only bother others, maybe even discourage them' (Ivo).

They used this repertoire similarly in situations where they mentioned having to do some jobs when their partner is not at home. They used the necessity repertoire to explain why then women, for example, do typically 'male' work (such as physically demanding jobs). The necessity repertoire occurred in the household in analogous cases – for example when the female partner was not at home. Some male entrepreneurs thus said that, when needed, they can cook or run the household, but it was conditioned by the necessity principle. In that case, interlinkage between the repertoires or linkage with other repertoires was not clear. Similarly to the preceding repertoires, there was also a specific feature here in recognition of the other person's work. If a partner was seen as doing some tasks only because the business could not work without them, and because no one else would do them, they were regarded as selfless and deserving of appreciation. As mentioned in functional repertoire, this recognition of the other partner's work was not connected with less work at home for women.

Collective Repertoire

The final repertoire was the collective one, based on the notion of the enterprise as a complete whole involving both the partners (and other people, if any). The argument was that the enterprise is shared so everyone has to participate. A typical feature was the application of this principle to other family members involved in the enterprise. Work in the enterprise was seen as a collective task that has to be done collectively (not necessarily together simultaneously; the jobs might be divided). Since the enterprise was interpreted as a joint project in the collective repertoire, the decision making and overview of the business was also seen as naturally inherent to both partners. It is interesting that this repertoire did not occur as often in the home sphere. Partnership (or family) was thus rather understood as a collective unit in the work area, while responsibilities in the household were based more often on the traditional repertoire. An example of using the collective repertoire is Lubica's family, where 'we've always had everyone cooking, including the kids and my husband'. The declared reason was that they all shared the same household so they each had to pull their own weight. For the copreneurs, partnership was an opportunity for trust and reliance on which they can depend, and therefore they make decisions together. They typically did not allow the broader family to make decisions, because as Pavol put it: 'There's nothing worse than having to argue with someone. You have an idea, he has an idea, and you should try to agree' (Pavol).

Agreeing with a female partner did not pose such pitfalls.

INTERPRETATION AND CONCLUSION

The research identified five different repertoires that were utilized in the division of both work and family responsibilities. The research results reveal not only the form of the repertoires but also their gendered nature. The second step of the analysis, looking into usage of repertoires, also reveals how this gendered nature is reproduced ('done') (West and Zimmerman, 1987) or challenged. The repertoires were largely gendered. The traditional repertoire not only attributed to women and men 'naturally' different positions in business and in the household, but also very often indicated different values of the male and female contributions (for details see Connell, 2005; Williams, 2001). A strong embeddedness in the traditional internalized values of Slovak society (Bútorová, 2008; Výrost, 2011) manifested itself here. The traditional repertoire was so strong that it justified the women's role in the household even in cases where the men were not the breadwinners. For example, the man regarded her as dependent on his decisions. Here we can see a connection with the fact that Slovak men more often see their work contribution as unsubstitutable with women's work (Bútorová, 2008). The gendered nature of the repertoires was also manifested in the fact that the man perceived the woman's contribution as less important than she perceived it herself (similarly to McAdam and Marlow, 2012). Thus women are also contributing to the symbolically less valuable position of women in business. The repertoire concept also showed that their use between the domestic and work spheres may build on similar arguments, which nonetheless serve a different division of roles. The same repertoire – competence-based – led to a different level of work participation of men in the enterprise and the household. In the household, this repertoire almost exclusively explained the men's lower level of participation in housework. This brings us back to the fact that in the Slovak setting, the division of men's and women's roles in the household setting is based on arguments of different biological dispositions (Bútorová, 2008). Not all the repertoires were necessarily gendered. For example, the competence-based one might lead partners to divide work based on their individual interests. However, it was shown that this method of division comes against the barriers of there being no one to whom to delegate the remaining activities that the partners do not or cannot do. Limiting factors typically voiced were the lack or unavailability (financial or spatial) of services that would cover these areas (for details, see for example Bodnárová et al., 2005). The setting conditions – particularly the perception of conditions for small and medium-sized enterprises as unfavourable, as mentioned in the introduction to this chapter (GEM, 2014) – formed the foundation for the necessity-based repertoire, which struggled with the state-imposed burden.

In some cases the combination of used repertoires caused conflicts, such as in cases where women used competence-based repertoire in the work sphere (they did a lot of work just because they wanted to) and at the same time traditional repertoire at home (they did household tasks because they were women). The conflict appeared either because they felt they did not devote enough time to one of the two spheres or because they were overworked (they experienced double burden) (True, 2003, p.39). Conflicts were not perceived just by women; men faced similar situations when they understood their role traditionally, as breadwinners, and worked outside the business and at the same time had a role in the business based on their interest. Those conflicts were mainly in cases where the gendered nature of repertoires met with more equal ways of justifying role division. The gendered nature of repertoires need not necessarily cause conflicts, for example in couples where both partners were identified with traditional roles. Those findings show the most problematic areas leading to conflicts in entrepreneurial couples. As copreneurs are the most important unit of many small and medium-sized businesses, avoiding those conflicts can help them function better.

One aspect specific to copreneurship was the 'partnership element', which was shown to be gendered, but also erasing gender boundaries. The partnership element was present in the repertoires in the form of expressed respect for the partner, appreciation of their contribution to interconnected spheres – enterprise and the household. At the same time, the partnership embodied an environment of mutual trust and discretion, which was seen as an advantage for the enterprise. However, the appreciation and respect for the other partner's role in business did not automatically mean that their contribution would be appreciated in the home sphere. Things appreciated included the male partner's equalist attitude in the household as something exceptional, while the woman's work in the household was mostly 'invisible'. Conversely, in cases where the woman's work in the household was appreciated, it was valued as equal to the man's work. On those results we can see how gender is done (West and Zimmerman, 1987) in copreneurial couples through talking about division of roles. Not only were the repertoires copreneurs used for arguing about division of roles gendered, but also the way they used them. Research also showed ways in which gendered structures are challenged.

The conclusions presented in this chapter give some insight into an issue not very much studied in the Slovak Republic. It has to be pointed out that due to the qualitative nature of the research, this may not be the finite form of all the repertoires used by copreneurs. At the same time, one has to bear in mind while reading the results that the use of repertoires overlapped in the entrepreneurs' testimonials, and that not everyone used a repertoire in the same way. Future research could compare copreneurs with conventional entrepreneurs to reveal the specificity and role of the 'partnership' element. It would also be appropriate to compare the results from the Slovak setting with analogous research from a different setting, which might reveal which characteristics are specific for this setting and which are shared interculturally. This could reveal interesting features or differences not only in cultural repertoires themselves, but also in differences in how they are used.

ACKNOWLEDGEMENTS

The author wishes to acknowledge funding in support of this research from the Czech Science Foundation for the research project 'Intersectionality in sociological research of social inequalities and the impact of the economic crisis on employment' (grant no. GA15-13766S).

NOTES

1. Reasons for starting a business are divided into necessity-driven and opportunity-driven.
2. Ethnographic research has been conducted on ongoing negotiation of gender and other roles in everyday interaction (Bruni et al., 2004).

REFERENCES

Aidis, R., F. Welter, D. Smallbone and N. Isakova (2007), 'Female entrepreneurship in transition economies: the case of Lithuania and Ukraine', *Feminist Economics*, **13** (2), 157–83.

Aldrich, H.E. and J. Cliff (2003), 'The pervasive effects of family on entrepreneurship: toward a family embeddedness perspective', *Journal of Business Venturing*, **18** (5), 573–96.

Amorós, J. and N. Bosma (2014), *Global Entrepreneurship Monitor 2013 Global Report: Fifteen Years of Assessing Entrepreneurship across the Globe*, Santiago, Chile: Global Entrepreneurship Research Association (GERA).

Bednárik, R. (2012), *Stav sociálnej ochrany na Slovensku*, Bratislava, Slovakia: Inštitút pre výskum práce a rodiny.

Berger, P.L. and T. Luckmann (1966), *The Social Construction of Reality*, 1st edn, Garden City, NY, USA: Anchor Books.

Berk, S.F. (1985), *The Gender Factory: The Apportionment of Work in American Households*, 1st edn, New York, USA and London, UK: Plenum Press.

Blenkinsopp, J. and G. Owens (2010), 'At the heart of things: the role of the "married" couple in entrepreneurship and family business', *International Journal of Entrepreneurial Behaviour & Research*, **16** (5), 357–69.

Bodnárová, B., J. Filadelfiová and D. Gerbery (2005), *Výskum potrieb a poskytovania služieb pre rodiny zabezpečujúce starostlivosť o závislých členov*, Bratislava, Slovakia: Stredisko pre štúdium práce a rodiny.

Bowman, D.D. (2009), 'The deal: wives, entrepreneurial business and family life', *Journal of Family Studies*, **15** (2), 167–76.

Bruni, A., S. Gherardi and B. Poggio (2004), 'Doing gender, doing entrepreneurship: an ethnographic account of intertwined practices', *Gender, Work and Organization*, **11** (4), 406–29.

Brush, C.G., A. de Bruin and F. Welter (2014), 'Advancing theory development in venture creation: signposts for understanding gender', in K.V. Lewis (ed.), *Women's Entrepreneurship in the 21st Century: An International Multi-level Research Analysis*, 1st edn, Cheltenham, UK: Edward Elgar Publishing Limited, pp.11–31.

Bútorová, Z. (2008), *Ona a on na Slovensku. Zaostrené na rod a vek*, 1st edn, Bratislava, Slovakia: Inštitút pre verejné otázky.

Čermáková, M. (1995), 'Gender, společnost, pracovní trh', *Sociologický časopis/ Czech Sociological Review*, **31** (1), 7–24.

Connell, R.W. (2005), 'A really good husband: work/life balance, gender equity and social change', *Australian Journal of Social Issues*, **40** (3), 369–83.

Danes, S. and P. Olson (2003), 'Women's role involvement in family businesses, business tensions, and business success', *Family Business Review*, **16** (1), 53–68.

Deutsch, F.M. (2007), 'Undoing gender', *Gender & Society*, **21** (1), 106–27.

Dlouhá, M., N.C. Jurik and A. Křížková (2014), 'Genderové inovace v malém podnikání: institucionální podmínky a dosahování genderové (ne)rovnosti v podnikatelských párech', *Gender, Rovné Příležitosti, Výzkum*, **15** (2), 87–100.

Dyer, W.G. (2003), 'The family: the missing variable in organizational research', *Entrepreneurship Theory and Practice*, **27** (4), 401–16.

Fitzgerald, M.A. and G. Muske (2002), 'Copreneurs: an exploration and comparison to other family businesses', *Family Business Review*, **15** (1), 1–16.

Garcia, M.-C.D. and F. Welter (2011), 'Gender identities and practices: interpreting women entrepreneurs' narratives', *International Small Business Journal*, **31** (4), 384–404.

GEM (2014), 'Bouncing back towards optimistic prospects', accessed 16 August 2016 at http://www.gemconsortium.org/country-profile/106.

Gioia, D.A., K.G. Corley and A. L. Hamilton (2012), 'Seeking qualitative rigor in inductive research: notes on the gioia methodology', *Organizational Research Methods*, **16** (1), 15–31.

Grznár, M., P.A. Beránková, L. Cerná and T. Samec (2014), 'Politická kultura v narativech: kulturní repertoáry vztahování se k současné politice', *Antropowebzin*, **3–4**, 139–150.

Heck, R. and E. Trent (1999), 'The prevalence of family business from a household sample', *Family Business Review*, **12** (3), 209–19.

Jurik, N.C., A. Křízková and M. Pospíšilová (Dlouhá) (2016), 'Czech copreneur orientations to business and family responsibilities: a mixed embeddedness perspective', *International Journal of Gender and Entrepreneurship*, **8** (3), 307–26.

Kamm, J.B. and A.J. Nurick (1993), 'The stages of team venture formation: a decision-making model', *Entrepreneurship: Theory & Practice*, **17** (2), 17–28.

Kelley, D.J., C.G. Brush, P.G. Greene and Y. Litovsky (2012), *Global Entrepreneurship Monitor 2012 Women's Report*, Boston, USA: The Center for Women's Leadership at Babson College and London Business School.

Křížková, A., N.C. Jurik and M. Dlouhá (2014), 'The divisions of labour and responsibilities in business and home among women and men copreneurs in the Czech Republic', in K. Lewis, C. Henry, E.J. Gatewood and J. Watson (eds), *Women's Entrepreneurship in the 21st Century: An International Multi-level Research Analysis*, 1st edn, Cheltenham, UK: Edward Elgar Publishing, pp.258–77.

Lamont, M. (1992), *Money, Morals, and Manners: The Culture of the French and the American Upper-middle Class*, 1st edn, Chicago, USA: University of Chicago Press.

Lamont, M. (1995), 'National identity and national boundary patterns in France and the United States studying national', *French Historical Studies*, **19** (2), 349–65.

Lamont, M. (1999), *The Cultural Territories of Race: Black and White Boundaries*, 1st edn, Chicago, USA: University of Chicago Press.

Lamont, M. and L. Thèvenot (eds) (2000), *Rethinking Comparative Cultural Sociology: Repertoires of Evaluation in France and the United States*, 1st edn, Cambridge, UK: Cambridge University Press.

Larsen, E.A. (2006), 'The impact of occupational sex segregation on family businesses: the case of American harness racing', *Gender, Work and Organization*, **13** (4), 359–82.

Lewis, K. and C. Massey (2011), 'Critical yet invisible: the "good wife" in the New Zealand small firm', *International Journal of Gender and Entrepreneurship*, **3** (2), 105–22.

Marshack, K.J. (1994), 'Copreneurs and dual career couples: are they different?', *Entrepreneurship: Theory and Practice*, **19** (1), 49–69.

Marshack, K.J. (1998), *Entrepreneurial Couples: Making it Work at Work and at Home*, 1st edn, Palo Alto, CA, USA: Davies-Black Publisher.

McAdam, M. and S. Marlow (2012), 'Sectoral segregation or gendered practices? A case study of roles and identities in a copreneurial venture', in K.D. Hughes and J.E. Jennings (eds), *Global Women's Entrepreneurship Research: Diverse Settings, Questions and Approaches*, 1st edn, Cheltenham, UK and Northampton, MA, USA: Edward Elgar, pp.189–203.

McDowell, L. (2011), 'Doing gender: feminism, feminists and research methods in human geography', *Transactions of the Institute of British Geographers*, **17** (4), 399–416.

Neergaard, H. (2007), 'Sampling in entrepreneurial settings', in H. Neergaard and J.P. Ulhøi (eds), *Handbook of Qualitative Research Methods in Entrepreneurship*, 1st edn, Cheltenham, UK: Edward Elgar Publishing Limited, pp.253–78.

Nentwich, J.C. and E.K. Kelan (2014), 'Towards a topology of "doing gender": an analysis of empirical research and its challenges', *Gender, Work & Organization*, **21** (2), 121–34.

Pilková, A., M. Holienka, J. Rehák and Z. Kovačičová (2015), *Podnikateľská aktivita a prostredie na Slovensku* (GEM Sloven.), Bratislava, Slovakia: Univerzita Komenského v Bratislave, KARTPRINT.

Redman, P. (2001), 'The discipline of love negotiation and regulation in boys' performance of a romance-based heterosexual masculinity', *Men and Masculinities*, **4** (2), 186–200.

Silber, I.F. (2003), 'Pragmatic sociology as cultural sociology', *European Journal of Social Theory*, **6** (4), 427–49.

Smith, C.R. (2000), 'Managing work and family in small "copreneurial" business: an Australian study', *Women in Management Review*, **15** (5/6), 283–9.

Strauss, A. and J. Corbin (1998), *Basics of Qualitative Research: Techniques and Procedures for Developing Grounded Theory*, Thousand Oaks, CA, USA: Sage.

Swidler, A. (1986), 'Culture in action: symbols and strategies', *American Sociological Review*, **51** (2), 273–86.

Swidler, A. (2001), 'What anchors cultural practices', in T.R. Schatzki, K. Knorr-Cetina and E. von Savigny (eds), *The Practice Turn in Contemporary Theory*, London, UK and New York, USA: Routledge, pp.83–101.

True, J. (2003), 'Mainstreaming gender in global public policy', *International Feminist Journal of Politics*, **5** (3), 368–96.

Výrost, J. (2011), *Rodina a zmena rodových rolí v optike údajov medzinárodného projektu ISSP* [International Social Survey Programme], Košice, Slovakia: Spoločenskovedný ústav SAV.

Weber, K. (2005), 'A toolkit for analyzing corporate cultural toolkits', *Poetics*, **33** (3–4), 227–52.

Welter, F. (2011), 'Contextualizing entrepreneurship – conceptual challenges and ways forward', *Entrepreneurship Theory and Practice*, **35** (1), 165–84.

Welter, F., D. Smallbone, E. Aculai, N. Isakova and N. Schakirova (2003), 'Female entrepreneurship in post Soviet countries', in J. Butler (ed.), *New Perspectives on Women Entrepreneurs*, Greenwich, CT, USA: Information Age, pp.243–69.

West, C. and D.H. Zimmerman (1987), 'Doing gender', *Gender and Society*, **1** (2), 125–51.

Williams, J. (2001), *Unbending Gender: Why Family and Work Conflict and What To Do About It*, Oxford, UK: Oxford University Press.

6. Do dreams always come true? Daughters' expectations and experience in family business succession

Francesca Maria Cesaroni and Annalisa Sentuti

INTRODUCTION

In family business (FB) studies, some scholars have focused their attention on the role of daughters in the succession process (Jimenez, 2009; Wang, 2010; Dumas, 2011; Gupta and Levenburg, 2013). However, literature on this topic remains limited (Wang, 2010). Understanding the challenges that daughters face in this context is important in order to comprehend why they still represent a minority in FB succession (MassMutual, 2010) and to avoid the possibility of worthy female successors being overlooked by predecessors (Byrne and Fattoum, 2015). Ahrens et al. (2015) verified that only 23 per cent of successors are females and that this number decreases to 19 per cent when both genders are represented among the younger generations. Results confirmed that there is still a preference for males. Even if female successors are equipped with higher levels of human capital in comparison to male successors, these last are chosen because of the predecessors' gender preferences in favour of male family heirs.

Contributions to this topic have focused on three main research areas: (1) daughters' motivations and reasons why they choose (or not) to join the FB and to realize a career from within; (2) daughters' roles; (3) conditions that facilitate (or hinder) the daughters' ability to take on the leadership. These investigations have established a significant, but not yet exhaustive, study on the subject (Jimenez, 2009; Al-Dajani et al., 2014). In particular, the link between daughters' goals and effective role played in their FB was not effectively analysed. Consequently, it is unclear whether the daughters' role in the FB is the result of a free or imposed choice.

This chapter focuses on daughters involved in their FB with different roles. The purpose is to understand how daughters' ambitions and expectations for their career contribute to determining their actual role in the FB and if this role is consistent with their previous goals. We present a multiple case study considering nine women, daughters of small or medium-sized FB owners, who are currently involved in their FB and take part in different governance and management roles. Based on the knowledge gained from these cases, we propose an empirically formulated typology of daughters' profiles, characterized by different combinations of alignment/misalignment between daughters' expectations and roles actually held in their FB. The empirical analysis was set in Italy where the growth of women in FBs has been particularly slow and quite insignificant (Corbetta and Minichilli, 2010; Corbetta et al., 2011). In addition, a high gender gap persists in regard to women's economic participation and opportunity (WEF, 2015). Even if some research conducted in Italy has underlined that FBs favour women's involvement (Gnan and Montemerlo, 2008), there are areas that are 'off limits', where they are absent or very few in number. Women are mainly involved as shareholders, co-owners or members of the board of directors and often hold managerial roles with functional responsibilities, but they very rarely have top management roles and entrepreneurial leadership (Gnan and Montemerlo, 2008). Thus, the Italian context is particularly suitable for gaining a more thorough understanding of the daughters' position in their FBs in order to comprehend whether they are forced to suffer decisions imposed on them from the outside or if they are able to follow their own personal goals.

The rest of the chapter is structured as follows. First, we present a theory overview on daughters' motivations, ambitions and roles in FBs succession. Next, the methodology is described, followed by the main results. Finally, we present our discussion and conclusions.

DAUGHTERS AND FAMILY BUSINESS SUCCESSION: A THEORY OVERVIEW

Several studies on daughters and FB succession have focused on: (1) daughters' motivations and reasons why they choose (or not) to join the FB and to realize a career from within; (2) different roles that daughters may assume; (3) conditions that facilitate (or hinder) the daughters' ability to take on the leadership.

In the first research area, early studies pointed out that several daughters do not aspire to plan a career in the FB but join the business to help the family in a time of crisis, or to fill a position that no other relative wants or because other options are less attractive (Dumas, 1989, 1992; Salganicoff, 1990). Several years later, Gatewood et al. (2003) maintained that daughters are driven by 'pull' or 'push' motivations for engagement within the FB. Daughters who have grown up to perceive the FB as their own, with a desire to play an active role in ensuring its continuity, exhibit 'pull motivations'. Daughters with more difficult contexts may form a reactive vision of the FB, not considering themselves 'true' potential successors, and they demonstrate 'push motivations' because they are often constrained by situations of necessity. Other authors (Vera and Dean, 2005) noticed a prevalent attitude of 'detachment' from the FB, which might be due to the daughters' awareness of not being appropriately considered. Therefore, daughters do not see their work in the FB as a professional career and do not aim to own the firm. Martin (2001) pointed out that sometimes daughters do not want to be involved in FB, especially if, since childhood, they have been oriented towards other professions, which are deemed more suitable for women (such as teaching).

More recently, Zellweger et al. (2011) analysed the career-choice intentions of students with a FB background and found that women display a higher likelihood to opt for employment and a lower inclination to be intentional founders. In their research on adolescents' motivations to join the FB, Schröder et al. (2011) and Schröder and Schmitt-Rodermund (2013) found that highly capable daughters are more likely to opt for becoming employees or founding a new business than to succeed in the FB.

Dawson et al. (2015) empirically tested Sharma and Irving's conceptual framework of commitment (2005), which analyses factors affecting second or later-generation family members' 'intention to stay' and continue their career in the FB. This framework identifies four bases of FB successor commitment: affective, normative, calculative and imperative. Affective commitment refers to a 'strong belief in and acceptance of the organization's goals, combined with a desire to contribute to these goals, and the confidence in one's ability to do so'. Normative commitment refers to 'feelings of obligation to pursue a career in the FB' in order to 'maintain good relationships with the senior generation'. Calculative commitment refers to 'successors' perceptions of substantial opportunity costs and threatened loss of investments or value if they do not pursue a career in the FB'. Finally, imperative commitment refers to 'a feeling of self-doubt and uncertainty of the ability to successfully pursue a career outside the FB'. This model is very useful as it helps us to understand different reasons why family members choose to maintain a career from within their FB, but it does not explain how younger generations' 'intention to stay' takes shape with their effective involvement in the FB. In fact, the role that younger generations actually play in the FB is not considered in the model. As a result, it cannot be used to find out if younger members have the chance to join the FB, taking on a role consistent with their goals and expectations.

Finally, they found that gender was significantly related to normative commitment, with women reporting a feeling of higher obligation concerning the FB. In the authors' interpretation, this might be considered as an extension of societal expectations for women to take care of family on all dimensions. However, they call for further research on gender differences and normative commitment. At the same time, recent research maintained that firms whose successors experience affective commitment are more likely to achieve their goals and that this type of commitment is the most desirable from the viewpoint of both the first and second generation (McMullen and Warnick, 2015).

The second research area addressed the issue of the daughters' role in FBs. Several scholars analysed daughters' involvement in ownership, leadership and management within the FB and some of them proposed useful typologies. For instance, Curimbaba (2002) analysed daughters' roles as FB managers and three daughters' experiences were described: professional heiresses, invisible heiresses and anchors. Cesaroni and Sentuti (2014) focused on roles that women (mostly daughters but not limited to) can play within their FBs when the leader is a man. They found three profiles: completely invisible women; figurehead women; manager women. Other research has extensively shown that: daughters are often involved in FBs with marginal roles, few responsibilities and little decision-making roles (Constantinidis and Cornet, 2008; Barrett and Moores, 2009); they face greater difficulties in being chosen as successors and in being involved in FBs with a leadership role (Jimenez, 2009; Wang, 2010).

The third research area focused on conditions that facilitate (or hinder) the daughters' ability to take on leadership. Some authors have underlined that FBs offer better and more career opportunities to daughters (Salganicoff, 1990; Cole, 1997; Gnan and Montemerlo, 2008). However, it is widely recognized that the gender of the successor is the main factor that hinders the daughters' path towards a leadership role (Jimenez, 2009). Many studies have demonstrated that predecessors rarely consider their daughter as a real potential successor (Francis, 1999; Martin, 2001; Lee et al., 2003; Jimenez, 2009; Wang, 2010). On the other hand, some research has demonstrated that daughters often never consider themselves potential successors, seeing their involvement in the FB as simply a job opportunity, without leadership ambition (Vera and Dean, 2005). Daughters can assume the leadership of the FB only in 'special circumstances' (Wang, 2010) such as: all siblings are female and the family has no male heirs (sons or son-in-laws) (Dumas, 1998; Curimbaba, 2002; García-Álvarez et al., 2002; Haberman and Danes, 2007); no male family member is interested in running the business (Dumas, 1998; Vera and Dean, 2005); the family or the business is going through a tough time (for example, a predecessor's sudden illness, a risk of failure for the business) (Dumas, 1998; Curimbaba, 2002); conflicts between family members (Barrett and Moores, 2011); the daughter has a close relationship with the predecessor (Curimbaba, 2002). Concerning the latter point, Smythe and Sardeshmukh (2013) found that early socialization within the FB, better communication between father–daughter and a deeper understanding of the 'father's shadow', favoured the negotiation of the leadership role for the daughter. Some authors (Aronoff, 1998; Gersick et al., 1999) have affirmed that many families choose to create a team of siblings – sons and daughters – to share leadership and ownership in the future so that all descendants are potential successors, regardless of gender. But even in these cases, the effective leader is very often the eldest son (García-Álvarez et al., 2002).

Summarizing, even if these studies are very useful for the description of daughters' expectations and experiences within their FB, the relationship between these two dimensions is lacking. On one hand, several authors have considered intentions, motivations and reasons why daughters choose (or not) to join their FB and to realize a career from within. On the other hand, several scholars have analysed different roles that daughters may assume within the FB, including conditions that may facilitate (or hinder) them to take on leadership. However, they have not been jointly investigated by putting in relationship daughters' goals with the roles actually held within the FB. In our opinion, this is an important gap. This research examines the roles that daughters may assume within the FB, trying to understand if they actually have the chance to play a role consistent with their previous goals or if they are given a limited choice.

METHODOLOGY

Research Method

To answer the research question, a qualitative analysis based on a multiple case study (Eisenhardt and Graebner, 2007; Miles et al., 2014) was carried out. This method is particularly suited to the study of FBs, as deemed appropriate to 'penetrate the veil of the family' (Litz, 1997). This is especially true when the succession process is being analysed, as a number of variables – main actors' goals, preferences and personal choices, family relationships and behaviours – can deeply affect succession and its outcome (Nordqvist et al., 2009). A qualitative research is therefore particularly consistent with our research aim.

Case Selection and Data Collection

A purposeful sampling was employed (Patton, 2002). In line with our research question, we looked for FBs involving at least one daughter as a successor leading the company or holding a managerial role. As a result, daughters working in their FB with marginal roles and no decision-making power (for example, a secretary) were excluded. Similarly, daughters without a role in their FB, completely excluded from the succession, were not considered in our analysis. Thanks to authors' personal knowledge, contacts from previous studies and information provided by business associations, we selected nine Italian women, daughters of small or medium-sized FB owners. The sample has a high internal variance. Selected daughters are between 35 and 55 years old and work in very different FBs when it comes to size, industry, generation in control and number of sisters/brothers involved in the FB (Table 6.1). Focusing on these cases helped us to reach a satisfactory level of 'theoretical saturation', as additional learning from new cases was deemed minimal (Eisenhardt, 1989).

Nine in-depth, face-to-face, semi-structured interviews were carried out encouraging a flexible and informal dialogue (Qu and Dumay, 2011). Direct interviews with selected daughters took place at the sites of the FBs between autumn 2011 and spring 2015. They varied in length from two to four hours, were recorded and transcribed verbatim. Respondents were initially asked to introduce themselves and were let free to talk about their experience in the FB and the reasons and circumstances that caused them to follow the FB and to take on their current role. In the second part of the interviews, attention was primarily focused on daughters' expectations and ambitions before entering the FB and on their current opinions and evaluations about their actual role. Emerging themes were explored with more specific questions, based on information disclosed by interviewees. Interviews were the primary source of data, while other sources provided contextual information about the business. Secondary data was collected from business documents and websites, newspaper articles and online news. We also collected field notes to record interviewees' behaviour and the context of the interviews. Finally, where possible, we interviewed at least one other family member (predecessor or sibling) in order to receive more information about the context and confirm daughters' statements. These multiple sources of data were collected in order to triangulate the data, confirm emergent themes and avoid inconsistencies in the data (Miles and Huberman, 1994).

Table 6.1 Daughters and firms' profiles

	Name	Age	Interviewees' role in the FB	Brothers/ Sisters	Brothers/ Sisters' role in the FB	Firm size	Generation in control	Industry
FB1	Diane	38	Chief legal officer	An elder brother	Chief buyer and future CEO	Medium	1st (the father)	Plastic manufacturers
FB2	Marcie	40	CEO	No brother or sister	---	Small	2nd	Footwear
FB3	Titty	47	HR manager	A younger brother	CEO	Medium	2nd	Machinery manufacturers
FB4	Vanessa	46	Chief legal officer	An elder sister	CEO	Small	2nd	Engineering
FB5	Sylvia	35	CEO	A younger brother	None	Small	2nd	Hotel
FB6	Vicky	49	CEO	A younger sister	HR manager	Small	2nd	Engineering
FB7	Sophia	55	CEO and marketing manager	Two younger sisters	Production manager / public relations manager	Small	2nd	Spirits
FB8	Helen	42	CEO	An older sister and a younger brother	None	Small	3rd	Publishing
FB9	Keira	38	Accounting and finance manager	An elder brother	CEO and production manager	Medium	2nd	Machinery manufacturers

Data Analysis

In line with the requirements for qualitative research, the data analysis followed an iterative approach. As long as the interviews and empirical material were analysed, a structure of theoretical statements progressively took shape. It provided a partial answer to our research question, while also providing a stimulus to move forward with further analysis, ending up with the definition of a definitive interpretative framework (Emerson, 2004; Nordqvist et al., 2009). As is typical in multiple case research (Miles and Huberman, 1994), data was initially analysed in order to build individual case study summaries and to compare differences and similarities within and across cases, providing empirical evidence of specific contexts and the daughters' experience. Subsequently, the interviews passed through a two-step thematic analysis process.

The first step was aimed to identify daughters' professional expectations before entering the FB. To this end, transcribed interviews were analysed in order to identify daughters' professional goals. The authors read the empirical material independently and categorized the stream of words into meaningful categories, relating them to the research question. Patterns of meaning associated to each category were then identified and labelled, to create second-order themes (Miles et al., 2014). In cases of disagreement in the coding between the authors, the material was jointly reanalysed and themes were discussed to reach a consensus. The final data structure, with representative data and themes, is presented in Table 6.2. This first stage identified three groups of goals that the interviewed daughters pursued regarding their career. Next, the daughters' goals were crossed with their actual roles in their FB. This resulted in a 2 x 2 matrix, where four daughters' profiles were identified, corresponding to different combinations between ambitions and actual roles in their FB (Figure 6.1).

A second phase of analysis was necessary in order to answer research questions that had not been identified at the beginning of the research, since they were raised by results of the first phase. In particular, we wondered what the reasons were that led some daughters to accept a role that was inconsistent with their original goals. To answer these questions, their interviews underwent a second phase of coding, carried out as described in the first phase. The resulting data structure is presented in Table 6.3.

In the following sections, each step of the interviews' analysis is analytically described, along with the intermediate results obtained during this process. Finally, the daughters' profiles emerging from such analysis are labelled, described and discussed, together with reasons behind situations of misalignment between daughters' expectations and their role actually played in FBs.

Table 6.2   Daughters' goals and professional ambitions

Representative data	Goals and professional ambitions
'Since I was very young, my idea was "I want to work with Dad"' (Vicky)	Take on the leadership of the FB
'I grew up here, and when I was a baby I could see myself in this role. It's a part of me, it was all very natural' (Marcie)	
'From the beginning I hoped to take the place of my father at the helm of the company' (Titty)	
'I would have so much wanted to run the company' (Keira)	
'I didn't care to lead the company. Doing my job is enough for me [. . .] I've carved out my own space [. . .] I have time for my family and also some free time' (Vanessa)	Work in the FB with a minor role
'I'm happy that my brother led the company. I've two kids [. . .] I need time for my family' (Diane)	
'I wanted to become an interpreter and I was attending a degree in oriental languages' (Sylvia)	Have a professional career outside the FB
'I was studying geology. I had never thought about working in the family business' (Helen)	

FINDINGS

The Daughters' Expectations and Experience (Mis)match

Three groups of professional goals pursued by the selected daughters before entering their FB were identified (Table 6.2):

- succeed their parents and take on the leadership of the FB;
- work in the FB with a minor role, less demanding and with less responsibilities compared to the entrepreneurial role;
- pursue other career paths, outside of the FB.

The analysis in Table 6.2 presented our first important finding: not all daughters are interested in taking on the leadership of the FB. In fact, some daughters, while willing and keen to work in the FB, do not have leadership ambitions. They think of FB as an opportunity because it offers

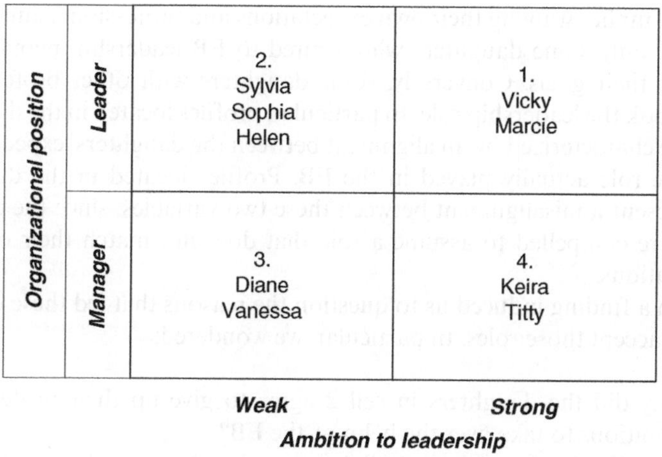

		Weak	Strong
Organizational position	*Leader*	2. Sylvia Sophia Helen	1. Vicky Marcie
	Manager	3. Diane Vanessa	4. Keira Titty

Weak   **Strong**

Ambition to leadership

Figure 6.1   Daughters' professional ambitions and actual roles in FBs

a satisfactory job with less responsibility, therefore allowing them to have enough time for their private life. Other daughters do not aspire to work in the FB and wish to pursue an independent professional career.

As our aim was to know whether the daughters' role in their FB is consistent with their professional ambitions, a 2 x 2 matrix (Figure 6.1) was created by combining together the following variables:

1. *Daughters' ambition to assume the FB leadership.* Based on the findings from the interviews, we made a distinction between *strong* and *weak ambition* to take on a top leadership position. We classified as daughters with *strong ambition* those who explicitly expressed the desire to lead the FB, while those without such an ambition were classified as *weak ambition* daughters, because they prefer a minor role in the FB, or desire to work outside of the FB.
2. *Organisational role daughters actually play* in the FB. Considering that daughters can hold roles characterized by different responsibility and power, we made a distinction between *leadership roles* and *managerial roles*. The term 'managerial role' is here used to identify various organizational positions, with decision-making power, but overall with less responsibility and power than the 'leadership role'.

Each cell in Figure 6.1 represents a different combination of daughters' expectations and their actual roles. Based on its characteristics, each case was associated to a specific cell. This matrix allowed us to note that not all daughters are able to achieve their goals and for some of them entering the FB implies waiving their own expectations and professional ambitions. In fact, only some daughters who aspired to FB leadership managed to achieve their goals. Conversely, some daughters with other professional goals took the leadership role. In particular, profiles located in the diagonal 1–3 are characterized by an alignment between the daughters' expectations and the role actually played in the FB. Profiles located in the diagonal 2–4 present a misalignment between these two variables, since the daughters were compelled to assume a role that does not match their original expectations.

Such a finding induced us to question the reasons that led these daughters to accept those roles. In particular, we wondered:

1. Why did the daughters in cell 2 agree to give up their professional ambitions to take over the helm of the FB?
2. Why did the daughters in cell 4 agree to continue working in the FB, content with a less important role, thus putting aside their dream of leading the FB?

The second phase of thematic analysis identified the reasons behind the daughters' decision to accept their actual role (Table 6.3).

The results, as a whole, allowed us to label the cells previously identified and gave rise to a typology of daughters' profiles with particular emphasis on reasons for misalignment (Figure 6.2).

These profiles – in terms of distinctive characteristics, daughters' professional goals and ambitions, opinions/perceptions about their actual role and reasons for misalignment – are described and discussed in the following section, along with excerpts from the interviews and stories of interviewed daughters.[1] These testimonies are useful to better understand the meaning that daughters give to their role and to identify critical issues associated with their experiences. Proper names and details have been altered for privacy reasons.

Daughters' Profiles

Leaders by choice
'Leaders by choice' are daughters who have taken over the leadership of the FB, achieving their goals and fulfilling a dream. Often leaders by choice have desired, since they were young, to follow in their father's footsteps and take the helm of the FB. They have clearly always had their future in the company in mind and tried to prepare as much as possible to gain the necessary skills. Their strong interest in the FB stems from the deep bond with their parents, especially their father, often seen as a model to follow.

Table 6.3   Reasons for misalignment between daughters' expectations and actual role in the FB

Representative data	Reasons
Compelled leader (Cell 2)	
'I was worried about the future of the company' (Helen)	Need to ensure FB continuity
'I finally chose the company. I did it for my mother and my family' (Sylvia)	Moral obligation
'My father suddenly died. I couldn't leave my mother alone with the company' (Sophia)	Gratitude and loyalty toward parents and family
'My grandfather had created it, and my father had devoted his entire life to the company. I didn't feel like giving up everything' (Helen)	
'In the beginning, I had to make myself like it. I knew that my family was counting on me' (Sylvia)	Desire not to disappoint family's expectations
Compelled manager (Cell 4)	
'My priority was the continuity of the family business' (Titty)	Desire to contribute to FB continuity
'My main concern now is that my brother and I get on well and share the same vision of the firm, as family unit is more important' (Titty)	Strong attachment to the family
'This didn't surprise me' (Titty) 'It is natural that it is so' (Keira)	Awareness that brother/sister division of roles cannot be questioned
'I accepted my father's decision' (Titty) 'I was forced to do it. My father put me to do that' (Keira)	Respect for father's decision

This, for example is Vicky's experience. She got a degree in economics and worked as an accountant for three years before joining the FB. After a period of training in the company, she began working alongside her father, with growing power and responsibility. Her father retired after a few years and Vicky took the leadership role. Her words clearly reveal Vicky's admiration for her father and her desire to follow in his steps:

I have a sister, Valery, and a 'brother': the product created by my father. When he started the business I was a kid, so I was growing up with this business. I was

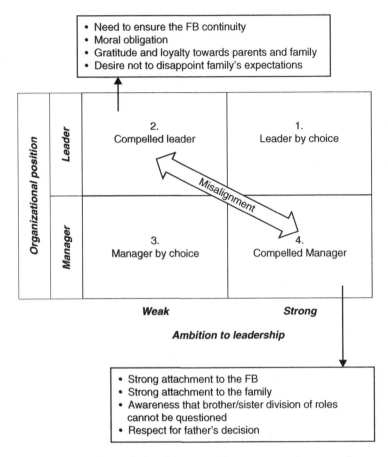

Figure 6.2   A typology of daughters' profiles in FBs and reasons for misalignment

always with Dad [. . .] Since I was very young, my idea was 'I want to work with Dad.' And I made all my choices based on the idea of working in our FB.

Marcie is the current leader of a small FB. Her experience is similar to that of Vicky's. After taking a degree in marketing, she joined the FB and started a period of training, working in various business departments. She succeeded her father several years later. Marcie has always desired to work with him and in her words strong ties with the FB also emerge:

I'm the daughter of an entrepreneur who has always owned a factory. I grew up here, and when I was a baby I could see myself in this role. It's a part of me, it was all very natural.

These cases clearly show that, for 'leaders by choice', leading the FB is the ultimate goal of a process that they have tenaciously pursued, attracted by the desire to be the new leader of their business. Some main factors allowed them to fulfil their ambitions:

- support and esteem from their parents, who strongly believed in the ability of their daughters and promoted their involvement and their legitimacy in the company;
- their solid preparation and qualification;
- their deep bond with their parents and with the FB.

However, we noted that there were no males present in younger generations. Vicky only has a sister, who joined the company but preferred a minor role, without entrepreneurial responsibilities. Marcie is an only child. They did not need to compete with anyone else.

Compelled leaders
'Compelled leaders' became entrepreneurs not by ambition, but for the need to ensure FB continuity, since no other family members were concerned or likely to lead the company. They were sometimes forced by unforeseen circumstances, which 'pushed' them to assume the leadership, even though they aspired to have a career outside of the FB. Sometimes their role is the result of choices made under conditions of highly emotional involvement, which forces them to give up their own goals and replace their predecessor, who is seriously ill or has prematurely died. This is Sylvia's case. She succeeded her mother at the helm of their hotel after her mother's premature death:

> I wanted to become an interpreter and I was working towards a degree in oriental languages when my mother was ill. In just a few months, I had to decide: sell everything or take the situation into my own hands. My brother had just started another career and he wasn't interested in the firm at all. I had taken a different road but I decided to give up my studies and take over the hotel. I found myself in the middle of a building site, with two gigantic mortgages to be paid. I had the strong feeling that I didn't really know where to start. Today I'm very devoted to the firm, but in the beginning I had to make myself like it.

Sylvia's decision was strongly influenced by the emotions provoked by her mother's death. She felt torn between her professional ambitions and her desire to respect her ailing mother's wishes. In the end, she said that she felt 'entangled into the situation' and chose the company for her mother and her family.

Sophia was also forced suddenly to abandon her studies, and enter the

FB after her father's death. Sophia's mother remained alone with three daughters and took over the firm. Sophia, the eldest daughter, was forced to begin working with her and later took on the company's leadership.

As shown by these cases, 'compelled leaders' are the result of forced choices, not because they were coercively imposed, but because they stemmed from a 'moral obligation'. Daughters in this group suffered from the idea of closing or selling the company. They showed a strong loyalty towards their family and a great gratitude towards their father/mother.

Such an attitude is clear in Helen's story. She worked as a geologist for some years, without any interest in the FB. When Helen realized that her brother and sister were not suitable to lead the FB she began to worry about its future, thinking back to her career choices. She decided to give up her professional activity and joined the firm. Her main concern was the survival of the FB, since her grandfather had created it and he and her father had dedicated their lives to it.

These stories recount the forced choices made in great emergency or need, mainly caused by the daughters' sense of responsibility towards their families and their desire not to disappoint their parents' expectations, to the point of giving up their ambitions and career aspirations.

Managers by choice

Daughters in this group show no leadership ambition. They work in the FB with task roles, characterized by limited power and responsibility (for example, accounting manager, marketing manager) and have spontaneously left the leadership to their siblings. 'Managers by choice' see the FB as an opportunity to do a job consistent with their studies and professional interests, while also having free time for their private and family life, which they consider as equally or more important.

Diane, for example, works in her FB as chief of the legal office. She got a degree in law, got married the day after graduation and in a few years had two children. A few years later, Diane joined the FB where her elder brother Daniel was employed as chief buyer. Currently, Diane is in charge of the legal office and heads up HR. The company's ownership was equally divided between brother and sister, but Daniel will be the future leader. Diane agreed with this solution, as it allows her to spend time with her family and cultivate her interests.

Vanessa, after graduating in law, practised as a lawyer. Years after, her needs changed because of the family, so she decided to join the FB, in charge of the legal office. When her father passed the leadership to Vanessa's older sister, Vanessa was pleased because she has never cared to lead the FB. She desired a rewarding profession, but her unquestioned priority was time for her family:

When I was younger, I didn't think about working in the FB. Then I got married, had a child, and said to myself: 'Let's try it.' I didn't care about leading the company. Doing my job is enough for me. Now I'm happy. I've carved out my own space. I'm satisfied with my work. I have time for my family and also some free time.

Vanessa and Diane both work in the FB without a leadership role, but they do not see their position as a waiver or as exclusion. On the contrary, they feel reassured by the presence of another family member at the helm of the company and are both satisfied with their role, as it allows them to satisfy their professional ambitions and have a good work–life balance.

Compelled managers

This group includes daughters who desired to take on the leadership of the FB but were forced to give up their ambitions and to be content with a minor role, leaving the company's leadership to another family member, typically male. Daughters in this position work in the FB as a manager or play the role of co-leader, a component of the entrepreneurial teams, with other siblings. In this case, however, another family member has the role of official leader, often a brother. This is Titty's experience. She joined the firm immediately after graduating, in order to help her father who was very ill. A few years later, her brother also joined the firm. Titty began to head up HR, while her brother headed up sales and marketing. They worked together for over 20 years but when their father retired, he left the leadership to Titty's brother. She accepted the role as co-leader – an important role, although it was subordinate to her brother – because of her great concern for the family unit and her strong desire to personally contribute to the continuity of the FB:

> I accepted my father's decision. It didn't surprise me. I accepted a supporting role. My main concern now is that my brother and I get along well and share the same vision for the firm, as the family unit is more important.

'Compelled managers' consider their secondary role in the FB as a waiver, because they know that their dreams will never come true. However, it also reflects the daughters' awareness that their brother's leadership cannot be questioned. They know that the division of roles between brother and sister is a compromise, often tacit, between predecessors and heirs and that it is the only possible solution. Keira seems to be very aware of this and says: 'it is natural that it is so'. She has an elder brother and she joined the firm when she was 20, after receiving a diploma in accounting. Since then she has always handled the finance and accounting office. This was a choice that was practically forced upon her because that was what everyone, her father above all, expected from her:

> I was forced to do it. I was forced to make that choice. It is easier to see a woman working in accounting. So my father gave me that job. First, he demanded I attended a technical high school. Then he forced me to manage the accounts.

Keira's brother succeeded their father and she regrets not having the leadership role, because even if she is her brother's 'right-hand man' and shares the important decisions with him, she has a subordinate role.

Compelled managers accept this role because of their strong attachment to family and the FB. The latter is considered a family asset, not only from a financial point of view, but also as a legacy of culture, traditions and values, and is considered an integral part of family identity. In the name of this objective, considered a priority, they accepted their parents' choices, and in the end they really think that 'this is the right thing to do' (Titty).

DISCUSSION AND CONCLUSIONS

The issue of daughters in FB succession has received an increasing amount of attention during the last decades (Jimenez, 2009; Wang, 2010; Gupta and Levenburg, 2013). Several scholars have analysed intentions, motivations and reasons why daughters choose (or not) to join their FB and to realize a career from within (Gatewood et al., 2003; Zellweger et al., 2011; Schröder and Schmitt-Rodermund, 2013; Dawson et al., 2015). Other research has examined the different roles that daughters may assume within the FB (Curimbaba, 2002; Cesaroni and Sentuti, 2014), including conditions that may facilitate (or hinder) taking on the leadership (Wang, 2010). However, an analysis of the daughters' expectations and experience (mis)match is missing.

This chapter has investigated the role that daughters may assume within the FB, trying to understand whether they have the chance to actually play a role consistent with their previous goals and ambitions or not. We have identified four daughters' profiles, based on the alignment/misalignment between daughters' expectations and experience. Finally, we have analysed reasons behind daughters' decision to accept a role inconsistent with their previous goals.

This study makes several important contributions. First, our analysis combines daughters' expectations and experience and, to our knowledge, we are the first to directly compare these two dimensions. Evidence shows that alignment between daughters' expectations and roles played in the FB is not always possible. In other words, not all daughters' dreams come true. In some cases, daughters who aspired to take on the leadership had to accept a minor role, mainly because – according to Ahrens et al. (2015) – gender preferences in favour of male family heirs still persist; and growing up with this awareness seems to persuade daughters to accept their subordinate role with conscious resignation. In other cases, daughters became leaders 'despite themselves', because no other family members were concerned or likely to lead the FB (Wang, 2010). In both cases, daughters accepted a role inconsistent with their previous goals because they were pressured by the family expectations and moral obligation towards their parents or, in the words of Sharma and Irving (2005) and Dawson et al. (2015), by a high normative commitment. Our results highlighted that daughters are characterized by a strong normative commitment. In this perspective, as we come to the second contribution, we found that the normative commitment plays an important role not only as a predictor of daughters' intention to stay in their FB (as affirmed by Dawson et al., 2015) but also as the main reason to give up their dreams and accept a role inconsistent with their previous goals. Although we did not carry out a comparative analysis between daughters and sons, we can suppose that strong normative commitment could also be the case for the sons who are socialized into the company, and have no choice but to accept the FB leadership. So this issue could be an avenue for further research in FB successions.

Third, our analysis indicates that some daughters are satisfied with their secondary position, because it allows them to focus on their family and interests. This result gives rise to conflicting reflections. On one hand, it suggests that the marginal role of daughters in FBs is not always the result of gender discrimination: daughters are not always 'victims' of stereotyping, forced to operate in a secondary position, but sometimes voluntarily choose a limited involvement. Contrastingly, this result could be the effect of a difference between the socialization of sons and daughters in the FB. It is widely recognized that when both genders are represented among younger generations, daughters are socialized differently and this has been identified as a key factor to the daughters' exclusion from leadership roles (Dumas, 1998; Constantinidis, 2010; Byrne and Fattoum, 2015). Their desire to join (or not) the FB, as well as to play (or not) a leadership role, in fact, could have been formed in a non-completely deliberate and spontaneous way. They may have been influenced by the time they spent in the company during their childhood and by the encouragement, stimuli and suggestions they received from family concerning their future career. These aspects could have indeed been key contributors to the daughters' career choices, and even what seems to be a free choice could be affected by gender differences in socialization.

On a practical level, these results draw FB owners' attention to advocate more support for daughter succession, in order to avoid 'sub-optimal choices of successors' (Wang, 2010). A greater awareness of these issues could help predecessors to better plan the career of younger generations, helping daughters to use their talent. Our findings suggest that it is also crucial to sensitize predecessors to consider daughters as potential successors and rethink socialization and leadership selection processes as a means to favour a change within FBs toward gender equality. At the same time, according to Dawson et al. (2015), 'it may be wise for family firm owners to proceed cautiously before attempting to create a sense of obligation in family members that [. . .] may inadvertently make them feel trapped in the firm'. On the contrary, predecessors should promote affective commitment in successors 'by supporting their psychological needs for competence, autonomy, and relatedness within the FB' (McMullen and Warnick, 2015).

This chapter has several limitations. First, this analysis is based on case studies. Consequently, results allow for analytical generalization but they are not statistically generalizable (Yin, 2003). Second, we selected cases from one single country. This choice limited opportunities to illuminate the relevant impact of cultural factors on daughters' ambitions and roles in the FBs. Future research should compare daughters' expectations and experiences across countries. Third, the daughters' expectations and experience (mis)match should be better analysed with longitudinal research. We recommend future research on this topic through the adoption of this method in order to verify how and why daughters' motivations/ambitions/reasons, their involvement in the FBs and their combinations change over time. Also a comparison between sons and daughters is suggested. Fourth, we did not consider daughters who were completely excluded from succession, without any role in the FB. Future research should include these daughters in order to better understand their goals and ambitions and the reasons behind their exclusion. Finally, quantitative studies could verify the relationship between daughters' expectations and experience in FBs and the factors that may affect their alignment/misalignments over time.

NOTE

1. The daughters involved in our research are not native English speakers. To ensure that verbatim quotations reported in the chapter properly reflect the meaning intended by the daughters interviewed, a native English speaker translated the interviews.

REFERENCES

Ahrens, J.P., A. Landmann and M. Woywode (2015), 'Gender preferences in the CEO successions of family firms: family characteristics and human capital of the successor', *Journal of Family Business Strategy*, **6** (2), 86–103.

Al-Dajani, H., Z. Bika, L. Collins and J. Swail (2014), 'Gender and FB: new theoretical directions', *International Journal of Gender and Entrepreneurship*, **6** (3), 218–30.

Aronoff, C.E. (1998), 'Megatrends in family business', *Family Business Review*, **11** (3), 181–5.

Barrett, M. and K. Moores (2009), *Women in Family Business Leadership Roles: Daughters on the Stage*, Cheltenham, UK: Edward Elgar.

Barrett, M. and K. Moores (2011), 'Australia: the challenge of father–daughter succession in family business: a case study from the land down under', in D. Halkias, P.W. Thurman, C. Smith and R.S. Nason (eds), *Father Daughter Succession in Family Business: A Cross-Cultural Perspective*, England: Gower Publishing, pp.285–93.

Byrne, J. and S. Fattoum (2015), 'The gendered nature of family business succession: case studies from France', in R. Blackburn, U. Hytti and F. Welter (eds), *Context, Process and Gender in Entrepreneurship: Frontiers in European Entrepreneurship Research*, Cheltenham, UK: Edward Elgar, pp.127–52.

Cesaroni, F.M. and A. Sentuti (2014), 'Women and family businesses: when women are left only minor roles', *The History of the Family*, **19** (3), 358–79.

Cole, P.M. (1997), 'Women in family business', *Family Business Review*, **10** (4), 353–71.

Constantinidis, C. (2010), 'Entreprise familiale et genre', *Revue française de gestion*, **1**, 143–59.

Constantinidis, C. and A. Cornet (2008), 'Daughters taking over the family business: a gender analysis', 31st ISBE Conference, Conference CD, Belfast, North Ireland, 5–7 November.

Corbetta, G. and A. Minichilli (2010), *Osservatorio AUB*, II° Rapporto Aidaf-Unicredit-Bocconi.

Corbetta, G., A. Minichilli and F. Quarato (2011), *Osservatorio AUB*, III° Rapporto Aidaf-Unicredit-Bocconi.

Curimbaba, F. (2002), 'The dynamics of women's roles as family business managers', *Family Business Review*, **15** (3), 239–52.

Dawson, A., P. Sharma, P.G. Irving, J. Marcus and F. Chirico (2015), 'Predictors of later-generation family members' commitment to family enterprises', *Entrepreneurship Theory and Practice*, **39** (3), 545–69.

Dumas, C. (1989), 'Understanding of father–daughter and father–son dyads in family-owned businesses', *Family Business Review*, **2** (1), 31–46.

Dumas, C. (1992), 'Integrating the daughter into family business management', *Entrepreneurship Theory and Practice*, **16** (4), 41–56.

Dumas, C. (1998), 'Women's pathways to participation and leadership in the family-owned firm', *Family Business Review*, **11** (3), 219–28.

Dumas, C. (2011), 'How did all this get started?', in D. Halkias, P.W. Thurman, C. Smith and R.S. Nason (eds), *Father–Daughter Succession in Family Business: A Cross-Cultural Perspective*, England: Gower Publishing, pp.9–14.

Eisenhardt, K.M. (1989), 'Building theories from case study research', *Academy of Management Review*, **14** (4), 532–50.

Eisenhardt, K.M. and M.E. Graebner (2007), 'Theory building from cases: opportunities and challenges', *Academy of Management Journal*, **50** (1), 25–32.

Emerson, R.M. (2004), 'Working with "key incidents"', in C. Seale, G. Gobo, J.F. Gubrium and D. Silverman (eds), *Qualitative Research Practice*, London, UK: Sage.

Francis, A.E. (1999), *The Daughter Also Rises: How Women Overcome Obstacles and Advance in the Family-owned Business*, San Francisco, USA: Rudi.

García-Álvarez, E., J. López-Sintas and P.S. Gonzalvo (2002), 'Socialization patterns of successor in first- to second-generation family businesses', *Family Business Review*, **15** (3), 189–204.

Gatewood, E., N. Carter, C. Brush, P. Greene and M. Hart (2003), *Women Entrepreneurs, Their Ventures, and the Venture Capital Industry: An Annotated Bibliography*, Stockholm, Sweden: ESBRI.

Gersick, K.E., I. Lansberg, M. Desjardins and B. Dunn (1999), 'Stages and transitions: managing change in the family business', *Family Business Review*, **12** (4), 287–97.

Gnan, L. and D. Montemerlo (2008), *Le PMI familiari in Italia tra tradizione e novità*, Milano, Italy: Egea.

Gupta, V. and N.M. Levenburg (2013). 'Women in family business: three generations of research', in K. Smyrnios, P. Poutziouris and S. Goel (eds), *Handbook of Research on Family Business*, Cheltenham, UK: Edward Elgar, pp.346–67.

Haberman, H. and S.M. Danes (2007), 'Father–daughter and father–son family business management transfer comparison: family FIRO model application', *Family Business Review*, **20** (2), 163–84.

Jimenez, R.M. (2009), 'Research on women in family firms: current status and future directions', *Family Business Review*, **22** (1), 53–64.

Lee, D.S., G.H. Lim and W.S. Lim (2003), 'Family business succession: appropriation risk and choice of successor', *Academy of Management Review*, **28** (4), 657–66.

Litz, R. (1997), 'The family firm's exclusion from business school research: explaining the void; addressing the opportunity', *Entrepreneurship Theory and Practice*, **21** (3), 55–71.

Martin, L. (2001), 'More jobs for the boys? Succession planning in SMEs', *Women in Management Review*, **16** (5), 222–31.

MassMutual (2010), *Kennesaw State University and Family Firm Institute, American Family Business Survey*, Springfield, MA: Massachusetts Mutual Life Insurance Company.

Miles, M.B. and A.M. Huberman (1994), *Qualitative Data Analysis: An Expanded Sourcebook*, London, UK: Sage.

Miles, M.B., A.M. Huberman and J. Saldana (2014), *Qualitative Data Analysis: A Methods Sourcebook*, 3rd edn, London, UK: Sage.

McMullen, J.S. and B.J. Warnick (2015), 'To nurture or groom? The parent-founder succession dilemma', *Entrepreneurship Theory and Practice*, **39** (6), 1379–412.

Nordqvist, M., A. Hall and L. Melin (2009), 'Qualitative research on family businesses: the relevance and usefulness of the interpretive approach', *Journal of Management and Organization*, **15** (3), 294–308.

Patton, M.Q. (2002), *Qualitative Research & Evaluation Methods*, Thousand Oaks, CA, USA: Sage.

Qu, S.D. and J. Dumay (2011), 'The qualitative research interview', *Qualitative Research in Accounting & Management*, **8** (3), 238–64.

Salganicoff, M. (1990), 'Women in family business: challenges and opportunities', *Family Business Review*, **3** (2), 125–37.

Schröder, E. and E. Schmitt-Rodermund (2013), 'Antecedents and consequences of adolescents' motivations to join the family business', *Journal of Vocational Behavior*, **83** (3), 476–85.

Schröder, E., E. Schmitt-Rodermund and N. Arnaud (2011), 'Career choice intentions of adolescents with a family business background', *Family Business Review*, **24** (4), 305–21.

Sharma, P. and P.G. Irving (2005), 'Four bases of family business successor commitment: antecedents and consequences', *Entrepreneurship Theory and Practice*, **29** (1), 13–33.

Smythe, J. and S.R. Sardeshmukh (2013), 'Fathers and daughters in family business', *Small Enterprise Research*, **20** (2), pp.98–109.

Vera, C.F. and M.A Dean (2005), 'An examination of the challenges daughters face in family business succession', *Family Business Review*, **18** (4), 321–45.

Wang, C. (2010), 'Daughter exclusion in family business succession: a review of the literature', *Journal of Family and Economic Issues*, **31** (4), 475–84.

WEF (2015), 'Global Gender Gap Report 2015'.

Yin, R. (2003), *Applications of Case Study Research*, London, UK: Sage.

Zellweger, T., P. Sieger and F. Halter (2011), 'Should I stay or should I go? Career choice intentions of students with family business background', *Journal of Business Venturing*, **26** (5), 521–36.

7. Building dynamic capabilities – chairperson's leadership, knowledge and experience in SMEs

Daniel Yar Hamidi

INTRODUCTION

Innovation is central to growth and competitiveness for small and medium-sized enterprises (Love and Roper, 2015; Parrilli and Elola, 2012), while firms' capabilities to innovate are more important than ever in order for firms to survive in the current competitive global markets (Covin and Slevin, 1991; Zahra and Covin, 1995; Huse et al., 2005b). It is argued that firms' abilities to innovate can best be implemented by developing dynamic capabilities within the firm (Katkalo et al., 2010; Teece, 2014; Teece et al., 1997; Augier and Teece, 2009; Eisenhardt and Martin, 2000; Teece, 2012). Dynamic capability is defined as higher-level competences that determine the firm's ability to integrate, build and reconfigure internal and external resources/competences to address, and possibly shape, rapidly changing business environments (Teece and Freeman, 1990; Teece et al., 2012; Teece et al., 1997). While the importance of the ability to innovate is a well-established fact in research on firms in general, it is even more critical for small and medium-sized enterprises (SMEs) to develop and maintain these abilities (Borch and Huse, 1993; Brunninge et al., 2007).

SMEs are characterized by inherent constraints with respect to resources and capabilities. SMEs generally employ fewer people, possess fewer resources and operate in fewer markets (Mazzarol and Reboud, 2009). These characteristics are often predicted to create size disadvantages, usually referred to as 'liabilities of smallness', which in turn create difficulties for SMEs in securing staff and financial capital (Winborg and Landstrom, 2001). As a consequence, SMEs suffer from the inability to capture economies of scale and bargaining power with key stakeholders (Strotmann, 2007) and are notoriously vulnerable to changes in their environment (Blake and Saleh, 1992).

A growing number of scholars are studying the role and effect of SMEs' boards of directors on strategy development and the encouragement of innovation (Neville, 2011; Gabrielsson, 2007; Brunninge et al., 2007). In this context, the board is seen as an important governance mechanism that can influence and add to the governance and performance of the firm (Neville, 2011). Further, research suggests that SMEs can benefit from active board work when it comes to a number of strategic issues such as building trust and extending the firm's strategic networks (Borch and Huse, 1993), discovering and exploiting new market opportunities (Borch et al., 1999; Zahra et al., 2000) and building and establishing organizational processes that support and encourage innovation, business renewal and strategic change (Zahra et al., 2000; Brunninge et al., 2007; Borch et al., 1999). These processes and actions, when embedded in firms, determine the firms' dynamic capabilities (Eisenhardt and Martin, 2000). Thus, there seems to be general consensus on the impact of an effective board of directors on setting small firms' strategic direction and thereby contributing to firms' long-term development and value-creation (Fiegener, 2005; Knockaert et al., 2015; Huse, 2000) while building firms' dynamic capabilities.

The creation of effective boards is, however, about creating well-functioning teams, at the apex of the firm's organization, that are responsible for decision making and control (Brunninge et al., 2007; Fama and Jensen, 1983). In trying to answer questions about antecedents for board effectiveness, scholars have been increasingly paying attention to board processes and board-member behaviours rather than structural aspects of the board (Forbes and Milliken, 1999; Finkelstein and Mooney, 2003). By focusing on board processes and, more specifically, on chairperson leadership and qualifications, this study investigates the effects of chairperson leadership, knowledge and experience on firms' abilities to build dynamic capabilities. Very few studies have examined the role of board leadership in SMEs, despite the fact that globally the majority of firms are small and medium-sized enterprises (ACCA, 2010).

Furthermore, the extant research on board leadership usually leans towards exploring the antecedents for, and outcomes of, structural leadership characteristics, such as CEO-duality (Daily and Dalton, 1992b; Daily and Dalton, 1993; Yar Hamidi and Gabrielsson, 2012), without considering board processes and board chairpersons' actual behaviour and qualifications (Huse and Gabrielsson, 2012; Gabrielsson et al., 2007). This chapter thus adds to this body of knowledge in at least three ways. First, it is an answer to the call for using primary data, rather than relying on archival data as has often been the case in extant research on boards of directors (Daily et al., 2003; Huse, 2000). By using first-hand survey data on chairperson leadership, knowledge and experience, this chapter moves from using archival data about structural aspects of board leadership to focus on the actual work of chairpersons of boards and its effect on boards' work and abilities to develop firms' dynamic capabilities. Second, in contrast to the main body of research on boards of directors, which often considers the boards from an external perspective, this chapter applies alternative theoretical perspectives to the prevailing agency theory by using the resource-dependency perspective to interpret the effect of board leadership. Board leadership is defined as the leadership exerted by the chairperson of the board. Third, this chapter is considered a response to the call for more theoretical and empirical research on board leadership in SMEs, and as such will furnish practitioners with applicable knowledge about board leadership in small and medium-sized enterprises.

The remainder of the chapter is structured as follows. Following a brief introduction to the relevant literature on the perspectives applied in this study, the theoretical approach of the study will be presented and hypotheses to be examined are developed. The following section will present the sample and discuss methodological choices, including variable measurements, data collection and the analysis method. Next, following the presentation of the results, a discussion about their implications for research and practice and suggestions for further research will conclude the chapter.

THEORETICAL BACKGROUND AND HYPOTHESES

Governance of Firms

Corporate governance has been researched in many fields of scholarly work and from various theoretical perspectives. During the 1970s and the early 1980s, a tradition of managerial hegemony dominated the debate on corporate governance and the role of boards of directors (Wolfson, 1984; Herman, 1982). This perspective perceived boards of directors primarily as serving managerial interests in their pursuit of organization-wide corporate goals and objectives, and considered boards primarily as 'ornaments on the corporate tree' whose relevance was limited to a purely legalistic perspective (Mace, 1971). Since the late 1980s, two other perspectives have been emerging and dominating the corporate governance debate: these are the shareholder supremacy and stakeholder perspectives.

The shareholder supremacy perspective, supported mainly by agency theoretic influences (Jensen and Meckling, 1976; Fama and Jensen, 1983), argues that boards are elected to be agents in the service of shareholders, and thus should be independent against managerial influences. Value-creation in the firm and from a board perspective is about maximizing shareholder returns and the close monitoring of managers to enable the distribution of value created in the firm to the shareholders. However, the agency theoretical perspective has not been without criticisms (Huse, 2005a; Huse, 2005b; Daily et al., 2003; Roberts et al., 2005). One important weakness of the large body of research using agency theory is the over-looking of younger entrepreneurial companies that struggle with liabilities of newness and smallness (Zahra and Filatotchev, 2004), and the misfit of some key assumptions of agency theory when applied to the context of small and medium-sized enterprises (Huse, 2005b; Forbes and Milliken, 1999), such as the fact that in many cases ownership and management coincide in the same individuals (Nordqvist and Melin, 2002) and the agency problem as conceived by agency theory is absent.

The recent attention to stakeholder perspectives in the research on boards of directors (Huse and Rindova, 2001; Sacconi, 2007) is a reaction to the dominant prevalence of the shareholder supremacy perspective in corporate governance research. Stakeholder perspectives generally argue that the survival and success of a firm depend on the firm's ability to create value for all stakeholders (Jawahar and McLaughlin, 2001) – not only the shareholders. Boards are thus accountable to a broad variety of stake-holders, which includes the shareholders as a group, and must continually assess which stakeholders are the most important for the firm at each stage of the firm's development and keep them engaged in the firm's business (Jawahar and McLaughlin, 2001).

Both of these views have a firm external perspective and focus on how actors external to the firm (such as shareholders and external stakehold-ers) can benefit from the work of the board of directors. This leaves the firm internal perspective on boards and governance with limited scholarly attention in the extant research on boards of directors. This chapter is concerned with how boards and their members contribute to firms' value-creation by building dynamic capabilities in the firm. Value-creation con-cerns the whole value chain, and thus goes beyond measures of earnings or firms' financial performance, and includes a larger set of parameters, such as innovation and the development of firms' resources (Huse et al., 2005a). Building firms' capabilities is about developing a set of current or potential activities that use the firm's resources effectively to make and/or deliver products and services (Teece, 2014). It is within this firm internal perspective that we find most of the strategic management literature on boards of directors. Examples are the resource-dependency theory (Pfeffer and Salancik, 1978; Hillman and Dalziel, 2003) and the resource-based view of the firm (Zahra and Filatotchev, 2004). Nevertheless, these theor-ies do not explicitly discuss the role of the board of directors in strategic decision-making towards innovation in the firm; boards are seen rather as a resource or as resource providers to the firm.

This chapter aims theoretically and empirically to balance firm internal and external perspectives on the work and leadership of the board by building on and extending the prevailing agency theory in an empirical setting relevant to the SME context. This will advance our understanding of the effects of board leadership on developing small firms' dynamic capabilities. More precisely, I will draw on resource-dependency theory (Pfeffer and Salancik, 1978; Hillman et al., 2000; Hillman and Dalziel, 2003) and dynamic capabilities (Augier and Teece, 2009; Katkalo et al., 2010; Teece, 2014; Teece et al., 1997; Eisenhardt and Martin, 2000) to examine the effects of board leadership on SMEs' abilities to create dynamic capabilities and to innovate.

Boards in Small Firms: a Resource-dependency Perspective

Research on boards of directors has often had its focus on large public companies and has predominantly used an agency theoretical perspective (Huse, 2005b; Daily et al., 2003; Yar Hamidi and Gabrielsson, 2014). However, when relaxing some of the core assumptions of agency theory and the context of large public corporations, such as the perception of managerial opportunism and the separation of control and ownership (Fama, 1980; Fama and Jensen, 1983; Jensen and Meckling, 1976), we will need alternative theoretical perspectives to explain the governance of small and medium-sized enterprises and board behaviours (Roberts et al., 2005; Machold et al., 2011). Challenging and relaxing some of agency theory's basic assumptions might lead to new research traditions and new perspectives on research on boards and corporate governance (Huse et al., 2011a). An alternative and appropriate theoretical perspective in this context is the resource-dependency theory as presented by Pfeffer and Salancik (1978).

The resource-dependency perspective focuses on boards' use of their human and social capital in the provision of resources to the firm and includes a variety of activities, including providing advice and counsel, bringing legitimacy and providing access to important constituents outside the firm, serving as channels of communication between the firm and its environment and aiding the management in strategy formulation (Pfeffer and Salancik, 1978). This perspective is widely adopted by stakeholder traditions (Hillman and Dalziel, 2003).

The concept of board capital as the sum of human and social capital of board directors, and as a representation of the board's ability to provide resources to the firm and to engage in board activities, was introduced by Hillman and Dalziel (2003). Board capital and utilizing it are central aspects in the resource-dependency perspective discussing boards of directors.

In the SME context – where overlap between management and ownership, a lack of a formalized managerial structure (Brunninge and Nordqvist, 2004) and a greater need to bring critical resources to the firm (Cowling, 2003) are conditions that must be considered – the resource-dependency perspective and the board capital construct are appropriate perspectives to adopt in order to understand boards' and directors' contributions to building dynamic capabilities in the firm.

Board Leadership and Building Dynamic Capabilities

The fundamental question for firms and research on firms is how firms can achieve and sustain competitive advantages (Teece et al., 1997). Winners in the current global market demonstrate timely responsiveness and an ability to innovate, coupled with the capability to co-ordinate internal and external competences. As discussed above, board capital is a proxy for the board's ability to manage its tasks (Haynes and Hillman, 2010). In this context, the chairperson of the board is expected to lead the board and its discussions and develop the board's working processes, in a method characterized by sharing knowledge and opposing viewpoints (Gabrielsson et al., 2007). This might be the most critical resource presented by the board of directors (Forbes and Milliken, 1999; Zahra and Filatotchev, 2004). Board leadership in small firms is likely to be especially visible and important for co-ordinating the board's resources to fulfil its tasks as an effective board (Daily and Dalton, 1992b), capable of developing the firm's dynamic capabilities. To ensure positive board outcomes, the board chairperson is expected to lead the board members to 'meld the board into a cohesive group, and to make each individual director feel that he or she is equal' (Huse, 2007, p.201) in order to realize the full potential of what Haynes and Hillman (2010) refer to as board capital breadth, consisting of occupational, functional and interlocking heterogeneities.

This is about the chairperson's leadership efficacy and the ability to motivate and use each board member's competence in order to utilize the board's capital. The chairperson should lead board discussions (Gabrielsson et al., 2007) and formulate proposals for decisions, while summarizing discussions and constantly working with developing the board's working processes (Neubauer, 1997), as well as preparing well for meetings and working effectively and trustfully with the CEO (Roberts, 2002). Hence, it is expected that the chairperson's leadership efficacy is positively associated with the firm's ability to foster dynamic capabilities. The first hypothesis can thus be formulated as follows:

H1: There is a positive association between chairperson leadership efficacy and building dynamic capabilities in SMEs.

Boards' knowledge and skills are especially important to small firms (Zahra and Filatotchev, 2004). Board members' firm-specific knowledge can be a complement to firms' internal knowledge and the skills base provided by managers, and a cost-efficient way of securing advice and new ideas without hiring external consultants (Machold et al., 2011). Previous research has shown that intra-industry differences in revenues are greater than inter-industry differences in revenues, which strongly suggests the importance of firm-specific factors and the relative unimportance of general industry effects (Rumelt, 1991). What is distinctive about firms is their way of organizing and getting things done based on the competence and capabilities of the firm and its constituencies (Teece et al., 1997).

An important issue for board leadership is ensuring that board members have knowledge relevant to the firm (Forbes and Milliken, 1999; Hillman and Dalziel, 2003). Thus, the chairperson's firm-specific knowledge might be crucial in examining and securing relevant knowledge among board members and also as a means of preventing 'process losses' associated with highly interdependent and episodic teams serving as the boards of directors (Forbes and Milliken, 1999). This is also referred to as the 'gap minding' task of the board chairperson in SMEs (Yar Hamidi, 2016).

While the essence of competences and capabilities is embedded in organizational processes, the content of these processes and the opportunities they can offer for developing competitive advantages are shaped by the assets the firm possesses and the evolutionary path it has adopted (Teece et al., 1997; Teece, 2012). Hence, the chairperson's firm-specific knowledge and an understanding of the firm's evolution are important elements in order to understand and explain the core of the firm's dynamic capabilities and its development of competitive advantages.

Forbes and Milliken (1999) underline two dimensions of knowledge that are most relevant to the board of directors. These are, first, functional area knowledge and skills and, second, firm-specific knowledge and skills. Firm-specific knowledge relates to the information about the firm itself and an intimate understanding of its challenges, operation and managerial issues.

Hence, it is expected that the chairperson's firm-specific knowledge is positively associated with the firm's ability to foster dynamic capabilities. The second hypothesis can therefore be formulated as follows:

H2: There is a positive association between chairperson firm-specific knowledge and building dynamic capabilities in SMEs.

The provision of knowledge and skills may directly affect the firm's value-creating capabilities. This is the case especially if the knowledge and skills are industry-specific, including knowledge of critical technology and the industry's characteristics, competition, features and products, as well as market developments (Kaufman and Englander, 2005). As mentioned, Forbes and Milliken (1999) emphasize two dimensions of knowledge relevant to the board of directors: (1) functional area knowledge and skills; and (2) firm-specific knowledge and skills. Firm-specific knowledge was commented on and discussed above when formulating the second hypothesis. Functional area knowledge and skills, however, comprise and refer to general and traditional domains of business, including marketing and finance, but also to the interaction of the firm with its environment and the logic of the firm's industry. Knowledge and experience from relevant industries and the firm's challenges, relevant networks and information-gathering channels are thus important parts of this knowledge and skill dimension. The chairperson's earlier experience in the firm's industry is therefore expected to be of value in guiding the board's activities towards building dynamic capabilities by accessing resources relevant to the firm (Eisenhardt and Martin, 2000) in the firm's environment.

Further, the chairperson's relevant industry experience and professional competence seem to be a source of legitimacy for the chairperson in his or her position as the leader of the board of directors (Pick, 2007). Hence, it is expected that the chairperson's industry experience is positively associated with building dynamic capabilities in small and medium-sized enterprises. The third hypothesis can thus be formulated as follows:

H3: There is a positive association between chairperson industry experience and building dynamic capabilities in SMEs.

METHODS

Sample and Data Collection

The data set used in this chapter to test the hypotheses is data collected from the Norwegian value-creating board surveys conducted in Norway between 2005 and 2006. The use of this data set is motivated by the demand from previous research for first-hand data and the lack of process data on behavioural aspects of boards of directors in previous research on boards (Forbes and Milliken, 1999; Huse, 2005b). By doing this, the current study avoids using secondary archival data on board structure as a proxy for board processes (Finkelstein and Mooney, 2003). Access to process data has been called one of the major empirical challenges for researchers on boards of directors and corporate governance (Daily et al., 2003); however, the value-creating board-survey data set makes it possible to conduct this study.

The constructs and scales related to behavioural aspects and processes of actual board work in this study have been developed by corporate governance scholars in several countries over many years (Huse, 2007; Huse, 2009; Gabrielsson et al., 2007; Minichilli and Hansen, 2007; Zona and Zattoni, 2007; Pugliese and Wenstop, 2007; van Ees et al., 2008). Using clear questions with simple words and expressions, this survey avoids ambiguous formulations that can lead to misinterpretations (Dillman, 2011). The original survey targeted respondents in different subsets of firms to allow control over contingencies such as industry and firm size. A full review and discussion of the background and development of the Norwegian value-creating board survey can be found in Huse (2009).

In the initial sample frame for this study, the European Community's definition of SMEs is followed as a guideline. The category of SMEs is made up of firms that employ fewer than 250 people and have an annual turnover not exceeding EUR 50 million and/or an annual balance-sheet total not exceeding EUR 43 million (European Commission, 2003). These criteria resulted in an initial sample of 520 firms. However, the current study's research interest in chairperson leadership also requires a board of directors with at least two members. Thus, firms with just one official board member were excluded. Finally, all cases with missing or incomplete data in one or several variables of interest in this study were excluded. The final sample includes 315 cases with complete and accurate data. This corresponds to 60 per cent of the initial sample of SMEs included in the data set.

The Norwegian context is of special interest to this research since SME boards in Norway are traditionally active (Huse, 1990). The corporate governance system in Norway has both differences from and similarities to other countries and contexts (Shleifer and Vishny, 1997). State ownership of companies in Norway is larger than in Anglo-American countries, which gives the state a greater influence in the industry sector (Machold et al., 2011). This is manifested in legislation and high state ownership of publicly held corporations. However, there are also parallels. The Norwegian code of practice for corporate governance shows many similarities to other international codes regarding board structures and the division of responsibilities among boards, shareholders and management (NUES, 2014).

Variables and Measures

Building dynamic capabilities, the dependent variable, is based on a multi-item Likert-type scale to gauge a firm's ability to build dynamic capabilities. In line with Gabrielsson (2007), CEOs are considered the best source of information regarding strategic issues in SMEs in the current study. Consistent with the dynamic capability framework, it is contended that firms' capabilities need to be understood not in terms of the profit-and-loss account, but chiefly in terms of the organizational structures and managerial processes that nurture productive activities (Teece et al., 1997). This touches upon how organizational innovation has been constructed and measured in previous studies (Torchia et al., 2011; Zahra et al., 2000). Following this stream of research, CEOs were asked in the survey to assess the extent to which they agree (7 = strongly agree; 1 = strongly disagree) to statements regarding the firm being characterized by: (1) being the first firm in the industry to develop innovative management systems; (2) being the first firm in the industry to introduce new business concepts and practices; (3) changing the organization structure considerably to facilitate innovation; and (4) implementing development programmes for personnel to facilitate creativity and innovation. A higher score on this scale indicates a higher ability to build dynamic capabilities in the firm. Cronbach's alpha for this construct is .85.

Independent Variables

The theoretical framework of the study involves three independent variables related to chairperson leadership efficacy (Hypothesis 1), firm-specific knowledge (Hypothesis 2) and industry experience (Hypothesis 3). Chairpersons' firm-specific knowledge and industry experience were each gauged by single-item measures based on responses from CEOs, where they were asked to assess on a Likert-type scale to what extent they agree (7 = strongly agree; 1 = strongly disagree) that the board chairperson has extensive knowledge of the firm (main operations, key competence, products etc.) or extensive, relevant industry experience. A higher score on each measure indicates, respectively, more firm-specific knowledge or more industry experience.

Chairpersons' leadership efficacy was measured with a multi-item Likert-type scale based on the theoretical and empirical work of Gabrielsson et al. (2007). Following this source, the variable was measured by asking board members to what extent they agree (7 = strongly agree; 1 = strongly disagree) that their chairperson is excellent on aspects such as: (1) motivating and using each board member's competence; (2) formulating proposals for decisions and summarizing conclusions at board meetings; (3) leading board discussions; (4) working well with the CEO; (5) working constantly to develop boards' working processes; (6) performing open and trustworthy leadership; and (7) always being very well prepared for board meetings. Cronbach's alpha for this variable is .86.

Control Variables

Following previous research, two sets of control variables were included in the research model. The first set of variables aims to control for industry and firm characteristics that might potentially influence boards' involvement in strategy (Golden and Zajac, 2001; Haynes and Hillman, 2010; Judge Jr and Zeithaml, 1992; Machold et al., 2011). Firm industry belongingness was gauged by a nominal dichotomous variable identifying the company's main industry as either manufacturing (industry = 1) or other (industry = 0). A dichotomous variable indicating whether the firm was a high-technology firm (no = 0; yes = 1) was also included, since board involvement in strategy is particularly manifested in these firms (Carpenter et al., 2003). Moreover, the analysis controls for firm size and firm age, measured by the number of employees and the number of years the firm had existed. Both of these variables were transformed using a logarithmic transformation to adjust for the skewed distribution in the data. Finally, a dichotomous variable indicating whether the CEO considers the firm to be a family firm (no = 0; yes = 1) was included, since strategic involvement on board level could be different in family firms (Brunninge et al., 2007; Brunninge and Nordqvist, 2004).

The second set of variables aims to control for a set of board characteristics frequently used in board research. These are often referred to as the 'usual suspects' (Finkelstein and Mooney, 2003). These variables are expected to influence various board- or firm-level outcomes. Board size was measured as the total number of board members. This variable was transformed using logarithmic transformation to adjust for the skewed distribution in the data. Outsider ratio was measured as the percentage of outsider (non-executive) directors out of the total number of board members (Mallette and Fowler, 1992). Shareholder ratio was measured by dividing the number of directors holding shares in the firm by the total number of directors on the board. CEO-duality was measured as a dichotomous variable, coded 1 if the CEO was also the chairperson of the board and 0 otherwise. Chair tenure was measured with a continuous variable indicating how many years the chairperson had been working in this position.

ANALYSIS AND RESULTS

Since metric and binary measures were used regarding our dependent and independent variables, a linear multiple regression analysis was applied to test the hypotheses of the study. The linear regression analyses for the three models were conducted in steps to capture the contribution of each set of variables to the model significance. The F-changes for models I and III are significant for all the changes displayed in Table 7.1, which shows descriptive data, including mean, minimum, maximum and standard deviation, for all the variables used in the analysis.

Before running the analysis, potential problems in the distribution of the variables were examined by conducting residual analysis to verify the assumptions of the hierarchical regression analysis. No results were found that indicated a need for a change of the main conclusions in the analysis. In the hypothesis testing, the interpretation of the F-change results in the linear regression was combined with the beta coefficients in the models and with correlation coefficients. Correlations for all variables are presented in Table 7.2.

Table 7.1   Descriptive statistics for relevant variables

	N	Minimum	Maximum	Mean	Std deviation
High-tech firm	468	0.00	1.00	0.31	0.46
Firm size (Ln employees)	508	0.00	5.48	3.78	1.14
Firm age	512	0.00	181.00	42.71	40.73
Family firm	509	0.00	1.00	0.28	0.45
Firm industry (manufacturing)	515	0.00	1.00	0.35	0.48
Number of board members (Ln)	507	.69	2.30	1.66	0.30
Outsider ratio	487	0.00	1.00	0.78	0.31
Shareholder ratio	467	0.00	1.00	0.32	0.34
CEO-duality	490	0.00	1.00	0.08	0.28
Chair tenure	446	0.00	40.00	5.60	5.71
Chairperson leadership	488	1.00	7.00	5.16	1.04
Chairperson firm-specific knowledge	506	1.00	7.00	5.94	1.12
Chairperson industry experience	505	1.00	7.00	5.32	1.57
Building dynamic capabilities	477	1.00	6.50	3.74	1.39
Valid N (listwise)	315				

Table 7.2 Correlation analysis

	1	2	3	4	5	6	7	8	9	10	11	12	13	14
1 High-tech firm	1													
2 Firm size (Ln employees)	.186**	1												
3 Firm age	.030	.287**	1											
4 Family firm	-.130**	.015	.172**	1										
5 Firm industry (manufacturing)	.105*	.190**	.064	.037	1									
6 Number of board members (Ln)	.086	.354**	.181**	-.208**	-.052	1								
7 Outsider ratio	.189**	.187**	.073	-.225**	.006	.363**	1							
8 Shareholder ratio	-.064	-.263**	.004	.214**	-.019	-.223**	-.360**	1						
9 CEO-duality	-.068	-.109*	.024	.190**	-.002	-.199**	-.303**	.222**	1					
10 Chair tenure	-.200**	-.089	.034	.309**	.014	-.182**	-.286**	.271**	.272**	1				
11 Chairperson leadership	.024	-.008	.034	-.004	-.024	-.021	.072	.067	.032	.028	1			
12 Chairperson firm-specific knowledge	-.056	-.074	-.047	.041	.047	-.233**	-.120*	.029	.199**	.095*	.076	1		
13 Chairperson industry experience	-.046	-.025	-.106*	.076	.146**	-.172**	-.102*	-.049	.154**	.051	.094*	.635**	1	
14 Building dynamic capabilities	.084	.280**	-.022	-.047	-.125**	.156**	.120*	-.166**	-.070	-.070	.186**	.027	.007	1

Notes:
** Correlation is significant at the 0.01 level (2-tailed).
* Correlation is significant at the 0.05 level (2-tailed).

Table 7.3   Regression analysis for building dynamic capabilities

	Model I	Model II	Model III
Industry and firm characteristics			
High-tech firm	0.02	−0.02	−0.04
Firm size (Ln employees)	0.41***	0.42***	0.43***
Firm age	0.00**	−0.01**	−0.01**
Family firm	0.03	0.10	0.22
Firm industry	−0.39**	−0.40**	−0.34**
Board characteristics			
Number of board members (Ln)		−0.37	−0.16
Outsider ratio		0.46	0.45
Shareholder ratio		−0.04	−0.14
CEO-duality		0.19	0.08
Chair tenure		−0.01	−0.01
Chairperson characteristics			
H1 Chairperson leadership			0.27***
H2 Chairperson firm-specific knowledge			0.23**
H3 Chairperson industry experience			−0.11†
R	.346	.362	.437
Adjusted R2	.105	.102	.156
F (sign) Full model	8.382***	4.576***	5.472***
F-change	8.382***	0.798	7.483***
N	315	315	315

Notes:
† .10-level ; * .05-level; ** .01-level; *** .001-level.

There are generally low levels ($r < .70$) of correlation (Nunnally, 1978) among the predictors used in the analysis and the dependent variable. Based on this preliminary analysis, variance inflation factor analyses (VIF) were conducted after each regression to check for multicollinearity. The VIF values range from 1.1 to 1.96, thus clearly indicating that multicollinearity is not a problem in the current study (Kutner, 2005; Neter et al., 1990).

The regression analyses are shown in Table 7.3. Model I includes the first set of control variables relating to industry and firm characteristics. Model II includes the control variables for board characteristics, while in model III the independent variables are included.

In the first model, firm size ($p < .001$) and firm industry ($p < .01$) have a significant effect; while firm size has a positive significant effect, firm industry has a reverse relation. Model II shows continuous significant effects regarding industry characteristics (firm size $p < .01$ and firm industry $p < .01$) but no significant association with board characteristics. Model III includes the chairperson variables and tests hypotheses 1–3. The first hypothesis (H1) is supported in the analysis ($p < .001$), indicating that there is a strong positive association between chairperson leadership efficacy and the formation of dynamic capabilities in SMEs; this is in line with the assumptions of the study. The second hypothesis (H2) is also supported ($p < .01$) and indicates that there is a robust positive association between chairpersons' firm-specific knowledge and the formation of dynamic capabilities in SMEs. However, the third hypothesis (H3) is not supported by the analysis as the regression analysis in the model indicates a moderate reverse relation between chairpersons' industry experience and the formation of dynamic capabilities in SMEs. The beta coefficient for this measure is -0.11 and, together with the lower significance level ($p < .10$), indicates a moderate inverse effect by chairpersons' industry experience.

DISCUSSION

Boards of directors are seen as important – but often untapped – resources in SMEs (Huse et al., 2011b; Daily and Dalton, 1992a; Whisler, 1988). However, most of the research on boards takes a firm external perspective and focuses on how actors external to the firm (such as shareholders and external stakeholders) might benefit from the work of the board of directors. This leaves the firm internal perspective on boards and governance with limited scholarly attention on the extant research on boards.

An important issue when developing boards of directors in SMEs relates to the chairperson's position on the board. However, despite the chairperson being emphasized as playing a critical role in influencing board effectiveness (Roberts et al., 2005; Leblanc, 2005), previous research has rarely investigated chairpersonship in this context in any detail. Rather, the dominant focus in research on board leadership has been on the structural conditions of the firm, most notably in studies of the causes and consequences of combined CEO/chairperson leadership (CEO-duality) and often in the context of large, publicly held companies (Yar Hamidi and Gabrielsson, 2014).

By examining theoretically driven hypotheses on the effects of chairpersons' leadership efficacy, knowledge and experience on firms' abilities to build dynamic capabilities in 315 Norwegian SMEs, this study adds to the current scholarly knowledge of chairpersonship's effect on firms' ability to develop competitive advantages by its dynamic capabilities. The results show that chairperson leadership has a strong significant effect on firms' abilities to build dynamic capabilities. It is also demonstrated in the analysis that chairpersons' firm-specific knowledge has a robust positive association with their firm's ability to build dynamic capabilities.

However, the results also reveal that chairpersons' industry experience has a moderate reverse effect on firms' abilities to build dynamic capabilities. This counterintuitive and surprising finding needs a closer examination. Extensive industry experience on the part of chairpersons, especially from successful firms, may convince individuals that superior organizational performance is a result of conformity to the dominant logic of the industry. This might therefore limit the use of boards' knowledge when the industry's taken-for-granted measures are accepted by the chair. It might also affect the discussion of the board by posing as 'the rules of the game' (Cliff et al., 2006). Spender (1989) suggests that managers and entrepreneurs operating in the same industry develop a set of shared beliefs, or 'industry recipes', which imposes order on their logic and limits their information processing. The common understanding of the industrial environment and solutions among firms producing similar products thus triggers the acceptance of taken-for-granted behaviour through socialization processes. Gabrielsson and Politis (2012) found in their study of entrepreneurs' work experience that deep industry work experience shows a negative significant association with the number of new business ideas. This suggests that where entrepreneurs have operated for longer within an industry they are less likely to come up with new business ideas (Gabrielsson and Politis, 2012). This might be the effect of an institutionalization of beliefs and widely shared views that may be developed within industries (Cliff et al., 2006; Spender, 1989).

These arguments are in line with Haynes and Hillman's (2010) arguments on board capital depth and breadth and their findings that greater board capital breadth leads to more strategic change, while greater board capital depth leads to less strategic change following resource-dependency logic.

CONCLUSION

This study contributes to the scholarly research and literature on board leadership in at least three ways. First, this study uses first-hand survey data on leadership, knowledge and experience of board chairpersons in SMEs. In so doing, the current study moves from using archival data about structural aspects of board leadership to focus instead on the actual work of the chairperson of the board and its effect on building dynamic capabilities. Second, in contrast to the main body of research in the field, which often considers the external perspective on board work, this study applies a resource-dependency perspective and insight from strategic management to interpret the effect of chairpersonship on firm internal aspects, such as resource provision and building dynamic capabilities in SMEs. Third, this study is a response to the call for more theoretical and empirical research on board leadership in SMEs and to furnish practitioners with applicable knowledge about board leadership in SMEs.

There are various directions for future research. First, this study's results emphasize the chairpersonship's role in building dynamic capabilities. A potentially fruitful path may be to further link research in the board process tradition with that of strategic management (Andrews, 1981; Ansoff, 1957; Teece, 2012; Covin et al., 2001; Zahra and Garvis, 2000). This might illuminate how boards' work can benefit from firms' strategic development and create a more distinctive focus on firm internal contributions by boards.

Second, longitudinal design and process studies on boards of directors would contribute significantly to our understanding of board work and the chairpersons' effect on the building of dynamic capabilities in SMEs. Nevertheless, it should be admitted that there are difficulties in accessing that kind of process data (Daily et al., 2003); this type of study needs to advance the scholarly field of corporate governance (Huse, 2005b).

Finally, further examination of the board capital construct developed by Haynes and Hillman (2010) in combination with the concepts of ordinary and dynamic capacities developed by Teece (2014) might create a fertile ground for developing new insights on boards and the formation of dynamic and ordinary capabilities in firms.

REFERENCES

ACCA (2010), *Small Business: A global agenda*, London, UK: Association of Chartered Certified Accountants.

Andrews, K.R. (1981), 'Corporate strategy as a vital function of the board', *Harvard Business Review*, **59**, 174–84.

Ansoff, H.I. (1957), 'Strategies for diversification', *Harvard Business Review*, **35**, 113–24.

Augier, M. and D.J. Teece (2009), 'Dynamic capabilities and the role of managers in business strategy and economic performance', *Organization Science*, **20**, 410–21.

Blake, C.G. and S.D. Saleh (1992), 'A model of entrepreneurial venture performance', *Journal of Small Business & Entrepreneurship*, **9**, 19–26.

Borch, O.J. and M. Huse (1993), 'Informal strategic networks and the board of directors', *Entrepreneurship: Theory & Practice*, **18**, 23–36.

Borch, O.J., M. Huse and K. Senneseth (1999), 'Resource configuration, competitive strategies, and corporate entrepreneurship: an empirical examination of small firms', *Entrepreneurship Theory and Practice*, **24**, 49–70.

Brunninge, O. and M. Nordqvist (2004), 'Ownership structure, board composition and entrepreneurship: evidence from family firms and venture-capital-backed firms', *International Journal of Entrepreneurial Behaviour & Research*, **10**, 85–105.

Brunninge, O., M. Nordqvist and J. Wiklund (2007), 'Corporate governance and strategic change in SMEs: the effects of ownership, board composition and top management teams', *Small Business Economics*, **29**, 295–308.

Carpenter, M.A., T.G. Pollock and M.M. Leary (2003), 'Testing a model of reasoned risk-taking: governance, the experience of principals and agents, and global strategy in high-technology IPO firms', *Strategic Management Journal*, **24**, 802–20.

Cliff, J.E., P.D. Jennings and R. Greenwood (2006), 'New to the game and questioning the rules: the experiences and beliefs of founders who start imitative versus innovative firms', *Journal of Business Venturing*, **21**, 633–63.

Covin, J.G. and D.P. Slevin (1991), 'A conceptual model of entrepreneurship as firm behavior', *Entrepreneurship: Theory & Practice*, **16**, 7–25.

Covin, J.G., D.P. Slevin and M.B. Heeley (2001), 'Strategic decision making in an intuitive vs. technocratic mode: structural and environmental considerations', *Journal of Business Research*, **52**, 51–67.

Cowling, M. (2003), 'Productivity and corporate governance in smaller firms', *Small Business Economics*, **20**, 335–44.

Daily, C.M. and D.R. Dalton (1992a), 'Financial performance of founder-managed versus professionally managed small corporations', *Journal of Small Business Management*, **30**, 25–34.

Daily, C.M. and D.R. Dalton (1992b), 'The relationship between governance structure and corporate performance in entrepreneurial firms', *Journal of Business Venturing*, **7**, 375–86.

Daily, C.M. and D.R. Dalton (1993), 'Board of directors leadership and structure: control and performance implications', *Entrepreneurship: Theory & Practice*, **17**, 65–81.

Daily, C.M., D.R. Dalton and A.A. Cannella, Jr. (2003), 'Corporate governance: decades of dialogue and data', *Academy of Management. The Academy of Management Review*, **28**, 371–82.

Dillman, D.A. (2011), *Mail and Internet Surveys: The Tailored Design Method – 2007 Update with New Internet, Visual, and Mixed-Mode Guide*, New York, USA: Wiley.

Eisenhardt, K.M. and J.A. Martin (2000), 'Dynamic capabilities: what are they?', *Strategic Management Journal*, **21**, 1105–21.

European Commission (2003), 'Commission recommendation of 6 May 2003 concerning the definition of micro, small and medium-sized enterprises'.

Fama, E.F. (1980), 'Agency problems and the theory of the firm', *The Journal of Political Economy*, **88**, 288–307.

Fama, E.F. and M.C. Jensen (1983), 'Separation of ownership and control', *Journal of Law & Economics*, **26**, 301–26.

Fiegener, M.K. (2005), 'Determinants of board participation in the strategic decisions of small corporations', *Entrepreneurship Theory and Practice*, **29**, 627–50.

Finkelstein, S. and A.C. Mooney (2003), 'Not the usual suspects: how to use board process to make boards better', *The Academy of Management Executive*, **17**, 101–13.

Forbes, D.P. and F.J. Milliken (1999), 'Cognition and corporate governance: understanding boards of directors as strategic decision-making groups', *Academy of Management Review*, **24**, 489–505.

Gabrielsson, J. (2007), 'Boards of directors and entrepreneurial posture in medium-size companies: putting the board demography approach to a test', *International Small Business Journal*, **25**, 511–37.

Gabrielsson, J., M. Huse and A. Minichilli (2007), 'Understanding the leadership role of the board chairperson through a team production approach', *International Journal of Leadership Studies*, **3**, 121–39.

Gabrielsson, J. and D. Politis (2012), 'Work experience and the generation of new business ideas among entrepreneurs: an integrated learning framework', *International Journal of Entrepreneurial Behavior & Research*, **18**, 48–74.

Golden, B.R. and E.J. Zajac (2001), 'When will boards influence strategy? Inclination x power = strategic change', *Strategic Management Journal*, **22**, 1087–111.

Haynes, K.T. and A. Hillman (2010), 'The effect of board capital and CEO power on strategic change', *Strategic Management Journal*, **31**, 1145–63.

Herman, E.S. (1982), *Corporate Control, Corporate Power: A Twentieth Century Fund Study*, Cambridge, UK: Cambridge University Press.

Hillman, A.J., A.A. Cannella and R.L. Paetzold (2000), 'The resource dependence role of corporate directors: strategic adaptation of board composition in response to environmental change', *Journal of Management Studies*, **37**, 235–56.

Hillman, A.J. and T. Dalziel (2003), 'Boards of directors and firm performance: integrating agency and resource dependency perspectives', *Academy of Management Review*, **28**, 383–96.

Huse, M. (1990), 'Board composition in small enterprises', *Entrepreneurship & Regional Development*, **2**, 363–74.

Huse, M. (2000), 'Boards of directors in SMEs: a review and research agenda', *Entrepreneurship & Regional Development*, **12**, 271–90.

Huse, M. (2005a), 'Accountability and creating accountability: a framework for exploring behavioural perspectives of corporate governance', *British Journal of Management*, **16**, 65–79.

Huse, M. (2005b), 'Corporate governance: understanding important contingencies', *Corporate Ownership & Control*, **2**, 41–50.

Huse, M. (2007), *Boards, Governance, and Value Creation: The Human Side of Corporate Governance*, Cambridge, UK: Cambridge University Press.

Huse, M. (ed.) (2009), *The Value Creating Board: Corporate Governance and Organizational Behaviour*, New York, USA: Routledge.

Huse, M. and J. Gabrielsson (2012), 'Board leadership and value creation: an extended team production approach', in T. Clarke and D. Branson (eds), *The SAGE Handbook of Corporate Governance*, London, UK: Sage.

Huse, M., R. Hoskisson, A. Zattoni and R. Viganò (2011a), 'New perspectives on board research: changing the research agenda', *Journal of Management & Governance*, **15**, 5–28.

Huse, M., A. Minichilli, M. Nordqvist and A. Zattoni (2011b), 'Board tasks in small firms: the importance of motivation and evaluations', *Sinergie rivista di studi e ricerche*.

Huse, M., A. Minichilli and M. Schøning (2005a), 'Corporate boards as assets for operating in the new Europe: the value of process-oriented boardroom dynamics', *Organizational Dynamics*, **34**, 285–97.

Huse, M., D.O. Neubaum and J. Gabrielsson (2005b), 'Corporate innovation and competitive environment', *International Entrepreneurship and Management Journal*, **1**, 313–33.

Huse, M. and V. Rindova (2001), 'Stakeholders' expectations of board roles: the case of subsidiary boards', *Journal of Management and Governance*, **5**, 153–78.

Jawahar, I.M. and G.L. McLaughlin (2001), 'Toward a descriptive stakeholder theory: an organizational life cycle approach', *Academy of Management Review*, **26**, 397–414.

Jensen, M.C. and W.H. Meckling (1976), 'Theory of the firm: managerial behavior, agency costs and ownership structure', *Journal of Financial Economics*, **3**, 305–60.

Judge, W.Q., Jr. and C.P. Zeithaml (1992), 'Institutional and strategic choice perspectives on board involvement in the strategic decision process', *Academy of Management Journal*, **35**, 766–94.

Katkalo, V.S., C.N. Pitelis and D.J. Teece (2010), 'Introduction: on the nature and scope of dynamic capabilities', *Industrial & Corporate Change*, **19**, 1175–86.

Kaufman, A. and E. Englander (2005), 'A team production model of corporate governance', *Academy of Management Executive*, **19**, 9–22.

Knockaert, M., E.S. Bjornali and T. Erikson (2015), 'Joining forces: top management team and board chair characteristics as antecedents of board service involvement', *Journal of Business Venturing*, **30**, 420–35.

Kutner, M.H. (2005), *Applied Linear Statistical Models*, New York, USA: McGraw-Hill Irwin.

Leblanc, R. (2005), 'Assessing board leadership', *Corporate Governance: An International Review*, **13**, 654–66.

Love, J.H. and S. Roper (2015), 'SME innovation, exporting and growth: a review of existing evidence', *International Small Business Journal*, **33**, 28–48.

Mace, M.L. (1971), *Directors: Myth and Reality*, Cambridge, MA, USA: Harvard Business School Press.

Machold, S., M. Huse, A. Minichilli and M. Nordqvist (2011), 'Board leadership and strategy involvement in small firms: a team production approach', *Corporate Governance: An International Review*, **19**, 368–83.

Mallette, P. and K.L. Fowler (1992), 'Effects of board composition and stock ownership on the adaption of "poison pills"', *Academy of Management Journal*, **35**, 1010–35.

Mazzarol, T. and S. Reboud (2009), *The Strategy of Small Firms: Strategic Management and Innovation in the Small Firm*, Cheltenham, UK: Edward Elgar.

Minichilli, A. and C. Hansen (2007), 'The board advisory tasks in small firms and the event of crises', *Journal of Management and Governance*, **11**, 5–22.

Neter, J., W. Wasserman and M.H. Kutner (1990), *Applied Linear Statistical Models: Regression, Analysis of Variance, and Experimental Designs*, New York, USA: Irwin.

Neubauer, F. (1997), 'A formal evaluation of the chairman of the board', *Corporate Governance: An International Review*, **5**, 160–65.

Neville, M. (2011), 'The role of boards in small and medium sized firms', *Corporate Governance: the International Journal of Effective Board Performance*, **11**, 527–40.

Nordqvist, M. and L. Melin (2002), 'The dynamics of family firms: an institutional perspective on corporate governance and strategic change', in D. Fletcher (ed.), *Understanding the Small Family Business,* London, UK: Routledge.

NUES (2014), 'The Norwegian code of practice for corporate govern-ance', accessed 24 February 2015 at www.nues.no/filestore/Dokumenter/Anbefalingene/2014/2014-10-30Code2014ENGweb.pdf.

Nunnally, J.C. (1978), *Psychometric Theory,* Columbus, USA: McGraw-Hill.

Parrilli, M.D. and A. Elola (2012), 'The strength of science and technology drivers for SME innovation', *Small Business Economics,* **39**, 897–907.

Pfeffer, J. and G.R. Salancik (1978), *The External Control of Organizations: A Resource Dependence Perspective,* California, USA: Stanford Business Books.

Pick, K. (2007), 'Around the boardroom table: interactional aspects of govern-ance', 3265061, Harvard University.

Pugliese, A. and P.Z. Wenstop (2007), 'Board members' contribution to strategic decision-making in small firms', *Journal of Management and Governance,* **11**, 383–404.

Roberts, J. (2002), 'Building the complementary board. The work of the plc chair-man', *Long Range Planning,* **35**, 493–520.

Roberts, J., T. McNulty and P. Stiles (2005), 'Beyond agency conceptions of the work of the non-executive director: creating accountability in the boardroom', *British Journal of Management,* **16**, 5–26.

Rumelt, R.P. (1991), 'How much does industry matter?', *Strategic Management Journal,* **12**, 167–85.

Sacconi, L. (2007), 'A social contract account for CSR as an extended model of corporate governance (II): compliance, reputation and reciprocity', *Journal of Business Ethics,* **75**, 77–96.

Shleifer, A. and R.W. Vishny (1997), 'A survey of corporate governance', *The Journal of Finance,* **52**, 737–83.

Spender, J.-C. (1989), *Industry Recipes: The Nature and Sources of Managerial Judgement,* Oxford, UK: Basil Blackwell.

Strotmann, H. (2007), 'Entrepreneurial survival', *Small Business Economics,* **28**, 87–104.

Teece, D.J. (2012), 'Dynamic capabilities: routines versus entrepreneurial action', *Journal of Management Studies,* **49**, 1395–401.

Teece, D.J. (2014), 'The foundations of enterprise performance: dynamic and ordinary capabilities in an (economic) theory of firms', *Academy of Management Perspectives,* **28**, 328–52.

Teece, D.J. and C. Freeman (1990), 'Profiting from technological innovation: impli-cations for integration, collaboration, licensing and public policy', *The Economics of Innovation,* International Library of Critical Writings in Economics, No. 2, Aldershot, UK and Brookfield, VT, USA: Edward Elgar Publishing.

Teece, D.J., H. Landstrom and F.T. Lohrke (2012), 'Profiting from techno-logical innovation: implications for integration, collaboration, licensing and public policy', *Intellectual Roots of Entrepreneurship Research,* Elgar Research Collection, International Library of Entrepreneurship, Vol. 23, Cheltenham, UK and Northampton, MA, USA: Edward Elgar Publishing.

Teece, D.J., G. Pisano and A. Shuen (1997), 'Dynamic capabilities and strategic management', *Strategic Management Journal,* **18**, 509–33.

Torchia, M., A. Calabrò and M. Huse (2011), 'Women directors on corporate boards: from tokenism to critical mass', *Journal of Business Ethics,* **102**, 299–317.

van Ees, H., G. van der Laan and T.J.B.M. Postma (2008), 'Effective board behavior in the Netherlands', *European Management Journal*, **26**, 84–93.

Whisler, T.L. (1988), 'The role of the board in the threshold firm', *Family Business Review*, **1**, 309–21.

Winborg, J. and H. Landstrom (2001), 'Financial bootstrapping in small businesses: examining small business managers' resource acquisition behaviors', *Journal of Business Venturing*, **16**, 235–54.

Wolfson, N. (1984), *The Modern Corporation: Free Markets Versus Regulation*, New York, USA: Free Press.

Yar Hamidi, D. (2016), 'Governance for innovation – board leadership and value creation in entrepreneurial firms', PhD thesis, Halmstad University.

Yar Hamidi, D. and J. Gabrielsson (2012), 'Trends in corporate governance research on board leadership: implications for research and practice', paper presented to the EURAM conference, Rotterdam, 7–9 June.

Yar Hamidi, D. and J. Gabrielsson (2014), 'Developments and trends in research on board leadership: a systematic literature review', *International Journal of Business Governance and Ethics*, **9**, 243–68.

Zahra, S.A. and J.G. Covin (1995), 'Contextual influences on the corporate entrepreneurship-performance relationship: a longitudinal analysis', *Journal of Business Venturing*, **10**, 43–58.

Zahra, S.A. and I. Filatotchev (2004), 'Governance of the entrepreneurial threshold firm: a knowledge-based perspective', *Journal of Management Studies*, **41**, 885–97.

Zahra, S.A. and D.M. Garvis (2000), 'International corporate entrepreneurship and firm performance: the moderating effect of international environmental hostility', *Journal of Business Venturing*, **15**, 469–92.

Zahra, S.A., D.O. Neubaum and M. Huse (2000), 'Entrepreneurship in medium-size companies: exploring the effects of ownership and governance systems', *Journal of Management*, **26**, 947–76.

Zona, F. and A. Zattoni (2007), 'Beyond the black box of demography: board processes and task effectiveness within Italian firms', *Corporate Governance: An International Review*, **15**, 852–64.

8. Co-creating strategy between independent consultants in a micro-firm context

Tanja Lepistö, Satu Aaltonen and Ulla Hytti

INTRODUCTION

Today, value creation is not solely in the hands of a single service provider but instead usually involves networks of other companies, such as suppliers or retailers (Ballantyne et al., 2011). The current business environment has amplified the need to consider not only how to address consumer needs more perceptively but also how partners can be incorporated into the practice of creating value propositions. Success relies on building a strategy capable of integrating this networked way of doing business that involves interaction, and collaboration. Such a strategy should also be reflected through the firm's processes and marketing communications in order to attract customers, and co-creating value can support that. The co-creation of value is a new approach to value, one that highlights the importance of the joint creation of value by the company and the customer (Prahalad and Ramaswamy, 2004), but also with other stakeholders (Vargo and Lusch, 2008). Co-creation differs from traditional conceptions emphasizing the construction of value by companies within their corporate structure and for the consumer (Vargo and Lusch, 2004; Alves, 2013), because value co-creation involves both clients and suppliers acting as co-creators of value. Suppliers apply their knowledge and skills in the production and branding of the product and the clients apply their knowledge and capacities in their everyday utilization practices (Vargo et al., 2008).

Although there is a vast amount of research on co-creation, there are still gaps in the current literature. First, current literature exhibits a strong focus on co-creation between service provider and customer (Fosstenløkken et al., 2003; Payne et al., 2008; Aarikka-Stenroos and Jaakkola, 2012; Rasmussen, 2012) and thus more research focusing on other stakeholders is necessary. Second, studies focusing on co-creation tend to discuss it on an abstract level (Gummesson, 2008: Vargo et al., 2008). Although there are studies focusing on, for example, client–consultant interaction (such as Nikolova et al., 2009; Sieg et al., 2012) and managing professional service relationships (such as Hirvonen and Helander, 2001), there is a need to focus more precisely on the practices of co-creation in order to understand how resources, like knowledge and expertise, are integrated in co-creation. Finally, co-creation is largely examined in the marketing context, such as in service co-creation, but we suggest that the concept can be extended to other contexts, such as the co-creation of strategy. In our opinion, focusing on strategy work between partners offers a new and interesting perspective on strategizing and strategy work in small and micro-sized firms.

This chapter directs attention to the co-creation between partners in a micro-firm context. To address the research gap, this study answers the research question: how is strategy constructed in a dialogue between independent consultants in a partnership? Since the objective is to study how the actors really *co-strategize*, the current research adopts a practice-based view and scrutinizes dialogue among partners (Orlikowski, 2010). Practice research views organizations 'as constituted by the shared practices that actors draw on to act and interpret other actors' actions' (Orlikowski, 2007; Echeverri and Skålén, 2011). In this study, dialogue between partners relating to strategy is seen as practice. In line with the strategy-as-practice approach, we understand strategy as being developed, produced and negotiated continuously in everyday activities.

The chapter begins with an examination of the strategy-as-practice approach and co-creating strategy through social construction. Following that, the methodological choices are explained. In the findings section, we present the dialoguing practices identified in our qualitative study,[1] through which strategy is co-created between the partners. The chapter concludes with a discussion, its implications, its limitations, and some ideas for future research.

LITERATURE REVIEW

The Strategy-as-practice Approach

Practice perspectives have been developed in the social sciences and managerial disciplines (Whittington, 2006). Adopting a practice perspective in research has ontological and epistemological consequences, which can be explained by describing the three ways to study practices (Orlikowski, 2010). First, scholars might adopt an empirical focus on how people act in organizational contexts. Accordingly, the practice is seen as a phenomenon and the aim is to answer a '*what*' question by describing everyday activity. The second way is to adopt a theoretical focus on understanding relations between the actions people take and the structures of organizational life. This approach answers a '*how*' question, and thus aims to explain the dynamics of everyday activity and enhance understanding of how practices are produced, reinforced and changed, while also taking account of the intended and unintended consequences of those actions. The third way is to adopt a philosophical focus on the constitutive role of practices in producing organizational reality. The perspective is that social reality is made up of practices and the social world is brought into being through everyday activity (Orlikowski, 2010). The three alternative approaches are important because those studying practices are interested in how knowledge is produced. Practice perspective views acquiring knowledge as equating to doing, and knowing and doing are not seen as entirely separate options, and nor are knowing and working. There is knowing in everything people do (Gherardi, 2015).

Strategy-as-practice is a research approach utilized especially in studies on strategic management, organizational decision making, and managerial work focusing on the micro-level social activities, processes and practices characterizing organizational strategy and strategizing. It is an approach that enables in-depth analysis of what takes place in activities dealing with strategies within organizations. Through the concept of practice, researchers are able to conduct a dialogue with practitioners and thus to advance theoretical understanding by offering practical implications to managers and other organization staff (Golsorkhi et al., 2010). Under the practice perspective, strategy is seen not just as a property of an organization, but as something people do with people from both within the organization and from outside it (Whittington, 2006).

For a practice to be a practice, it must be seen as such by its practitioners, and is therefore socially sustained. This means that it is recurrent and it is recurrent because it is institutionalized (there are certain values, beliefs, norms, habits and discourses accepted, understood and shared by the members of the group/organization). Although the practice is recurrent it does not mean that everything is always repeated in exactly the same way, so there is room for development, change and learning (Gherardi, 2011). The results of practice-based studies are especially important to practitioners themselves, because through research (like using video material as data) it is possible to shed light on the tacit, interactional, discursive and embedded production of organizational practice and learning (Gherardi, 2011). Such results also highlight the importance of the actions of all participants in generating organizational outcomes (Feldman and Orlikowski, 2011).

Jensen Schau et al. (2009) offer a general outline of the characteristics of practices as comprising understandings, procedures and engagements. Understandings are defined as the practice-related knowledge (expertise) skills and experiences of each resource-integrating actor. Procedures are the practice-related rules, principles and cultural norms of each resource-integrating actor, and engagements are the practice-related wants and needs, goals and purposes to which each resource-integrating actor is committed (Jensen Schau et al., 2009; Kowalkowski et al., 2012). These characteristics form a background on which each actor taking part in strategy work draws and which affects the knowledge exchange between actors (in that it may both enable and delimit it) (Kowalkowski et al., 2012). A slightly broader view would define practices as accepted ways of doing things, which are embodied and materially mediated, and both shared between actors and routinized over time (Reckwitz, 2002; Vaara and Whittington, 2012). A definition of strategy from a strategy-as-practice perspective is, 'a situated, socially accomplished activity', whereas strategizing means 'actions, interactions and negotiations of multiple actors and practices that they draw upon in accomplishing that activity' (Jarzabkowski et al., 2007, pp.7–8).

This chapter relies on a strategy-as-practice approach to focus on the micro-level interaction between individual practitioners in strategizing (Jarzabkowski and Spee, 2009), in this case in workshops. Workshops as a mode of doing strategy can be seen as practices. They are in a way 'concentrated episodes in the wider strategy praxis, a sort of episodic strategy practices' (Jarzabkowski and Spee, 2009, p.83).

Social Construction of Strategy

The chapter contributes to current discussions on value co-creation (Payne et al. 2008, Grönroos and Voima 2013) and service development (Vargo and Lusch 2008, Ballantyne et al. 2011) by focusing on the strategy dialogue in co-creation workshops between partnering consultants. The value co-creation literature emphasizes collaboration with customers and other stakeholders and learning from them in order to be adaptive to their individual and dynamic needs (Vargo and Lusch, 2004; Vargo and Lusch, 2008). This collaboration with other actors, or influenced by them (Jaakkola, Helkkula and Aarikka-Stenroos, 2015), is seen as co-creation, which can be defined as the joint creation of offerings (Hoyer et al., 2010) or value, and occurring through the exchange and integration of resources (Vargo and Lusch, 2008). Resources (such as knowledge, skills, and motivation) do not create value in themselves, but only during the process of integrating and implementing them (Lusch et al., 2010). Resources are therefore 'building blocks of the social that practices integrate into service'

(Skålén et al., 2015; Ballantyne et al., 2011; Echeverri and Skålén, 2011; Grönroos, 2011).

The co-creation takes place, not only with customers (which was the starting point of the co-creation discussion; see Prahalad and Ramaswamy, 2004), but also with other stakeholders. The context of the discussion has therefore changed from being based on networks to encompassing service ecosystems. The institutions – norms, rules, symbols, meanings and so on – can be seen as co-ordination mechanisms for value creation and co-creation (Lusch and Vargo, 2014). Hence, the role of a service provider is to understand how the process of value creation is perceived by clients, to foster value creation opportunities, and manage the ways and means favouring the co-creation of value (Payne et al., 2008; Prahalad and Ramaswamy, 2004). Co-creation has also been discussed in the entrepreneurship literature, especially in the effectuation stream (Sarasvathy, 2001), where the focus has been on building and utilizing networks in new venture creation and internationalization (Galkina and Chetty, 2015). The emphasis is on adopting a more emergent view on strategy and forging co-operation relationships by pre-commitments to reduce uncertainty. In an effectuation context, experimentation is important to identify strategy and business models that work, as is flexibility and investing based on affordable loss (Chandler et al., 2011). This means that entrepreneurs adopting effectuation, who start by assessing the means available and the acceptable level of downside risk, can open themselves up to surprises when they seek and determine goals with their stakeholders (Dew et al., 2009).

The co-creative practice of formulating a value proposition involves knowledge exchange between resource-integrating actors whose knowledge is situated in their respective practice (Kowalkowski et al., 2012). The current study focuses on the co-creation of strategy between independent, partnering consultants. The focus is on the dialogue arising during strategy workshops facilitated by researchers. The study was motivated by the authors' practical experience with entrepreneurs and consultants offering professional services, and the fact that service providers are today often involved in interactions not only between themselves and their customers in a dyad, but in networks comprising customers and other stakeholders.

Dialogue is one of the building blocks of co-creation. In the context of co-creation, dialogue implies interactivity, engagement and a propensity to act. Dialogue refers to equal and reciprocal discussion, where even the topic and the aim of the discussion are open for discussion, the opinions of others are respected and the discussants are ready to question their own opinions and premises. The aim of the dialogue is to find a solution that is acceptable to each participant. The process of dialogue embraces the idea of a willingness to learn from others and commit to finding a solution

(Ellinor and Gerard, 1998; Heikkilä and Heikkilä, 2001). Dialogue entails many forms of learning, but perhaps most importantly, learning how to collaborate (cf. Ballantyne, 2004). A (true) dialogue is challenging for the participants (Vähämäki, 2008).

The current research adopts a relational constructionist view (Fletcher, 2006). That approach involves constructing a joint strategy as a relational activity, where actors' resources, experiences, understandings and interests are interwoven in a dialogue through which strategy emerges. In these dialogical episodes, reality is socially constructed based on the participants' previous understandings, experiences and personality (ibid.). The relational constructionist view emphasizes the relationality and co-ordination between people and their contexts, and the relationality between people and their past and future, as well as the implications of those relations for the perceived spheres of opportunity (Bouwen and Steyaert, 1990; Fletcher, 2006).

RESEARCH DESIGN AND METHODS

Case Selection

In addressing its research question on how strategy is co-created between the partners, and in conducting a detailed data analysis to form an understanding of the case context, the current research utilizes a two-case study. Case study research is empirical research in which diverse information acquired by different methods is used to study present events or human behaviour in a given environment (Yin, 2009). Therefore, the focus in a case study is often on understanding the dynamics present within certain settings (Eisenhardt, 1989, p.534). A purposive sampling strategy (Miles and Huberman, 1994) was used to select the cases offering the best opportunity to study the social construction of strategy by analysing dialogue. In case studies, case selection and defining the case are critically important (Eriksson and Kovalainen, 2008).

In this research, the case is the strategy dialogue in co-creation workshops between the partnering consultants. As is typical of strategy-as-practice research, human actors and their actions and interactions take centre stage (Jarzabkowski and Spee, 2009). The study is conducted in two micro-sized firms operating in professional services. Here the firms are called the *Competence Management Company* and the *Consultancy Group*. Large firms have established processes for strategy work whereas micro-sized firms rely more on informal and less explicit processes (Kohtamäki, Kraus et al., 2008; Kohtamäki, Tornikoski et al., 2008), making them interesting environments in which to study strategy work. These particular firms were selected because they both (1) demonstrated a need for strategy work and a common vision and (2) were willing to engage in co-creation with the partnering consultants to develop their strategy and in providing joint professional services to customers. The cases differ however in their organization: the Competence Management Company is a small owner-manager-led firm that co-operates with independent self-employed experts. The Consultancy Group is a limited company formed by seven independent self-employed consultants wishing to develop and offer joint services for customers. In both of these firms all the actors are engaged in strategy development and execution.

The Competence Management Company was founded in 2009 and the business idea is based on the academic work of the owner-manager on developing the qualification classification system for working-life skills and knowledge. The company aims to support its customers' processes by focusing on the management of expertise; analysing the competences and qualifications of personnel through competence surveys, and mapping the gaps in organizational skill profiles. The software for competence management is at the heart of the firm's supply of services. In addition, the firm sells licences for the software and offers turnkey solutions for human relations management, such as support for annual development discussions or various training events and courses. The competence analysis and the mapping of gaps in organizational skills is tailored to each customer and involves co-creation, because the strategic expertise areas in the customer company are defined in co-operation with the customer.

Strategy development became topical within the case organization especially because the firm grew in late 2013. Prior to that the company employed two professionals in addition to the owner-manager, an IT specialist for software development and a customer manager. In autumn 2013 the company contracted three independent consultants to market its services. Those same people are also responsible for providing services to customers. The decision to focus on new business customer acquisition after launching the new software highlights the interest in growth, and the decision to partner with three consultants is important strategically. The company already had a well-established customer base of organizations in the education field and thus the acquisition of more business customers was the next step. This decision also poses challenges and induces changes in strategic management, not least, because the partners are located in different parts of the country. The self-employed consultants also have other customers. The initial meetings with the three consultants made it clear that the Competence Management Company needed to sharpen its marketing communications and redefine its strategy to make its value proposi-

Table 8.1   Participants and data collection: Competence Management Company workshop

Participant	Organization	Field of expertise
Owner-manager (Thomasina)	Owner, Competence Management Company	PhD in knowledge management, founder of the company
Customer manager (Sarah)	Employee, Competence Management Company	Marketing and customer management
Sales representative 1 (Haley)	Independent consultant	Human relations
Sales representative 2 (John)	Independent consultant	Sales skills
Sales representative 3 (Leeann)	Independent consultant	Building industry
Description of data collection	The workshop took place in May 2014, lasted three hours, and was recorded and later transcribed. A researcher was present and made field notes. The participants worked with flipcharts, which the researcher photographed for future reference

tion appealing to a new business-customer segment. The new marketing partners offered a different kind of expertise (see Table 8.1).

The Consultancy Group was founded in 2013 by a group of independent consultants operating in different parts of Finland. The group aimed to be able to tender for projects demanding more resources and more diverse expertise than any individual member could muster. The group selected a CEO from within its number and now offers consultancy services for customers from both the public and private sectors, with a special focus on supervising approaches. All the consultants have different areas of expertise and knowledge, in addition to their knowledge of supervisory approaches (see Table 8.2). Combining their expertise on coaching, supervision and training enables them to offer their customers tailored services and to facilitate development projects co-created with their customers and the customers' stakeholders.

The company was newly established at the time of the study and therefore the strategy work was ongoing. The firm aimed to convey its available expertise to potential customers, to productize its services, and to define the specific steps required to deliver on a jointly defined vision for the future of the company. The workshops organized in both firms were intended to promote strategy work. The workshops were attended by company

Table 8.2   Participants and data collection: Consultancy Group workshop

Participant	Organization	Field of expertise
Partner 1 (Hannah)	Independent consultant / CEO of Consultancy Group	Knowledge management, tacit knowledge, well-being at work, managerial work, public organizations
Partner 2 (Rose)	Independent consultant	Development of expertise, age management, mentoring, public organizations, SMEs
Partner 3 (Eric)	Independent consultant	Finding solutions to workplace challenges, supervisory approach, public and private organizations
Partner 4 (Susan)	Independent consultant	Physical education and well-being, managerial work, multidisciplinary co-operation, public organization, non-profit organizations
Partner 5 (Peter)	Independent consultant	Consulting service sector and industry, development of managerial work, capability development of personnel
Description of data collection	The workshop was organized in April 2015. Two researchers observed and noted the proceedings. The parts of the workshop where the participants described their ideas to the whole group were recorded. The results of the group work were recorded on flipcharts and a picture collage and were photographed by researchers for future reference.	

representatives and facilitated by an independent expert. Two researchers observed the workshops and collated the data underpinning the current research. The data collection methods they employed are detailed below.

Data Collection and Analysis

The data consist of both observational and recorded and transcribed material from two workshops. The workshop for the Competence Management Company lasted three hours and was recorded and later transcribed. The second workshop organized for the Consultancy Group also lasted three hours and was partly recorded. The latter workshop involved the participants working simultaneously in two groups, making recording all of the process very challenging. Accordingly, the two researchers chose to record and transcribe only those parts of the discussion involving all participants.

A review of the literature on co-creation and social construction and dialogue constitutes the conceptual framework of this study and has guided its analysis. The aim of the analysis was to broaden the existing understanding of strategy work in micro- and small-sized firms between partners, with the focus on co-creation of strategy in workshops from the practice perspective. The workshop data was analysed by focusing on the dialogue between the participants, in terms of its starting point and how the participants constructed the strategy. The intention was to focus on the interactions, experiences and sense-making processes of the people involved in the study (Eriksson and Kovalainen, 2008). Following the idea presented by Eisenhardt (1989), the within-case analysis initially used the data collected from both workshops in order to establish an overall picture of the nature of the workshops, before a subsequent cross-case analysis was conducted to illuminate the kind of practices recurring in both workshops.

The two researchers first analysed the data individually before comparing their findings to generate a rich set of possible interpretations and nuances in the analysis. The data from the two workshops was analysed through searching for the themes through which the participants co-constructed strategy, that is, what they talked about. The researchers analysed differences and similarities in the data concerning the phenomena (strategy co-creation through dialogue), and coded text segments with similar features under the same category (Miles and Huberman, 1994). Those categories included: referring to one's own background and expertise, discussing the customer, reflecting *who we are* and *what we do* (the participants), and discussing the required steps during the strategy formulation process. The text segments in each category were then checked and analysed further. Further analysis aids in conceptualizing the results and thus increases the abstraction level (Coffey and Atkinson, 1996).

The data collected from the two workshops provided different types of knowledge for the analysis. In the workshop organized for the Competence Management Company, the focus was more on defining and finding the right words to articulate the value proposition to the customer, whereas in the workshop for the Consultancy Group the starting point was the future vision. Therefore, we believe the two data sets complement each other and that analysing them enables us to form a more concise picture of strategy work undertaken by the partners, starting from the more abstract vision and moving towards concrete plans and decisions on what will be done next. Moreover, the members of the Consultancy Group are all independent consultants, who co-operate with each other, whereas the Competence Management Company features a CEO, two hired experts and three sales representatives. So it is evident that the power structures in these two workshops were different, which in turn affected the discussions in the workshops. Despite these differences between the two workshops, they both included the dialoguing practices identified in our analysis. These practices are outlined in the findings section below.

CASE FINDINGS

This chapter describes the co-strategizing between the partners, focusing on the dialogue observed during facilitated co-creation workshops. The analysis identified the following practices: (1) dialoguing about the customer; (2) dialoguing *who we are* and *what we do*; (3) dialoguing the utilization of a range of varied experience and knowledge in customer co-operation; (4) dialoguing the required steps regarding the future; and (5) dialoguing the need for a customer perspective. Table 8.3 below adds detail on the processes and provides excerpts from the data supporting specific practices.

To sum up, we identified five dialoguing practices occurring in the strategy co-creation workshops: dialoguing about the customer; about who we are and what we do; about the utilization of varied experience and knowledge in customer co-operation; about the steps required in the future; and on the need for a customer perspective. The partners draw from these practices in the course of strategizing in workshops. Our results indicate the actors' experiences and life world are eminently relevant to the dialogues taking place during co-strategizing. The different backgrounds of the actors become apparent when they discussed the productization of services and marketing, for example. Those varied backgrounds pose challenges to co-operation but also offer opportunities, because co-creative strategy work depends on being able to establish an understanding of others' needs and of the concepts and issues relevant to them.

DISCUSSION AND CONCLUSIONS

The current business environment has amplified the need to consider not only how to address consumer needs more perceptively but also how the firm's partners are invited to participate in strategy creation practices. Dialoguing practices relating to joint value propositions and strategy have been studied surprisingly rarely. The current chapter primarily tackles this omission by considering this dialogue between the independent, partnering consultants from a social constructivist perspective. The aim of this chapter was to increase the understanding of the dialoguing practices relating to joint strategy building employed by the partners. The cases presented were particular and therefore the strategy-building practices that

Table 8.3 Summary of the analysis

The practice	Examples of strategy dialogue from the workshops
Dialoguing about the customer	• Discussing the importance of new customer acquisition versus developing relationships with existing customers. The dialogue begins when the facilitator introduces the changes taking place in the marketing of professional services and points out the importance of building and maintaining lasting customer relationships. This leads to a discussion on the role and importance of existing customers.
	• The importance of new customer acquisition following the launch of the new software is evident: 'We are now clearly focusing on new customer acquisition. Before the launch of our latest software, we did not even attempt to acquire customers from the private sector. Naturally all the old customers using the old software are also important, but people present here today are responsible for new customer acquisition from the private sector.' (Thomasina, owner–manager)
	• A strong point is made focusing on the importance of existing customers providing the company with new leads and thus also shaping the future of the firm: 'But keeping the old customers [is important] too, because they are really loyal and good customers. One way to keep them committed is that they exchange experiences and then they tell how experienced they have become in using our software. It is a way to market our services and software really, that these new customers ask the old ones. Would it be possible to find new customers through these old ones? Would that guide how we will be in the future?' (Sarah, customer manager)
Dialoguing who we are and what we do	• The dialogue begins with a discussion of the challenge to define who the potential customers are, which also poses challenges for strategy work and then moves to the importance of knowing what the partners are good at, and using that understanding as a starting point to pinpoint who the customers could be.
	• The difficulty of pinpointing who could be a customer is reflected in the metaphor comparing trying to learn what the customer wants and needs to tramping through snow: 'There are two parts in this, one is our world inside the Consultancy Group and the other represents the world of the customers [. . .] This picture [jointly created in the workshop] is very telling – an eye opener – as we are trying to find our path in this new world, this picture where this girl is tramping through the snow, looking for her way forward. It is a bit like that for us too, not knowing what the solution will be.' (Hannah, CEO)

153

Table 8.3 (continued)

The practice	Examples of strategy dialogue from the workshops
	• Next, participants explored potential reasons for the challenges facing the firm. These included changes in the business environment and the notion that the time of traditional consulting is passed. In a changing world, different kinds of services and facilitation are needed to successfully serve customers, and identifying them entails finding a common vision: 'It is an interesting question, because we are self-employed consultants, each having different kinds of objectives, ideas, expectations and dreams, plus thoughts about what all this means. And on the other hand there is this joint venture, which can enable many things [. . .] Also the time for traditional training [has passed], and in my opinion, this picture does not describe an organization offering training. It tells us about an organization trying to find a new approach to development and also about constant development, albeit through small steps.' (Peter, partner 5) • Since a new type of expertise is seen as necessary, it is important to pick up on this and continue by defining the participants' expertise as trainer educators and their role in introducing a *'new and different'* take on consulting; not doing things for customers but engaging with and motivating them: 'It is often important to approach the customer very carefully. This idea applies to us in the Consultancy Group and our customers. It is our task to get people to act with good motivation, to get them to commit to their work and their work community. We are located here: between different worlds. We will be a market leader in facilitation. Because you said [referring to fellow partner, Peter] we are not consultants [in the traditional sense] and not trainers either. So we proceed with a facilitating approach as the first in our field.' (Susan, partner 4)
Dialoguing the utilization of varied expertise and knowledge in customer co-operation	• In discussing the need to know *who we are* and *what we do*, the fact that people coming from different backgrounds with different expectations for the co-operation may find it difficult to adjust their own objectives and expectations to those of others becomes evident. However, the different backgrounds of the participants can be very useful in joint projects, in encouraging customer co-operation, and also in the strategy workshops. The discussion between the partners who are at the early stages of formulating their joint identity unfolds as follows. The facilitator initiates the discussion by saying:

154

'This is also nice: the phrase [on a flipchart] which says that a human being is the only animal that can change from doggie paddle to breaststroke just like that.'

- This remark evokes the idea that the swimming metaphor could also be a description of the work that the partners in the Consultancy Group do. The key capability seems to be the ability to harness all the expertise and knowledge that the customer organization possesses for the customer's benefit:

'Yes, that is a bit like our job. Maybe the customers need something like that. Facilitation in order to recognize the multiplicity of expertise; that all the potential and possibilities needed can be found there' [in the customer organization and its network]. (Hannah, CEO)

- This is seen to be true especially in situations where they have been able to make a difference in the customer organization:

'I think we all have, because we have worked on professional guidance, experiences with the customer organization about wild situations, and one can only think how the things would have been if nothing had been done.' (Peter, partner 5)

- Based on the ideas proposed earlier, a different kind of perspective can be proposed: instead of trying to strategize from the inside out, it would be useful to start from the outside, and thus perhaps identify a role that would fit the expertise and interests of the partners as a group:

'So we could also approach thinking and ideation: what we would like the world to be like in five years, rather than thinking what we would like our firm to be like. And that challenges us to think, what might our role be in order to [for our part] help to create the world we have envisioned?' (Eric, partner 3)

- Taking a new perspective is seen as a good way to proceed, and it is proposed that they are already going in that direction as a group:

'I think we are on the way. Because, in my opinion there are now far more opportunities to find a way to reach our vision, because we are a group rather than if we were not together.' (Hannah, CEO)

- The discussion regarding drawing upon the variety of expertise available looks different when it takes place between members of an established firm and their fairly recently contracted sales representatives. The focus is on utilizing different backgrounds and expertise in making the initial contact with potential customers. This ideation starts from what the participants (sales representatives) are best at, and emphasizes supporting the process by which sales representatives become confident competence management experts.

Table 8.3 (continued)

The practice	Examples of strategy dialogue from the workshops
	'John, you can focus on sales personnel and contact both your current customers and also our potential ones' [John has expertise in sales]. 'And I could deliver you the results of the peer review' [a database of previously conducted competence and qualifications mappings in various organizations [. . .] And then there are results describing the competencies and skills of practical nurses. I could forward them to you [refers to Sarah, who has experience in co-operating with health-care organizations] [. . .] And if you, Haley could concentrate on managers, because you have a natural way to address managers and talk about human resources management. And for Leeann the building and construction industry firms and contacts.' (Thomasina, CEO)

- This division of '*tasks*' is accepted but it is also suggested that the owner-manager of the Competence Management Company could utilize the fact that the business idea and the software is based on her PhD research more than she had previously in discussions with potential customers, and also when marketing the firm's services and expertise:

'Somehow I can picture Thomasina calling [a potential customer] and saying that I have defended my thesis on competence management. And to say like this to a certain target group of course, like people in human resource management, addressing them and asking whether they have time to discuss it. Like referring to the expertise on such a high level.' (Haley, sales representative 1)

This suggestion is reaffirmed in the dialogue:

'And it would also show that you are conducting research on this subject and that you know what you are talking about. And that you are interested in hearing the opinions of people having expertise and experience on these matters in potential customer organizations too. That you could adopt the role of an expert, like John will have a role as the person knowledgeable about sales management.' (Sarah, customer manager)

- Partners bring their own experience to the strategizing process, but at this juncture it mostly affects the allocation of tasks and assigning different potential customer segments to each participant. There is no discussion on searching for the lowest common denominator of the experience and knowledge base of the participants or potential gains of synergies.

156

Dialoguing the required steps regarding the future

- In strategizing, the essential task is to build a bridge between the world of the customer and the world of the partners. To achieve this, it is necessary to decide on the steps that need to be taken in order to achieve this aim. The facilitator begins by eliciting from the consultants the kind of steps they think should be taken. This evokes a comment addressing the need to find a way to get the message on how the Consultancy Group could help and support them, through to the customers:

  'We need to be able to convey the message to the customers that we will be able to help them and support them in their processes.' (Susan, partner 4)

- How might that be achieved? It is essential to learn to speak the same language as the customers:

  'On reflection and having worked in two or three organizations somewhat similar to ours, we have to learn to speak the same language as the customer better than we do [. .] we have decided that support and facilitation, and finding customers that we find '*right*' for us are important, and it is nice to notice that we seem to be pondering over these things at the right time, there is a demand for our kind of expertise and the service we offer.' (Peter, partner 5)

- It is considered necessary to find a way to make the expertise and services offered more tangible. The Consultancy Group tackles quite broad themes when working with its customers and its areas of expertise may be quite difficult for a potential customer to grasp, and also challenging to encapsulate in a value proposition. Visualization, a tool used in productization, is suggested as one solution:

  'We have been talking about co-creation, a facilitating approach and a common vision. And we have these different services, but they are all a bit elusive and difficult to grasp [for customers]. I was thinking about selling images and using visualization, for example. And I find that we will need help and support for this kind of image creation. How can we put down in words what our services can do for customers? We need to think, who would help us?' (Susan, partner 4)

- The proposal is supported but the CEO raises the issue of pricing the services (Hannah, CEO). A solution is proposed in the form of co-operation:

  'We also develop when we co-create with customers, and not only customers, but other stakeholders too. Take this workshop, for example. It is essential for us to succeed to look for stakeholders and look for interactions, be it with a customer organization or other type of organization (business development for example), who could help us in our journey.' (Eric, partner 3)

157

Table 8.3 (continued)

The practice	Examples of strategy dialogue from the workshops
	• Another partner raises the issue of resources:
	'Then there is a need to talk about resources because we are all independent consultants, and we have our own customers in addition to the customers we serve together. How many joint customers and projects can we have and so on? And also there is a question of time devoted to our joint projects.' (Rose, partner 2)
	• The discussion about tangible steps continues before the facilitator concludes:
	'The most important actions to be taken according to your choices are: to find customers suitable to you, '*to put services down in words*' or images and seeking partners for co-operation, and also to find ways to listen to people in organizations, and tools to help do that. And finding the right words to convey the value proposition linked, with co-operation being the key element. It seems to me that these actions you have chosen are to the customer. And now, last but not least: what will be done first?'
Dialoguing the need for a customer perspective	• The lively discussion on this topic continues and customer narratives are introduced as a valuable tool '*to put the services down in words*'. There was discussion on co-operation with the local business development organization, the dialogue and ideation were ongoing. The strategy work will continue in both organizations.
	• Understanding the customers and trying to step into their shoes was noted in the workshops as a very important aspect of strategy work. In addition, the customers' stories and the successes could be a useful way to convey the value proposition of the firm to potential customers.
	• The current reality for the Competence Management Company, and a challenging one, is that it has few customer references to pass on:
	'Of course, when selling to them it is easy for us to show slides and refer to the customer base. But what is still a bit depressing, is selling to business customers, because when they ask we can offer hardly any references.' (Thomasina, owner-manager)

A solution is suggested:

- 'But what I have been thinking here, is that we could offer a case description even if we do not have any names to name. We could take an example, describe a problem that an organization had and state how we solved it. And how it resulted in many good things.' (Haley, sales representative 1)

- The discussion focuses on building lasting relationships with customers and experiences of the customers wanting to get close; sometimes even too close, maybe being overreliant or overdemanding. The facilitator suggests one explanation:

- 'But of course the organizations are quite – I mean, that they respond to their delivery networks differently. That is to say, that they might see them as more strategic than before.' (facilitator)

- The facilitator's statement elicits reflection and understanding:

- 'Okay, now I realize why they come so close [the customers]. That may be because we can go right to the core with our services. Like an organization providing training services we are involved in developing their core product.' (Sarah, sales manager)

- 'That is their core, that's true. Their processes are founded upon our stuff.' (Thomasina, owner-manager)

- The customer perspective presented in these dialoguing practices is indirect and mediated through the roles and interests of the partners taking part in the workshop. They recognize the importance of the customer perspective but do not introduce into the discussion real experiences gleaned from the customer encounters.

159

we were able to pinpoint are not necessarily generalizable. But although our examples are case specific, we believe that the ways in which strategy is jointly constructed – based on different resources, roles and experiences that the participants have – is common to many businesses (Kowalkowski et al. 2012). We also believe that other organizations would benefit from a relational constructivist analysis of their strategy work.

Although there is a vast body of research on the tools and methods relating to strategy making, and on how strategy work takes place and the role of the actors involved (Vaara and Whittington, 2012), there still is a need to increase understanding regarding strategy work, especially in micro firms and between the self-employed. Our cases illustrate the central role that co-creation and dialogue play in strategizing between the partners. Our analysis identifies dialoguing practices that the participants use during strategy workshops. The strategy work was based on dialoguing about the customer, who are the main important customers and the importance of knowing the customers. Traditionally this is considered a decision to be taken before the firm is established or in the early stages of developing a strategy (business plan) for the new venture. Our findings suggest that the dialogue concerning the (main) customer may be an important ongoing practice in co-strategizing. The dialoguing practice of who we are and what we do highlighted the varied expertise and experiences of the entrepreneurs. That variation can be both a challenge and an opportunity. The challenge is to reconcile the different expectations regarding co-operation, and the opportunities stem from finding new ways to integrate and use a range of expertise to open new commercial avenues. Here, it is possible to draw parallels with research focusing on organizational identity (Holmer-Nadesan, 1996), and the ways of constructing the identity (who we are) that are important.

Looking for ways to integrate resources in the form of knowledge and skills was emphasized in the dialogue about the utilization of varied experience and knowledge in customer co-operation. Thus, it is possible to understand co-strategizing as a highly effectual process (Sarasvathy, 2001) departing from who we are and what we can do as the basis of strategy. Our findings contribute by highlighting the dialogue and involvement of multiple partners in the dialogue. The examples presented in the chapter illustrated several occasions where different strategic options were discussed jointly between the partnering consultants and facilitators by surfacing and sharing assumptions, exploring underlying assumptions, and for developing common ground (Doz and Kosonen, 2010). Each participant utilized their personal and professional backgrounds and also their previous encounters with customers to formulate their opinions on opportunities, and that experience was clearly an element of the dialoguing practices observed.

Inviting partners to a strategy meeting means that knowledgeable people are integrated into the practice of strategizing. Furthermore, ensuring people can participate in decision making and present their own ideas can help overcome the challenges that hinder the emergence of strategic ideas. In the context of professional services, the challenge of getting to know the customer and adopting a customer perspective was emphasized in the dialogue. These practices also highlight the fact that institutional elements, the business environment, the need to know the competition and to differentiate the firm from its competitors are essential parts of strategy co-creation, and each participant evaluates these elements based on his or her own experience and expertise. Therefore, the way in which the strategy was evolving in the dialogue could be viewed as an outcome of social construction. The findings also emphasize the agility, meaning that there is an opportunity to move to negotiating the steps required in the future. What Jarzabkowski and Balogun (2009) refer to as co-strategizing is about integrating varied expertise, expectations and interests, and our findings confirm that integration flows from active dialogue and compromises made by the actors in strategic planning. The findings also indicate co-strategizing in micro firms is an iterative and ongoing process that needs time and space to develop in the midst of business as usual.

Dialogue is an essential element of co-creation (Prahalad and Ramaswamy, 2004); if the participants are not willing to listen and learn and to question their own premises, it is hard to devise a strategy that everyone will happily commit to. Therefore, this chapter contributes to strategy-as-practice literature by highlighting the strategy work conducted between equal and independent consultants in a partnership. The contribution to co-creation stems from adopting the strategy-as-practice approach and focusing on how different forms of knowledge and expertise are integrated in the co-strategizing conducted by different actors. Theoretically this study draws from aspects of the entrepreneurship, marketing and strategy literature.

Because this is a qualitative two-case study, the results cannot be empirically generalized to other companies. Nevertheless, detailed data and analysis of the dialoguing practices can be transferable when studying strategy formation in other contexts. This chapter reports on a particular occurrence in a specific context and with data that represents a snapshot from strategy work, and it would be interesting to study strategizing longitudinally, with follow-up workshops organized for the case firms. Another interesting approach would also be to focus on the role of the materials used in strategy workshops (such as making picture collages, as in this study) – doing so would focus attention on to material practices in strategizing (Jarzabkowski and Spee, 2009) in the entrepreneurial context.

The practical importance of this analysis lies in providing insights for firms in relation to why and how co-strategizing can prove beneficial. Overall, firms should understand both the importance and complexity of strategizing and see co-creation and workshops as valuable tools in strategy work. A practical implication arises from the finding that it is important for small firms to find the time to organize a workshop or a meeting with important partners and to set aside time for ideating on the future, for exchanging experiences and customer narratives, and to look for new ways to utilize the varied expertise at their disposal, instead of being focused purely on conducting business as usual. Perhaps the most important aspect for the future of small firms is the determination of tangible steps and activities to advance strategy implementation and the awareness that such steps can be small and involve experimentation if appropriate.

NOTE

1. See also Doz and Kosonen (2010) for the use of 'dialoguing' concept in strategy renewal processes as a practice of 'surfacing and sharing assumptions, understanding contexts, exploring underlying assumptions and hypotheses, not just conclusions, and for developing common ground'.

REFERENCES

Aarikka-Stenroos, L. and E. Jaakkola (2012), 'Value co-creation in knowledge intensive business services: a dyadic perspective on the joint problem solving process', *Industrial Marketing Management*, **41**, 15–26.

Alves, H. (2013), 'Co-creation and innovation in public services', *The Service Industries Journal*, **33** (7–8), 671–82.

Ballantyne, D. (2004), 'Dialogue and its role in the development of relationship specific knowledge', *Journal of Business & Industrial Marketing*, **19** (2), 114–23.

Ballantyne, D., P. Frow, R.J. Varey and A. Payne (2011), 'Value propositions as communication practice: taking a wider view', *Industrial Marketing Management*, **40** (2), 202–10.

Bouwen, R. and C. Steyaert (1990), 'Construing organizational texture in young entrepreneurial firms', *Journal of Management Studies*, **29**, 637–49.

Chandler, G.N., D.R. DeTienne, A. McKelvie and T.V. Mumford (2011), 'Causation and effectuation processes: a validation study', *Journal of Business Venturing*, **26**, 375–90.

Coffey, A. and P. Atkinson (1996), *Making Sense of Qualitative Data*, Thousand Oaks, CA, USA: Sage Publications.

Dew, N., S. Read, S.D. Sarasvathy and R. Whitbank (2009), 'Effectual versus predictive logics in entrepreneurial decision-making: differences between experts and novices', *Journal of Business Venturing*, **24**, 287–309.

Doz, Y.L. and M. Kosonen (2010), 'Embedding strategic agility: a leadership agenda for accelerating business model renewal', *Long Range Planning*, **43**, 370–82.

Echeverri, P. and P. Skålén (2011), 'Co-creation and co-destruction: a practice theory based study of interactive value formation', *Marketing Theory*, **11** (3), 351–73.

Eisenhardt, K. (1989), 'Building theories from case study research', *Academy of Management Review*, **14** (4), 532–50.

Ellinor, L. and G. Gerard (1998), *Dialogue: Rediscover the Transforming Power of Conversation*, New York, NY: Wiley.

Eriksson, P. and A. Kovalainen (2008), *Qualitative Methods in Business Research*, London, UK: Sage Publications.

Feldman, M.S. and W.J. Orlikowski (2011), 'Theorizing practice and practicing theory', *Organization Science*, **22** (5), 1240–53.

Fletcher, D.E. (2006), 'Entrepreneurial processes and the social construction of opportunity', *Entrepreneurship & Regional Development*, **18**, 421–40.

Fosstenløkken, S.M., B.R. Løwendahl and O. Revang (2003), 'Knowledge development through client interaction: a comparative study', *Organization Studies*, **24** (6), 859–79.

Galkina, T. and S. Chetty (2015), 'Effectuation and networking of internationalizing SMEs', *Management International Review*, April 2015, DOI: 10.1007/s11575-015-0251-x.

Gherardi, S. (2011), 'Organizational learning: the sociology of practice', in M. Easterby-Smith and M.A. Lyles (eds), *Handbook of Organizational Learning and Knowledge Management*, 2nd edn, Hoboken, NJ, USA: John Wiley.

Gherardi, S. (2015), 'Practice-based research . . . according to?', Presentation during the course 'practice-based research in business studies', Aalto University, School of Economics, Helsinki, Finland 26–28 August.

Golsorkhi, D., L. Rouleau, D. Seidl and E. Vaara (2010), 'Introduction: what is strategy as practice?', in D. Golsorkhi, L. Rouleau, D. Seidl and E. Vaara (eds), *Cambridge Handbook of Strategy as Practice*, Cambridge, UK: Cambridge University Press.

Grönroos, C. (2011), 'Value co-creation in service logic: a critical analysis', *Marketing Theory*, **11** (3), 279–301.

Grönroos, C. and P. Voima (2013), 'Critical service logic: making sense of value creation and co-creation', *Journal of the Academy of the Marketing Science*, **41**, 133–50.

Gummesson, E. (2008), 'Extending the service-dominant logic: from customer centricity to balanced centricity', *Journal of the Academy of Marketing Science*, **36** (1), 15–17.

Heikkilä, J. and K. Heikkilä (2001), *Dialogi: avain innovatiivisuuteen*, Porvoo, Finland: WSOY.

Hirvonen, P. and N. Helander (2001), 'Towards joint value creation processes in professional services', *The TQM Magazine*, **13** (4), 281–91.

Holmer-Nadesan, M. (1996), 'Organizational identity and space of action', *Organization Studies*, **17**, 49–81.

Hoyer, W.D., R. Chandy, M. Dorotic, M. Kraft and S.S. Singh (2010), 'Consumer cocreation in new product development', *Journal of Service Research*, **13** (3), 283–96.

Jaakkola, E., A. Helkkula and L. Aarikka-Stenroos (2015), 'Service experience co-creation: conceptualization, implications, and future research directions', *Journal of Service Management*, **26** (2), 182–205.

Jarzabkowski, P. and J. Balogun (2009), 'The practice and process of delivering integration through strategic planning', *Journal of Management Studies*, **46** (8), 1255–88.

Jarzabkowski, P., J. Balogun and D. Seidl (2007), 'Strategizing: the challenges of a practice perspective', *Human Relations*, **60**, 5–27.

Jarzabkowski, P. and A.P. Spee (2009), 'Strategy-as-practice: a review and future directions for the field', *International Journal of Management Reviews*, **11** (1), 69–95.

Jensen Schau, H., A.M. Muñiz Jr. and E.J. Arnould (2009), 'How brand community practices create value', *Journal of Marketing*, **73**, 30–51.

Kohtamäki, M., S. Kraus, T. Kautonen and E. Varamäki (2008), 'Strategy in small growth-oriented firms in Finland: a discourse analysis approach', *The International Journal of Entrepreneurship and Innovation*, **9** (3), 167–75.

Kohtamäki, M., E. Tornikoski and E. Varamäki, E. (2008), 'The strategic management competence of small and medium-sized growth firms', *International Journal of Entrepreneurship and Small Business*, **7** (1), 139–50.

Kowalkowski, C., O. Persson Ridell, J.G. Röndell and D. Sörhammar (2012), 'The co-creative practice of forming a value proposition', *Journal of Marketing Management*, **28** (13–14), 1553–70.

Lusch, R.F. and S.L. Vargo (2014), *Service-Dominant Logic: Premises, Perspectives, Possibilities*, Cambridge, UK: Cambridge University Press.

Lusch, R.F., S.L. Vargo and M. Tanniru (2010), 'Service, value networks and learning', *Journal of the Academy of Marketing Science*, **38** (1), 19–31.

Miles, M.B. and M. Huberman (1994), *Qualitative Data Analysis: An Expanded Sourcebook*, Thousand Oaks, CA, USA: Sage.

Nikolova, N., M. Reihlen and J. Schlapfner (2009), 'Client – consultant interaction: capturing social practices of professional service production', *Scandinavian Journal of Management*, **25** (3), 289–98.

Orlikowski, W.J. (2007), 'Sociomaterial practices: exploring technology at work', *Organization Studies*, **28** (9), 1435–48.

Orlikowski, W.J. (2010), 'Practice in research: phenomenon, perspective and philosophy', in D. Golsorkhi, L. Rouleau, D. Seidl and E. Vaara (eds), *Cambridge Handbook of Strategy as Practice*, Cambridge, UK: Cambridge University Press, pp.23–33.

Payne, A.F., K. Storbacka and P. Frow (2008), 'Managing the co-creation of value', *Journal of the Academy of Marketing Science*, **36** (1), 83–96.

Prahalad, C.K. and V. Ramaswamy (2004), 'Co-creation experiences: the next practice in value creation', *Journal of Interactive Marketing*, **18** (3), 5–14.

Rasmussen, S. (2012), 'Co-creation in professional service firms – problem solving processes as an opportunity for enhanced value creation and creative and innovative project solutions', master's thesis in 'pedagogikk; Kunnskap, Utdanning og Læring', Pedagogisk forskningsinstitutt, Utdanningsvitenskapelige fakultet, Universitetet I oslo.

Reckwitz, A. (2002), 'Toward a theory of social practices: a development in cultural theorizing', *European Journal of Social Theory*, **5** (2), 243–63.

Sarasvathy, S. (2001), 'Causation and effectuation: toward a theoretical shift from economic inevitability to entrepreneurial contingency', *Academy of Management Review*, **26** (2), 243–63.

Sieg, J.H., A. Fischer, M.W. Wallin and G. von Krogh (2012), 'Proactive diagnosis: how professional service firms sustain client dialogue', *Journal of Service Management*, **23** (2), 253–78.
Skålén, P., J. Gummerus, C. Koskull and P. Magnusson (2015), 'Exploring value propositions and service innovation: a service-dominant logic study', *Journal of the Academy of Marketing Science*, **43** (2), 137–58.
Vaara, E. and R. Whittington (2012), 'Strategy-as-practice: taking social practices seriously', *The Academy of Management Annals*, **6** (1), 285–336.
Vargo, S.L. and R.L. Lusch (2004), 'Evolving to a new dominant logic for marketing', *Journal of Marketing*, **68** (1), 1–17.
Vargo, S.L. and R.F. Lusch (2008), 'Service-dominant logic: continuing the evolution', *Journal of the Academy of the Marketing Science*, **36**, 1–10.
Vargo, S.L., P.P. Maglio and M.A. Akaka (2008), 'On value and value co-creation: a service systems and service logic perspective', *European Management Journal*, **26** (3), 145–52.
Vähämäki, M. (2008), 'Dialogi organisaation oppimisessa: itseohjautuvan muutoksen mahdollisuus tuotantotyössä' [Dialogue in organizational learning: a potential for autonomous change in industrial work], Dissertation, series A-2:2008, Turku: Turku School of Economics.
Whittington, R. (2006), 'Completing the practice turn in strategy research', *Organization Studies*, **27** (5), 613–34.
Yin, R.K. (2009), *Case Study Research – Design and Methods*, 4th edn, Applied Social Research Methods Series, Vol. 5, Thousand Oaks, CA, USA: Sage.

9. Empirical exploration of a cohort of new technology-based firms in Sweden: what happens to them during their early years?

Heikki Rannikko, Erno Tornikoski, Anders Isaksson, Hans Löfsten and Hanna Rydehell

INTRODUCTION

Within entrepreneurship research firm growth has received an increasing amount of attention in the last years. Henrekson and Johansson (2010), for example, found only 20 studies published after 1990 for their literature review on high-growth firms, whereas four years later Coad et al. (2014) could identify more than 100 papers in their Google scholar search on the topic. However, although new and small firms should be in the heart of entrepreneurial growth research, many growth studies deal with firms that are larger in size and thereby leave out a great deal of the entrepreneurial activity. For example, the seminal 'Arriving at high growth firm' article (Delmar et al., 2003) studied growth among firms larger than 20 employees and the widely applied OECD definition on high-growth firms, which was introduced in 2012, applies to firms that have more than ten employees. A general conclusion arises that there is a need to study growth among firms that are at the heart of entrepreneurship research, that is, new firms independent of their initial size. Small independent firms experience problems in developing their innovative resources due to the costs of market and technological development and incorporating or integrating knowledge. Few studies focus on new technology-based firms (NTBFs) and their survival. However, NTBFs are similar to other small businesses as they often have inexperienced management and may seek to address new markets with new or developing products (Löfsten, 2016). This chapter deals with NTBFs in Sweden and it could be suitable to refer to earlier Swedish studies in this field of research; some examples are Dahlstrand (1997);

Klofsten (1997); Rickne and Jacobsson (1999); Löfsten and Lindelöf (2002); Dahlstrand and Jacobsson (2003); Löfsten and Lindelöf (2005); and Löfsten (2010).

Another observation from firm growth research, related to the emphasis on larger firms, is that there still is confusion about measuring growth. Various researchers have argued, for example, that methodological differences, such as in terms of measurement, contribute to mixed results concerning firm growth theory (Davidsson and Wiklund, 2000; Shepherd and Wiklund, 2009; Weinzimmer et al., 1998). Therefore, it has been suggested that researchers should use several rather than a single measure. This would allow easier comparisons across studies, more substantial robustness checks, and qualitative investigation of the differences found between different quantitative indicators (Coad et al., 2014). Increased overall understanding, then, would facilitate knowledge accumulation in firm growth research, as pointed out by Shepherd and Wiklund (2009).

We take two previous shortcomings (lack of studies on new and small firm development, and confusion in measuring growth) as a motivation to our study and set out to investigate the development of new firms from establishment onwards. While previous studies have lacked focus on the left-hand tail of the growth rate distribution (Coad et al., 2014) we approach the phenomenon through detailed analysis of a representative sample and track down what happens to each firm (exit/survival/growth) during their first seven years.

As our empirical context we use the cohort 2006 of Swedish NTBFs. Among the overall firm population, it is NTBFs that are promoted to have more wealth-creation potential and this therefore makes it an especially interesting object of study. However, as such, the act of creating an NTBF is not what makes a difference: it is the post-entry performance of some of them that can lead to desired societal benefits. At the same time, empirical evidence points out that NTBFs do not necessarily possess higher probability of fast growth than other firms (see Almus, 2002) – in fact, technology and firm size just seem to increase survival chances (Giovannetti et al., 2011). While the survival and growth of newly founded firms is an integral part of entrepreneurship research, there are several gaps in the current research that hinder progress in understanding the post-founding performance of newly founded firms, and it seems that a more detailed analysis of the survival patterns of new firms is needed.

Our study makes original contributions to our current understanding about new technology-based firm growth. First, we find that surprisingly many firms (70 per cent) from the 2006 cohort of new technology-based firms still operate in the end of year 2014. This is a much higher share than what has been found in previous studies. Additionally we find that only very few firms experience high growth during their first seven years (0.6–3 per cent from the cohort) and that among high-growth firms employment growth and sales growth are highly correlated. As what comes to the growth measurement challenge of new and small firms we see that the 'kink-point' approach (Clayton et al., 2013) might be useful. By applying this approach researchers would capture much of the growth left out by, for example, the OECD measure.

This chapter is structured as follows. In the next section we review some of the existing literature on firm growth research in order to develop formal research questions for the study. Thereafter we detail our data set, the sampling procedure, the measures and our analytical techniques. The third section will present the results. Finally, we discuss our observations in the light of existing literature, highlight the contribution of this study, and discuss the implications and draw the main conclusions.

THEORETICAL DEVELOPMENT

Firm creation is widely embraced because new firms seem to contribute to the health of economies (Gallagher and Stewart, 1986). While new firms are exposed to high mortality rates (Dunne et al., 1988; Audretsch, 1995), it is also estimated that only a small minority of the surviving firms want to grow, and finally achieve enough growth to have a positive societal impact (Storey, 1994; Brüderl and Preisendörfer, 2000; Napier et al., 2012). It is these growing firms, and especially so-called high-growth firms, which have been the focus of policy makers and entrepreneurship researchers in recent years.

In order to analyse this growing interest in firm growth research we looked at some recent studies from Scopus research database. We searched with the term 'growth AND firm' all articles in social sciences since 2011. Since this resulted in over 4,000 results, we further restricted the search to the ten most appearing entrepreneurship or innovation journals. These were: on place 1 *Small Business Economics* (75 hits), on place 2 *Research Policy* (38), on place 3 *Industrial and Corporate Change* (37), on place 6 *Journal of Small Business and Enterprise Development* (32), on place 7 *International Journal of Entrepreneurship and Small Business* (29), on place 9 *International Small Business Journal* (29), on place 34 *Journal of Business Venturing* (16), on place 37 *International Journal of Entrepreneurial Behavior and Research* (15), on place 41 *Journal of Small Business Management* (14) and on place 46 *Entrepreneurship and Regional Development* (13). The publication years show the rising interest: there were 11 articles published in 2012; 11 in 2013; 13 in 2014; and 14 in 2015. These figures suggest that indeed the interest in growth studies has increased over the past few years. The journal *Small Business Economics* appears to be the leader, with *Research Policy* in the second position.

However, although firm growth research has grown in numbers, few problems have been noticed as what comes to research methodology. For example, Nightingale and Coad (2014), in their summary on methodological challenges of growth research, discuss five interrelated areas that may hamper the meaning of research findings. First, data quality might restrict possibilities for conducting studies due to missing data, bad quality data or unrepresentative data. Second, skewed statistics do not support the use of conventional regression strategies. Third, definitional flexibility, for example in defining entrepreneurial firms, causes difficulties in comparing different studies. Fourth, the phenomenon of 'regression to the mean' amplifies the growth impact of small firms in comparison to large firms. Fifth, definitional variability, for example in defining firm growth, may bias conclusions from firm growth studies.

In order to find out to what extent problem areas can be seen in existing research we further analysed studies that we found from the Scopus database, especially focusing on data coverage and operationalization of growth measures. From the previously mentioned 297 studies we further excluded irrelevant articles by looking through titles. If the title did not hint that empirical analysis of firm growth is in the focus, the paper was left out. After going through the titles we ended up with 80 articles. From these articles we analysed each abstract in order to find out whether the article deals with analysis of growth among population or subpopulation of firms, after which we were left with 45 studies.

Based on analysing sampling strategies of reviewed studies there seems to be three different approaches in recent growth research. The first category is studies that use a data set containing an entire population of firms (active) for a given timeframe across industries or in chosen industries. About 20 per cent of the studies represent this category. The second category is studies that use different kinds of samples, either representative or non-representative. To this category belongs the vast majority of reviewed studies, around 70 per cent of all. The third category is studies that concentrate on one or multiple cohorts of firms and follows their development for some number of years. To this category belongs only 10 per cent of the reviewed studies.

What comes to the role of firm age and firm size as sampling criteria it seems is that most often these are not explicitly considered. Self-evidently among cohort studies the focus is on new firms since the analysis focuses on the first years of new firms, which tend to be small. In population-level studies, however, and in studies based on samples, new or small firms are often excluded or the role of these in sampling is not mentioned. From the reviewed 45 studies (Table 9A.1 in Appendix), 13 studies impose a clear age limit and 13 studies impose a clear size limit in sampling, whereas for 15 studies it is clear that there is no age limit and for ten studies it is clear that there is no size limit. However, interestingly, for 17 studies the role of age concerning sampling is unclear, or one cannot even find descriptive age statistics in the study; and for 22 studies the role of age concerning sampling is unclear or one cannot find descriptive size statistics. When it comes to growth measures used, the most popular measure of growth seems to be in recent growth research the log difference of sales. Another observation is that in some cases additional measures, most typically employment change, have been used.

While a thorough review of recent growth studies is beyond the scope of this chapter, for our purposes two observations impose themselves from the above analysis. The first observation is that there is a lack of studies that explicitly consider new firms. In this chapter we add new knowledge to the field by adopting a cohort approach, which is underrepresented among existing research, to allow focus on new and small firms. Moreover, while only few studies consider simultaneously the development of growth firms and the development of not-so-high-growth-firms of a given population (Coad et al., 2014), in this chapter we go beyond decline, mortality and growth, and study why and when firms exit the new technology-based firm population and which firms remain in the population and thereby add new knowledge to the field. To guide our analysis we formally pose the first research question as: what happens to new technology-based firms in their first seven years?

Our second observation from existing research concerning high growth in specific firms is that due to measures and definitions used, new and small firms are largely missing from the high-growth analysis. Moreover, to cope with measurement challenge in general, it has been suggested that researchers should use several measures rather than a single measure in order to allow easier comparisons across studies, more substantial robustness checks, and qualitative investigation of the differences found between different quantitative indicators (Shepherd and Wiklund, 2009). Thus, in order to include new and small firms' growth in the analyses on one hand, and to increase our study's reliability on the other hand, we apply various different measures of growth in studying new technology-based firm growth. To guide our analysis we set the second research question as: how do surviving NTBFs grow when different measures of growth are applied?

DATA AND METHODOLOGY

Our empirical setting is the entire population of NTBFs founded in Sweden in the year 2006. To distinguish NTBFs from other firms we apply the Eurostat classification of technology sectors (high technology manufacturing, medium-high technology manufacturing, medium-low technology manufacturing, low technology manufacturing and knowledge-intensive high technology services). From these sectors we found 1,525 NTBFs that were founded in 2006. As the moment of the database search was at the end of year 2014 we concentrate our research to the period between 2007 and 2013. To answer research question one – 'what happens to new technology-based firms in their first seven years?' – we conduct an in-depth analysis through the firm registry. Sweden is known for its advanced firm registration system, making it a perfect context to carry out a cohort study. We identified firms using Retriever Business, a database that contains financial and other legal information on all businesses in Sweden.

Previous studies in the new technology-based firm context have sought to define 'high technology' (Markusen et al., 1986). According to Monck et al. (1988), there are two groups of indicators: (1) measures of resource inputs to high-technology activity, such as research and development (R&D) effort and R&D expenditure; and (2) the employment of qualified personnel and measures of output or performance, such as growth rates, patent records, copyrights and licences, and technological innovations. We use the Eurostat categorization of manufacturing and services industries according to technological intensity, which corresponds to the former approach.[1] Butchart (1987) pioneered the industry approach in the UK, which was widely applied thereafter (see, for example, Brown and Mason, 2014). Based on NACE revision 2 codes, we concentrate on firms in high technology, medium-high technology and knowledge-intensive high technology services.

To answer research question two – 'how do surviving NTBFs grow when different measures of growth are applied' – we conduct a growth analyis using various different growth measures for only those NTBFs that show full-time series of employment or sales information. In measuring growth we apply 50 per cent annual sales growth (Autio et al., 2000; Halabisky et al., 2006) threshold and the OECD definition, according to which in the beginning of the measurement period there needs to be at least ten employees and in a three-year period firms must have annually 20 per cent employee growth on average. To operationalize the former indicator we first calculated annual growth rates for each firm. Then from each three-year period, beginning in 2006, we picked up those firms that fulfilled the above-mentioned rule. As 2006 is the first year and 2013 the last year we have five three-year periods during which a firm may qualify as a high-growth firm. To pick up high-gowth firms accrding to the OECD definition, first their annual growth rates were calculated. From these, three-year averages were calculated. If the average was greater than 20 per cent, the firm was defined as a high-growth firm. As an addition to the OECD indicator we apply a 'kink point' approach (Clayton et al., 2013). According to this rule, small firms that have less than ten employees are included in the group of high-growth firms through applying growth at the ten employee threshold. Thus, for a firm with ten employees, high growth would mean 7.28 employees more over a three-year period. Consequently, for firms with less than ten employees, growth of eight or more is considered high growth. By considering OECD and kink-point approaches together we are able to have all firms from the cohort included in the analysis, independent of their initial size. Given that we are interested in new-firm growth, this is an important addition.

ANALYSIS AND RESULTS

In the analysis section we carry out two sets of analyses in order to answer research question one and two. First, our purpose is to find out how many firms are in operation at the end of the seven-year inspection period. Because during this exercise we also look at possible exit causes the analysis provides answers to research question one. Second, we look at growth among firms that are still in operation by the end of year 2014 through measures that were explained in the method section ('OECD approach', 'kink-point approach' and 'Autio approach'). Within this analysis we pay attention to share of high-growth firms and to the relationship between sales and employment growth in different groups of firms.

From analysing empirical data our first main observation is that surprisingly many firms from the 2006 cohort still operate at the end of year 2014. As a result of our search from the Swedish firm registry at the end of year 2014, we found 1,525 firms that could be classified as technology-based firms according to Eurostat industry classification and that were founded in the year 2006. From this set of firms 1,072 firms were operating at the end of year 2014, making the survival percentage 70 per cent. During the eight-year period (2006–14) 282 firms had been unregistered, that is, they had officially quit their operation. From the remaining 1,243 firms 63 had a process going that eventually led to exit (such as bankruptcy). Finally, thereafter, from the remaining 1,180 firms 109 firms were found that had no sales in any year during the inspection period. We suspect that these firms were not operative, and could not be counted as viable going

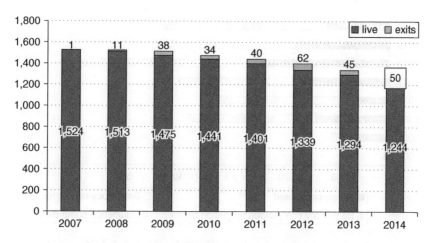

Figure 9.1   Annual exits from the 2006 cohort of NTBFs

concerns. In the end, thus, 1,072 were fully operative, making the survival rate 70 per cent from 2006 to 2014. Figure 9.1 displays with more detail how exits from the cohort of 2006 firms have taken place temporally. The main observation from the statistics is that after the year 2008 the annual number of exits rises to an average level of 40 exits per year. This rise coincides with the financial crisis that started in 2008. As Table 9A.2 in the Appendix shows, there is a great variety in exit/survival rates between different industries. However, if we look at only those industries (two-digit NACE code level) in which there were more than 20 start-ups in year 2006, the exit rate varies between 19 per cent and 40 per cent, with an average of 32 per cent. These groups are 26 (manufacture of computer, electronic and optical products), 47 (retail trade not in stores, stalls or markets), 58 (publishing activities), 59 (motion picture, video and television programme production, sound recording and so on), 61 (telecommunications), 62 (computer programming, consultancy and related services), 63 (information service activities), 70 (activities of head offices; management consultancy activities) and 72 (scientific research and development). Thus, looking at NTBF survival through those industries where the most firms are, survival is rather surprisingly evenly distributed.

What comes to exit causes it seems is that a 'forced' exit is more probable than a 'voluntary' one. As Figure 9.2 shows, there are four different categories to count for exit reasons. From these we consider as voluntary exit a merge with another company. As forced exit, on the other hand, we count those that are classified to bankruptcy or liquidation. From these categories on average over the eight-year period the most probable is a merge with

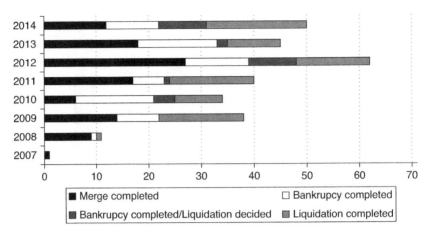

Figure 9.2   Annual exit causes from the 2006 cohort of NTBFs

another firm with 13 merges. In other categories, there are 22 cases in sum per year on average. Interesting in the development of exits is the slight upward trend in the number of forced exits. Whereas only two forced exits took place in year 2008, in year 2014 there were 38 forced exits. On the other hand, a similar growth trend for voluntary exits cannot be noticed.

Our second main observation from analysing empirical data is that, independent of the growth measure used, only a small minority of firms qualify as high-growth firms. However, between different measures there is inconsistency in how they capture the high-growth phenomenon. To make these observations an analysis was carried out for those firms that had not been excluded from the firm database by the end of year 2014 and which show positive sales for at least one year during the period 2007–13. As previously stated, to this group belong 1,072 firms. However, in visual check it was noticed that some of the firms were from the beginning too large to be considered as a new entrepreneurial firm and consequently these three firms were excluded from the analysis, leaving us 1,069 firms. As Table 9A.3 in the Appendix shows, these remaining firms have developed positively from 2007 to 2013. In 2007 the mean sales for the group was 2786Tkr and this grew to 7267TKr in year 2013. While the growth in mean sales is considerable, the growth in median sales during the same period is much less impressive: the median sales in 2007 was 982TKr and this grew to 1018TKr in 2013. The increasing spread between mean level of sales and median level of sales hints that there is a small group of firms that has managed to grow fast and is thus responsible for overall positive development.

The same development that can be seen from sales statistics can also be seen with employment statistics, but to a lesser extent (see Table 9A.4 in the Appendix). Whereas the average firm, measured through the median, remained as a one-person outlet during the entire period, the average firm, measured through mean, doubled its size from 2.3 employees to 4.6 employees. Again, this hints that a small number of growing firms have employed new people while most firms have remained at one employee level.

The above statistics reveal the aggregate development of the population of Swedish new technology-based firms from year 2006. In light of the presented figures the stylized fact that 'few high-growth firms are responsible for the bulk of economic benefits' holds true. However, within the whole NTBF population there are substantial differences between industries in sales performance.

In Table 9A.5 and 9A.6 in the Appendix we present sales and employment growth for those NACE two-digit groups among our NTBF population that had more than 20 firms established in year 2006. These groups are again 26 (manufacture of computer, electronic and optical products), 47 (retail trade not in stores, stalls or markets), 58 (publishing activities), 59 (motion picture, video and television programme production, sound recording and so on), 61 (telecommunications), 62 (computer programming, consultancy and related services), 63 (information service activities), 70 (activities of head offices; management consultancy activities) and 72 (scientific research and development).

As the tables show, the highest sales growth is found in the telecommunication sector (nace 61) where the mean sales of 15 firms grew by 543 per cent from 5056Tkr to 32115Tkr during the period. In that sector a significant change can be noticed also in median sales (1,192 per cent). Considering changes in both mean and median, the smallest growth figures can be found in the sector 47 (retail trade not in stores, stalls or markets). In this sector, growth in the mean was 33 per cent over the period whereas the median sales decreased by 49 per cent.

While sales growth figures show high volatility, the same cannot be noticed with employment figures. A typical NTBF in selected sectors has remained as a one- to two-person outlet. In eight sectors from nine, the median number of employees has remained at one, or at most has risen to two. At the highest in these eight sectors the mean number of employees in year 2013 was 6 in Computer programming, consultancy and related services (nace 62). These figures reveal that indeed typical NTBFs do not experience high employee growth in their first years. The only sector in which the mean employment size has risen to over ten employees is telecommunication (nace 61). As is evident through the analysis, growth of typical NTBFs is not a common phenomenon. In what follows we look more closely at these rare high-growth firms through three different statistics (as explained in the methods section). As with the previous tables, our focus is on the 1,069 entrepreneurial technology-based new firms from the cohort of 2006 in Sweden.

Concerning high-growth firms Table 9.1 shows how many growth firms there are according to two different measurement approaches in each three-year period starting from the period 2006–9 and ending with the period 2010–13. First, we have the OECD definition and kink-point approach, which are additive because the OECD definition considers only firms that have at least ten employees in the start year, while kink-point adds those firms that have less than ten employees to start with. The second approach is 'Autio approach', which considers as high-growth firms all firms that grow in sales over 50 per cent annually throughout a three-year period.

The first observation from the statistics is that the number of high-growth firms (HGFs) varies considerably between periods. For example, the number of HGFs according to the OECD definition varies between 1 and 18 firms. If we add firms that are high-growth firms according to the OECD to those that are high-growth firms according to the kink-point approach, the number of high-growth firms varies between 24 and 50 firms. On the other hand the number of high-growth firms varies from 10 to 24 when defined through the Autio et al. (2000) definition. Considering both definitions, the share of high-growth firms varies between 0.6 per cent and 3 per cent. The definitions are only partly overlapping: at most, 11 firms are jointly considered as HGFs according to both definitions (for the period 2007–10). For the remaining periods this number varies between two firms and four firms.

Moreover, employment high growth seems to persist to some extent while sales high-growth not similarly. Tables 9A.7a and 9A.7b in the Appendix display the number of firms that are classified as high-growth firms with the condition that a firm has been classified as a high-growth firm in the previous period. Statistics show that around 75 per cent of firms that were classified as high-growth firms according to joint OECD and kink-point approach in one period classify as high-growth firms the period after. However, this percentage shrinks sharply when the consequent periods are considered. For example, for those firms that were HGFs from 2006 to 2009 only 13 per cent classify as HGF in the period 2010–13. Furthermore, results are greatly different when the Autio et al. (2000) definition is applied. Table 9.2 below sheds more light on the persistence of high growth. It shows that indeed most firms have experienced only one growth period during our inspection period. Especially when the Autio et al. definition is used, the number of firms that have experienced more than one high-growth period differs greatly from the number of firms that have

Table 9.1   Number of high-growth firms among the 2006 cohort of Swedish NTBFs according to different measures

	Number of HGFs		Number of HGFs		Number of HGFs
		Sum OECD + KINK			
OECD_emp~09	1	KINK_emp_~09	23	Autio_sal~09	10
OECD_emp_~10	10	KINK_emp_~10	40	Autio_sal~10	24
OECD_emp_~11	16	KINK_emp_~11	29	Autio_sal~11	13
OECD_emp_~12	13	KINK_emp_~12	28	Autio_sal~12	10
OECD_emp_~13	18	KINK_emp_~13	19	Autio_sal~13	10

Table 9.2   Number of high-growth periods among the 2006 cohort of Swedish NTBFs according to different measures

Number of HG periods	Oecd_emp	Kink_emp	Autio_sal
1	17	17	42
2	9	11	8
3	5	6	3
4	2	2	0
5	0	0	0

experienced more than one high-growth period. Whereas, according to the Autio et al. definition, 42 firms experienced one growth period, eight firms experienced two growth periods and only three firms experienced three growth periods. When it comes to whether firms with two or more growth episodes experienced them as two consecutive episodes or as two isolated episodes it seems that growing through consecutive episodes is common. As Table 9A.8 in the Appendix shows, 26 out of 28 firms that experienced two high-growth periods experienced them as two consecutive episodes. The same observation applies to firms that experienced three or four high-growth periods.

Our third main observation from analysing empirical data is that the relationship between sales and employment growth are surprisingly stable for high-growth firms, especially when high growth is measured through combined OECD and kink-point approach. In Figure 9.3 we plot the development of mean and median sales and mean and median employment for three groups. The base is again those 1,069 firms that had survived until the end of year 2014, as explained earlier. From this, the first extracted group considers firms that are high-growth firms according to combined OECD and kink-point approach (89 firms). The second extracted group is high-growth firms according to the Autio et al. approach (49 firms); the third extracted group is firms that do not belong to either of these two groups and are part of the base (814 firms).

The first two graphs show that both the positive relationship between median sales and median employment, and the relationship between mean sales and mean employment, is stable among firms that classify as high-growth firms according to combined OECD and kink-point approach. In visual check, sales and employment seem to develop at almost exactly the same rate. This is an interesting observation when we bear in mind that definition is based on the employment growth. Cross-correlations for both pairs of time series are 0.99.

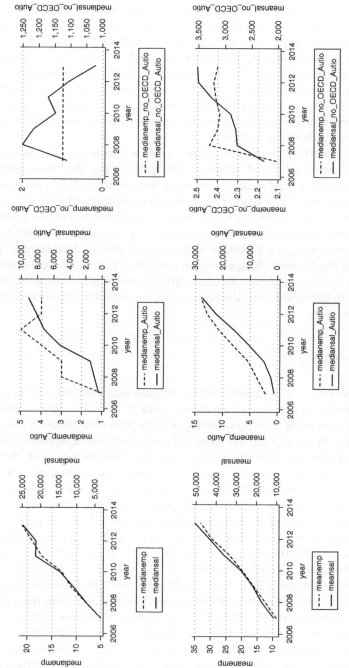

Figure 9.3   Development of median (mean) employment and median (mean) sales for three different groups among surviving Swedish cohort 2006 NTBFs

The graphs in the middle show the relationships between median sales and median employment, and the relationship between mean sales and mean employment, among firms that classify as high-growth firms according to the Autio et al. approach (from 2007 to 2013). For this group of firms the relationship is not as smooth as with the previous group. Especially in the case of median development, it seems that employment changes are driving changes in sales. This can also be seen from cross-correlations, which is 0.98 for the relationship between means and 0.79 for the relationship between medians.

Finally, the graphs at the bottom of Figure 9.3 show the relationships between median sales and median employment, and the relationship between mean sales and mean employment, among firms that do not classify as high-growth firms neither according to combined OECD and kink-point approach nor according to the Autio et al. approach. For this group of firms the observed relationships are not nearly as consistent as with the previous groups. Again, especially in the case of median development, it seems that employment changes are not associated to sales changes in any way. This can also be seen from cross-correlations, which are 0.70 for the relationship between means while no correlation exists for the relationship between medians.

DISCUSSION

This chapter was set to investigate two research questions, the first being 'what happens to new technology-based firms in their first seven years?' and the second being 'how do surviving NTBFs grow when different measures of growth are applied?' As empirical context we used a representative data set of Swedish technology-based new firms founded in year 2006. Concerning the first research question we find that surprisingly many firms from the 2006 cohort still operate at the end of year 2014. From the total of 1,525 firms established in year 2006, 1,070 firms were still operating at the end of year 2014, making the survival rate 70 per cent. This figure is much higher than what has been found in previous studies. Geroski et al. (2010) estimate survival after eight years to be 32–36 per cent for Portuguese firms founded between 1983 and 1985. This estimate is similar to Macdonald's (2012) study on the 2002 cohort of Canadian firms. In this study it was estimated that on average 35 per cent of firms from the 2002 cohort were alive after seven years on average, and that over different industries there was surprisingly little variation in survival. For example, in the sector 'professional, scientific and technical services', which may correspond partly to our sectors of interest, survival rate after seven years was

38 per cent. Moreover, Disney et al. (2003) present a table (p.97) on average cohort failure (survival) rates for firms in the UK, the USA, Canada, Portugal, France and Italy. Among these countries, survival rate after seven years varies between 52 per cent and 33 per cent. Finally, Santarelli and Vivarelli (2007) state that more than 50 per cent of new firms exit the market within the first five years of activity, according to econometric sectoral and microeconomic evidence. Thus, against these comparison results, survival among Swedish NTBFs seems high indeed.

Concerning the second research question our first observation is that, independent of the growth measure used, only a small minority of firms qualify as high-growth firms. This observation corresponds to earlier findings in the literature. Previously it has been found that firm growth rates follow Laplace distribution with its characteristic 'tent-shape' (Bottazzi and Secchi, 2006). This means that most firms are not growing at all and only few firms experience high growth. From the cohort 2006 of Swedish NTBFs we find that between 0.6 per cent and 3 per cent of firms are classified as high-growth firms. In comparison, the OECD report finds that in Sweden the rate of high-growth enterprises varied between 4 per cent and 6 per cent (OECD, 2015). However, the OECD's rate of high-growth enterprises measure estimates the number of high-growth enterprises as a percentage of the population of enterprises with ten or more employees. This is in contrast to our result that estimated the share of high-growth firms from the cohort. Moreover, OECD definition counts only those firms having more than ten employees, whereas we included also those firms having under ten employees through our combined OECD and kink-point approach. Concerning the second research question we additionally observe that sales growth and employment growth among high-growth firms are correlated, especially when employment-based growth measure is applied. This observation is counter to some earlier results in the literature. For example, Shepherd and Wiklund (2009) find in their study on correlations between different growth measures that employment and sales growth were only modestly correlated.

CONCLUSIONS

This chapter contributes to the current understanding of new technology-based firm growth. We find a surprisingly high survival rate (70 per cent) for the 2006 cohort of NTBFs at the end of 2014 and this rate is much higher than those reported in previous studies. Additionally, we find that very few firms experience high growth during their first seven years (0.6 to 3 per cent from the cohort) and that, among the high-growth firms, employment growth and sales growth are highly correlated. To address the challenges of measuring growth for new and small firms, we show the potential usefulness of the kink-point approach. Researchers can use this approach to capture much of the growth excluded in other measures, for example, the OECD measure.

NOTE

1. http://epp.eurostat.ec.europa.eu/statistics_explained/index.php/High-tech_statistics.

REFERENCES

Almus, M. (2002), 'What characterizes a fast-growing firm?', *Applied Economics*, **34**, 1497–508.
Anyadike-Danes, M., C. Bjuggren, S. Gottschalk, W. Hölzl, D. Johansson, M. Maliranta and A. Myrann (2015), 'An international cohort comparison of size effects on job growth', *Small Business Economics*, **44** (4), 821–44.
Anyadike-Danes, M., M. Hart and J. Du (2015), 'Firm dynamics and job creation in the United Kingdom: 1998–2013', *International Small Business Journal*, **33** (1), 12–27.
Audretsch, D.B (1995), 'Innovation, growth and survival', *International Journal of Industrial Organization*, **13**, 441–57.
Autio, E., P. Arenius and H. Wallenius (2000), 'Economic impact of gazelle firms in Finland', working papers series 2000:3, Helsinki University of Technology, Institute of Strategy and International Business.
Baptista, R. and M.T. Preto (2011), 'New firm formation and employment growth: regional and business dynamics', *Small Business Economics*, **36** (4), 419–42.
Bentzen, J., E.S. Madsen and V. Smith (2012), 'Do firms' growth rates depend on firm size?' *Small Business Economics*, **39** (4), 937–47.
Bertoni, F., M.G. Colombo and L. Grilli (2011), 'Venture capital financing and the growth of high-tech start-ups: disentangling treatment from selection effects', *Research Policy*, **40** (7), 1028–43.
Bos, J.W.B. and E. Stam (2014), 'Gazelles and industry growth: a study of young high-growth firms in The Netherlands', *Industrial and Corporate Change*, **23** (1), 145–69.
Bottazzi, G. and A. Secchi (2006), 'Explaining the distribution of firm growth rates', *Rand Journal of Economics*, **37** (2): 235–56.
Brenner, T. and A. Schimke (2015), 'Growth development paths of firms – a study of smaller businesses', *Journal of Small Business Management*, **53** (2), 539–57.
Brown, R. and C. Mason (2014), 'Inside the high-tech black box: a critique of technology entrepreneurship policy', *Technovation*, **34** (12), 773–84.
Brudel, J., P. Preisendorfer and R. Ziegler (1992), 'Survival chances of newly founded business organizations', *American Sociological Review*, **57** (2), 227–42.
Brüderl J. and P. Preisendörfer (2000), 'Fast-growing businesses: empirical evidence from a German study', *International Journal of Sociology*, **30** (3), 45–70.

Butchart, R. (1987), 'A new UK definition of the high technology industries', *Economic Trends*, **400** (February), 82–8.

Capasso, M., E. Cefis and A. Sapio (2013), 'Reconciling quantile autoregressions of firm size and variance-size scaling', *Small Business Economics*, **41** (3), 609–32.

Capasso, M., T. Treibich and B. Verspagen (2015), 'The medium-term effect of R&D on firm growth', *Small Business Economics*, **45** (1), 39–62.

Clayton, R.L., A. Sadeghi, D.M. Talan and J.R. Splezer (2013), 'High-employment-growth firms: defining and counting them', *Monthly Labor Review*, US Bureau of Labor Statistics.

Coad, A., S. Daunfeldt, D. Johansson and K. Wennberg (2014), 'Whom do high-growth firms hire?', *Industrial and Corporate Change*, **23** (1), 293–327.

Coad A., S.-E. Daunfeldt, H. Werner, D. Johansson and P. Nightingale (2014), 'High-growth firms: introduction to the special section: high-growth firms', *Industrial and Corporate Change*, **23** (1), 91–112.

Coad, A. and C. Guenther (2013), 'Diversification patterns and survival as firms mature', *Small Business Economics*, **41** (3), 633–49.

Coad, A., A. Segarra and M. Teruel (2016), 'Innovation and firm growth: does firm age play a role?', *Research Policy*, **45** (2), 387–400.

Coad, A. and J.P. Tamvada (2012), 'Firm growth and barriers to growth among small firms in India', *Small Business Economics*, **39** (2), 383–400.

Colombelli, A., J. Krafft and F. Quatraro (2014), 'High-growth firms and techno-logical knowledge: do gazelles follow exploration or exploitation strategies?', *Industrial and Corporate Change*, **23** (1), 261–91.

Corsino, M. and R. Gabriele (2011), 'Product innovation and firm growth: evidence from the integrated circuit industry', *Industrial and Corporate Change*, **20** (1), 29–56.

Cowling, M., W. Liu, A. Ledger and N. Zhang (2015), 'What really happens to small and medium-sized enterprises in a global economic recession? UK evidence on sales and job dynamics', *International Small Business Journal*, **33** (5), 488–513.

Cucculelli, M. and B. Ermini (2012), 'New product introduction and product tenure: what effects on firm growth?', *Research Policy*, **41** (5), 808–21.

Czarnitzki, D. and J. Delanote (2013), 'Young innovative companies: the new high-growth firms?', *Industrial and Corporate Change*, **22** (5), 1315–40.

Dachs, B. and B. Peters (2014), 'Innovation, employment growth, and foreign own-ership of firms: a European perspective', *Research Policy*, **43** (1), 214–32.

Dahlstrand, A.L. (1997), 'Growth and inventiveness in technology-based spin-off firms', *Research Policy*, **26** (3), 331–44.

Dahlstrand, A.L. and S. Jacobsson (2003), 'Universities and technology-based entrepreneurship in the Gothenburg region', *Local Economy*, **18** (1), 80–90.

Daunfeldt, S. and D. Halvarsson (2014), Are high-growth firms one-hit wonders? Evidence from Sweden', *Small Business Economics*, **44** (2), 361–83.

Davidsson, P. and J. Wiklund (2000), 'Conceptual and empirical challenges in the study of firm growth', in D. Sexton and H. Landström (eds), *The Blackwell Handbook of Entrepreneurship*, Oxford, MA, USA: Blackwell, pp.26–44.

De Faria, P. and J. Mendonça (2011), 'Innovation strategy by firms: do innovative firms grow more?', *International Journal of Entrepreneurship and Small Business*, **12** (2), 173–84.

Delmar, F., P. Davidsson and W. Gartner (2003), 'Arriving at the high growth firm', *Journal of Business Venturing*, **18** (2), 189–216.

Disney, R., J. Haskel and U. Heden (2003), 'Entry, exit and establishment survival in UK manufacturing', *The Journal of Industrial Economics*, **51** (1), 91–112.

Du, J. and Y. Temouri (2015), 'High-growth firms and productivity: evidence from the United Kingdom', *Small Business Economics*, **44** (1), 123–43.

Dunne, T., M.J. Roberts and L. Samuelson (1988), 'Patterns of firm entry and exit in the U.S. manufacturing industries', *RAND Journal of Economics*, **19** (4), 495–515.

Duschl, M. and S. Peng (2015), 'The patterns of Chinese firm growth: a conditional estimation approach of the asymmetric exponential power density', *Industrial and Corporate Change*, **24** (3), 539–63.

Eurostat-OECD (2007), 'Eurostat-OECD manual on business demography statistics', Luxembourg: Office for Official Publications of the European Communities.

Federico, J., R. Rabetino and H. Kantis (2012), 'Comparing young SMEs' growth determinants across regions', *Journal of Small Business and Enterprise Development*, **19** (4), 575–88.

Federico, J.S. and J. Capelleras (2014), 'The heterogeneous dynamics between growth and profits: the case of young firms', *Small Business Economics*, **44** (2), 231–53.

Gallagher, C. and H. Stewart (1986), 'Jobs and the business life-cycle in the UK', *Applied Economics*, **18** (8), 875–900.

García-Manjón, J.V. and M.E. Romero-Merino (2012), 'Research, development, and firm growth: empirical evidence from European top R&D spending firms', *Research Policy*, **41** (6), 1084–92.

Geroski, P., J. Mata and P. Portugal (2010), 'Founding conditions and survival of new firms', *Strategic Management Journal*, **31** (5), 510–29.

Giovannetti, G., G. Ricchiuti and M. Velucchi (2011), 'Size, innovation and internationalization: a survival analysis of Italian firms', *Applied Economics*, **43** (12), 1511–20.

Grilli, L. and S. Murtinu (2014), 'Government, venture capital and the growth of European high-tech entrepreneurial firms', *Research Policy*, **43** (9), 1523–43.

Halabisky, D., E. Dreessen and C. Parsley (2006), 'Growth in firms in Canada, 1985–1999', *Journal of Small Business and Entrepreneurship*, **19** (3), 255–68.

Henrekson, M. and D. Johansson (2010), 'Gazelles as job creators: a survey and interpretation of the evidence', *Small Business Economics*, **35** (1), 227–44.

Huber, P., H. Oberhofer and M. Pfaffermayr (2014), 'Job creation and the intra-distribution dynamics of the firm size distribution', *Industrial and Corporate Change*, **23** (1), 171–97.

Klofsten, M. (1997), 'Management of the early development process of technology-based firms', in D. Jones-Evans and M. Klofsten (eds), *Technology, Innovation and Enterprise: The European Experience*, London, UK: Macmillan.

Lawless, M. (2014), 'Age or size? Contributions to job creation', *Small Business Economics*, **42** (4), 815–30.

Lechner, C., B. Soppe and M. Dowling (2016), 'Vertical coopetition and the sales growth of young and small firms', *Journal of Small Business Management*, **54** (1), 67–84.

Lee, N. (2014), What holds back high-growth firms? Evidence from UK SMEs, *Small Business Economics*, **43** (1), 183–95.

Li, M., S.J. Goetz, M. Partridge and D.A. Fleming (2016), 'Location determinants of high-growth firms', *Entrepreneurship and Regional Development*, **28** (1–2), 97–125.

Link, A.N. and J.T. Scott (2012), 'Employment growth from the Small Business Innovation Research program', *Small Business Economics*, **39** (2), 265–87.

Löfsten, H. (2010), 'Critical incubator dimensions for small firm performance – a study of new technology-based firms localised in 16 incubators', *International Journal of Business Innovation and Research*, **4** (3), 256–79.

Löfsten, H. (2016), 'Business and innovation resources: determinants for the survival of new technology-based firms', *Management Decision*, **54** (1), 88–106.

Löfsten, H. and P. Lindelöf (2002), 'Science parks and the growth of new technology-based firms – academic-industry links, innovation and markets', *Research Policy*, **31** (6), 859–76.

Löfsten, H. and P. Lindelöf (2005), 'R&D networks and product innovation patterns – academic and non-academic new technology-based firms on science parks', *Technovation*, **25** (9), 1025–37.

Lööf, H. and P. Nabavi (2014), 'Survival, productivity and growth of new ventures across locations', *Small Business Economics*, **43** (2), 477–91.

Lopez-Garcia, P. and S. Puente (2012), 'What makes a high-growth firm? A dynamic probit analysis using Spanish firm-level data', *Small Business Economics*, **39** (4), 1029–41.

Macdonald, R. (2012), 'Firm dynamics: the death of new Canadian firms: a survival analysis of the 2002 cohort of entrants to the business sector', The Canadian Economy in Transition Series, Statistics Canada.

Markusen, A., P. Hall and A. Glasmeier (1986), *High Tech America: The What, How, Where and Why of the Sunrise Industries*, Boston, MA, USA: George Allen and Unwin.

Mazzucato, M. and S. Parris (2015), 'High-growth firms in changing competitive environments: the US pharmaceutical industry (1963 to 2002)', *Small Business Economics*, **44** (1), 145–70.

Monck, C.S.P., R.B. Porter, P. Quintas, D.J. Storey and P. Wynarczyk (1988), *Science Parks and the Growth of High Technology Firms*, London, UK: Croom Helm.

Napier, G., P. Rouvinen, D. Johansson, T. Finnbjörnsson, E. Solberg and K. Pedersen (2012), 'The Nordic growth entrepreneurship review 2012 – final report', *Nordic Innovation Report*, **25**, December, accessed 24 May 2013 at http://www.tem.fi/files/35549/The_Nordic_Growth_Entrepreneurhip_Review_2012.pdf.

Nightingale, P. and A. Coad (2014), 'Muppets and gazelles: political and methodological biases in entrepreneurship research', *Industrial and Corporate Change*, **23** (1), 113–43.

OECD (2015), *Entrepreneurship at a Glance 2015*, Paris, France: OECD Publishing.

Peric, M. and V. Vitezic (2016), 'Impact of global economic crisis on firm growth', *Small Business Economics*, **46** (1), 1–12.

Rickne, A. and S. Jacobsson (1999), 'New technology-based firms in Sweden – a study of their direct impact on industrial renewal', *Economics of Innovation and New Technology*, **8** (3), 197–223.

Santarelli, E. and M. Vivarelli (2007), 'Entrepreneurship and the process of firms' entry survival and growth', *Industrial and Corporate Change*, **16** (3), 455–88.

Shepherd, D. and J. Wiklund (2009), 'Are we comparing apples with apples or apples with oranges? Appropriateness of knowledge accumulation across growth studies', *Entrepreneurship Theory and Practice*, **33** (1), 105–23.

Sleuwaegen, L. and J. Onkelinx (2014), 'International commitment, post-entry growth and survival of international new ventures', *Journal of Business Venturing*, **29** (1), 106–20.

Storey, D. (1994) *Understanding the Small Business Sector*, London, UK: Routledge.

Tomczyk, D., J. Lee and E. Winslow (2013), 'Entrepreneurs' personal values, compensation, and high growth firm performance', *Journal of Small Business Management*, **51** (1), 66–82.

Uhlaner, L.M., A. van Stel, V. Duplat and H. Zhou (2013), 'Disentangling the effects of organizational capabilities, innovation and firm size on SME sales growth', *Small Business Economics*, **41** (3), 581–607.

Weinzimmer, L.G., P.C. Nystrom and S.J. Freeman (1998), 'Measuring organizational growth: issues, consequences and guidelines', *Journal of Management*, **24** (2), 235–62.

Xiao, J. (2015), 'The effects of acquisition on the growth of new technology-based firms: do different types of acquirers matter?', *Small Business Economics*, **45** (3), 487–504.

Yazdanfar, D. and P. Ohman (2015), 'Firm-level determinants of job creation by SMEs: Swedish empirical evidence', *Journal of Small Business and Enterprise Development*, **22** (4), 666–79.

Yazdanfar, D. and S. Turner (2013), 'The impact of internal finance on growth empirical evidence from Swedish firm level data', *International Journal of Entrepreneurship and Small Business*, **19** (1), 51–63.

APPENDICES

Table 9A.1 Recent studies regarding firm growth

	Article	Authors	Purpose	Method	Sample
1	Impact of global economic crisis on firm growth	Peric and Vitezic (2016)	Survival and growth in recession	Dynamic linear panel model, DV=ln(sal(t)), IV=ln(sal(t-1))	All Croatian firms in manufacturing and hospitality that survived 2008–13
2	Innovation and firm growth: does firm age play a role?	Coad et al. (2016)	Innovation and growth in different ages	Panel quantile regression, DV log differences (sal, emp, productivity)	+200 employee firms all, –200 firms from Spanish small firm sample between 2004 and 2012, new firms underrepresented (ten years old with caution)
3	Whom do high-growth firms hire?	Coad et al. (2014)	Employment and new hires among high-growth firms (HGFs)	Matching analysis of 1% or 5% fastest-growing firms in terms of sales or employment	During 1999–2002 active firms in knowledge-intensive industries in Sweden, firm age > three years
4	Innovation, employment growth and foreign ownership of firms, a European perspective	Dachs and Peters (2014)	How foreign-owned and domestically owned firms transform innovation into employment growth	Nominal sales growth	Data from CIS survey, firms with at least ten employees between 2002 and 2004

Table 9A.1 (continued)

	Article	Authors	Purpose	Method	Sample
5	High-growth firms in changing competitive environments: the US pharmaceutical industry (1963–2002)	Mazzucato and Parris (2015)	Under what conditions HGFs matter for translating R&D investments into economic growth and how this depends on firm-specific and industry-specific factors	Quantile regression, DV =log difference of sales, HGF 10% fastest-growing firms	Pharma firms trading on north American stock exchanges since 1950, age statistics not provided
6	What really happens to small and medium-sized enterprises in a global economic recession? UK evidence on sales and job dynamics	Cowling et al. (2015)	How small and medium-sized enterprises (SMEs) coped during the 2008 financial crisis	OLS regression, DV=relative sales and employment growth	Random sample of micro, small and medium-sized firms in UK, data from surveys, age information not provided
7	High-growth firms and productivity: evidence from the United Kingdom	Du and Temouri (2015)	Empirical link between total factor productivity (TFP) growth and HGFs	Panel regression analysis HGFs defined through OECD definition	26,313 firms in UK, covering the time period 2001–10, analysis restricted to firms having at least ten employees
8	An international cohort comparison of size effects on job growth	Anyadike-Danes et al. (2015)	Employment creation controlling for age, by comparing the cohorts of firms born in 1998 over their first decade to pin down size effects	Annual average growth rates	Cohorts of 1998 in different countries, sales and employees measured in 1998 and 2008, one cohort – two points of observation

	Title	Author	Research question	Method	Data
9	The effects of acquisition on the growth of new technology-based firms: do different types of acquirers matter?	Xiao (2015)	Whether acquisition, particularly that by multinational enterprises (MNEs), promotes the growth of NTBFs	Fixed-effects panel regression model combined with inverse-probability of treatment weights, log differences of ten sales or employees	A sample of Swedish NTBFs entering from 1997 to 2002 and being followed until 2009 that were acquired by foreign MNC (174 firms) or domestic MNC (87 firms); small and new firms included
10	Firm dynamics and job creation in the United Kingdom: 1998–2013	Anyadike-Danes et al. (2015)	What types of firms create the most jobs in the UK economy?	Analysis of growth performance of cohorts	Longitudinal firm-level data set in UK for 1998–2010; small and new firms included
11	The medium-term effect of R&D on firm growth	Capasso et al. (2015)	The effect of R&D expenditure on firm employment growth	Quantile regression techniques, transformed relative employment growth	Six waves of the innovation survey conducted between1996 and 2006 and matched with yearly data from the Business Register from 1996 to 2011; small and new firms included
12	Age or size? Contributions to job creation	Lawless (2014)	Job turnover and firm growth vary systematically across firm size groups and that smaller firms contribute to new job creation	Regression analysis, employment growth rate	Annual Employment survey in Ireland in manufacturing and internationally traded services; small and new firms included
13	Location determinants of high-growth firms	Li et al. (2016)	Understanding the local factors associated with fast-growth firms' emergence	Zero-inflated negative binomial regression	Inc. Magazine's published list of the 5,000 fastest-growing firms (INC5000) in terms of revenue; sample firm ages range from 4 to 193 years

	Article	Authors	Purpose	Method	Sample
14	Vertical coopetition and the sales growth of young and small firms	Lechner et al. (2016)	Examination of specific characteristics of vertical coopetition that affect the sales growth of young and small firms	Regression analysis, natural log transformation of average sales growth as dependent variable	Sample of 65 German firms that were VC financed firms and under ten years old
15	Growth development paths of firms – a study of smaller businesses	Bremner and Schimke (2015)	Whether firm characteristics that are related to firm growth in the literature are also related to the development path of firms	Relative growth indicator log differences of employees	Panel data on 178 German SME manufacturing firms over the period from 1992 to 2007; ages not reported
16	Reconciling quantile autoregressions of firm size and variance–size scaling	Capasso et al. (2013)	Aim of the paper is to understand what economic mechanisms may cause the Law of Proportionate Effect to break down for fast-growing and shrinking firms	Quantile regression techniques, log size	All the manufacturing firms present in the Business Register in the Netherlands from 1994 to 2004; includes firms with zero employees, referred to as self-employment
17	Influence of family ownership on small business growth; evidence from French SMEs	Hamelin (2013)	Paper uses a very large sample of French SMEs to explore the relationship between family ownership and small business growth	Regression analysis, sales growth, sustainable growth	French independent firms with annual sales higher than EUR 50 million and firms with annual sales lower than EUR 750,000, firms < 2 years old excluded

#		Authors		Method	
18	Diversification patterns and survival as firms mature	Coad and Guenther (2013)	We focus on the relationship between age and diversification patterns of German machine tool manufacturers in the post-war era	Regression analyses, Cox proportional hazard model	Approximately 2,000 firms that are active in the machine tool market between 1953 and 2002 in Germany; the age of a firm is approximated by using the year of the first observation within our analysis timeframe as the founding date
19	Disentangling the effects of organizational capabilities, innovation and firm size on SME sales growth	Uhlaner et al. (2013)	We test whether external sourcing and employee involvement in renewal activities predict sales growth, and if so, whether such effects are mediated by process and/or product innovation	OLS regression	Panel data of Dutch 229 SMEs, firms with < 4 employees removed
20	International commitment, post-entry growth and survival of international new ventures	Sleuwaegen and Onkelinx (2013)	We investigate the dynamics of commitment, growth and survival of different types of newly internationalizing Belgian firms	Regression analyses	Export and accounts data on Belgium SMEs for 1998–2005. Newness defined as firm starting exports within five years from inception
21	Government, venture capital and the growth of European high-tech entrepreneurial firm	Grilli and Murtinu (2014)	We assess the impact of government-managed (GVC) and independent venture capital (IVC) funds on the sales and employee growth of European high-tech entrepreneurial firms	Matching, fixed-effect regression and two-step system generalized method of moments	759 firms that have received VC finance, on average six years old

Table 9A.1 (continued)

	Article	Authors	Purpose	Method	Sample
22	What holds back high-growth firms? Evidence from UK SMEs	Lee (2014)	We consider the barriers faced by firms achieving high growth and those with the potential to do so	Propensity score matching and probit model, HGFs those with average annual growth of over 20% over a two-year period	Data for 4,858 UK SMEs with at least ten employees
23	Survival, productivity and growth of new ventures across locations	Lööf and Nabavi (2014)	We assess the impact of the location of genuinely new ventures and spinoffs on these firms' survival, productivity and growth	We first apply a discrete-time hazard model to study survival. Then, a dynamic panel-data approach is used to assess productivity and growth	Swedish data 5,195 unique entrants spawned by incumbent firms over the period 2000–2004 and 17,842 unique genuinely new firm entrants
24	The heterogeneous dynamics between growth and profits: the case of young firms	Federico and Capelleras (2014)	The present study investigates the dynamics between growth and profits of young firms by explicitly considering the endogeneity and heterogeneity aspects of the relationship	System GMM, DV difference in the logarithms of sales	A single cohort of young Spanish manufacturing firms (such as NACE Rev. 2 2-digit classification codes 10–33). All firms that were created from 1 January to 31 December 1996 and were followed over a 14-year period, from 1997 to 2010

25	Are high-growth firms one-hit wonders? Evidence from Sweden	Daunfeldt and Halvarsson (2014)	The research question is whether high-growth tends to persist	Autocorrelation functions, logarithmic difference in the number of employees or sales over a three-year period to measure firm growth	Our study covers all firms active during 1997–2008, no age information
26	What makes a high-growth firm? A dynamic probit analysis using Spanish firm-level data	Lopez-Garcia and Puente (2012)	This paper performs a multivariate analysis of the determinants of fast growth using a panel of Spanish firms	A probit model with correlated random effects, HGFs as those top 10% according to 'Birch–Schreyer indicator'	An unbalanced panel of 1,411 firms with at most six years of information; this sample bias towards medium- and large-sized firms, no age information
27	Do firms' growth rates depend on firm size?	Bentzen et al. (2012)	We have evaluated the validity of Gibrat's Law over the period 1990–2004	Panel data model	A sample of approximately 2,500 Danish firms representing all industries, no information on age
28	Venture-capital investor type and the growth mode of new technology-based firms	Bertoni et al. (2011)	The effect of independent venture capital on the growth mode of NTBF	Panel data models that control for endogeneity of IVC and CVC	A sample of 531 Italian new technology-based firms, no age limit
29	Entrepreneurs' personal values, compensation and high-growth firm performance	Tomczyk et al. (2013)	We tested whether high-growth firms' performance is related to the number of benefits offered and/or the values of the entrepreneur	We used regression analysis for each of the hypothesis tests	Data from 111 firms from the 2007 top 500 fastest-growing entrepreneurial firms in America, age from six to nine years

Table 9A.1 (continued)

	Article	Authors	Purpose	Method	Sample
30	Employment growth from the Small Business Innovation Research programme	Link and Scott (2012)	Employment growth in small firms funded by the US Small Business Innovation Research (SBIR) programme	Negative binomial model, retained employees	Data on SBIR-funded projects during 1992–2001, no matching
31	New firm formation and employment growth: regional and business dynamics	Baptista and Preto (2011)	This study examines differences in the effects of start-up rates on subsequent employment change. Two sources of such differences – types of start-ups and types of regions – are analysed	Panel regression, not firm-level analysis	All business units with at least one wage earner in the Portuguese economy between 1983 and 2000
32	Venture capital financing and the growth of high-tech start-ups: disentangling treatment from selection effects	Bertoni et al. (2011)	The aim of this work is to test whether VC investments have a positive treatment effect on the growth of employment and sales of NTBFs	We estimate Gibrat-law-type dynamic panel-data models augmented with time-varying variables that capture the VC status of firms	A ten-year longitudinal data set for 538 Italian NTBFs

33	Firm growth and barriers to growth among small firms in India	Coad and Tamvada (2012)	Empirical work on micro and small firms using census data (cross-sectional) in India	Cross-sectional regression. Log difference of gross output	We use firm-level data for the financial year 2002–3; 1.5 million Indian firms between 1 and 102 years of age
34	New product introduction and product tenure: what effects on firm growth?	Cucculelli and Ermini (2012)	The effect of product introduction on firm growth in a sample of Italian firms from 2000 to 2006	Fixed-effect panel data regression, the logarithmic difference of size as the dependent variable	186 Italian firms of which 3% have under 20 employees
35	Research, development and firm growth. Empirical evidence from European top R&D spending firms	García-Manjón and Romero-Merino (2012)	We present a model of endogenous firm growth with R&D investment as one of the main mechanisms of growth	OLS, quantile regressions, and GMM system estimators, logarithmic difference of size as the dependent variable	A sample of 754 European firms for the 2003–7 period, no size and age information
36	Comparing young SMEs' growth determinants across regions	Federico et al. (2012)	The authors propose an integrated model of venture growth where entrepreneurs' profile, firm resources and market characteristics are combined	This model is tested using three OLS regressions, one corresponding to each region	Sample of 1,443 young firms (between three and ten years old) of which 56 per cent (810) correspond to Latin American countries, 26 per cent (365) to South-East Asia and 18 per cent (268) to Mediterranean Europe

Table 9A.1 (continued)

	Article	Authors	Purpose	Method	Sample
37	Firm-level determinants of job creation by SMEs: Swedish empirical evidence	Yazdanfar and Ohman (2015)	Using a resource-based approach, the purpose of this paper is to examine the effects of the firm-level determinants financial leverage and liquidity on job creation at small and medium-sized enterprises (SMEs) in six industry sectors in Sweden	The generalized method of moments system model, log of number of employees as the dependent variable	The final sample comprised 26,721 SMEs with at least one but fewer than 200 employees
38	Gazelles and industry growth: a study of young high-growth firms in The Netherlands	Bos and Stam (2014)	This article examines to what extent and how the presence of gazelles, young high-impact firms, is related to the growth of industries over time	Panel vector autoregressive model	We analyse gazelles in The Netherlands over a 12-year period, annually from 1997 until 2008; we define a gazelle as a firm that is between five and ten years old with at least 20 employees
39	Innovation strategy by firms: do innovative firms grow more?	De Faria and Mendonça (2011)	This paper looks at the relationship between innovation and firm performance, distinguishing product and process innovation	A value-added Cobb-Douglas production function, dependent log difference in sales volume 2000–2003	Data from the third Community Innovation Survey (CIS III) and the Portuguese Quadros de Pessoal; 1,533 firms, average age 25 years

40	Young Innovative Companies: the new high-growth firms?	Czarnitzki and Delanote (2013)	This study investigates whether YICs grow more than other firms, both in terms of employment and in terms of sales	Ordinary least squares estimations and quantile regressions, annual relative sales and employment growth as dependent variables	Database of 3,537 Flemish firms during the years 2001–08, under six years old
41	The patterns of Chinese firm growth: a conditional estimation approach of the asymmetric exponential power density	Duschl and Peng (2015)	This article investigates the impact of ownership type on the entire growth rate distributional mass of Chinese firms	Conditional estimation approach of the asymmetric exponential power density; DVs: log growth rates based on two alternative size measures: number of employees and sales	Wide coverage data from the Chinese Industrial Enterprises Database conducted by the National Bureau of Statistics (NBS) of China for the years from 2001 to 2006. All firms with fewer than five employees are excluded
42	Product innovation and firm growth: evidence from the integrated circuit industry	Corsino and Gabriele (2011)	Exploiting a unique data set, we find that incremental product innovations commercialized in the immediate past positively affect the revenue streams of specialized business units operating in dynamic environments	Panel regression analysis, annual log differences in sales	Sample of 96 companies that account for 80% of total revenues from the IC industry and are representative of the population of IC producers

Table 9A.1 (continued)

	Article	Authors	Purpose	Method	Sample
43	Job creation and the intra-distribution dynamics of the firm size distribution	Huber et al. (2014)	We estimate firm-specific transition probabilities between size classes of the firm size distribution	We specify a three-equation Heckman-type model for the log sizes	The data set captures the universe of firms in the Austrian manufacturing industries between 1972 and 2004 (17,390 firms), at minimum five years old
44	High-growth firms and technological knowledge: do gazelles follow exploration or exploitation strategies?	Colombelli et al. (2014)	This article analyses the contribution of high-growth firms (HGFs) to the process of knowledge creation	Regression analyses of difference of sales as dependent	Our final data set is an unbalanced panel of 335 active companies listed on the main European financial market that submitted at least one patent application to the EPO in the period analysed, no age information, mostly large firms
45	The impact of internal finance on growth empirical evidence from Swedish firm-level data	Yazdanfar and Turner (2013)	This paper examines the impact of firms' internal liquidity access and related firm characteristics on the growth of Swedish micro firms	Seemingly unrelated regression model with four explanatory variables (for example, liquidity access, size, age and industry affiliation)	A database of over 62,000 observations covering 10,383 Swedish micro firms over the 2007–8 period

Table 9A.2   Survival rates in different nace two-digit categories

Nace1	N Original (2006)	N suvived 2014	Change	Change%
2	2	2	0	0 %
20	1	1	0	0
21	9	7	−2	−22 %
26	30	18	−12	−40 %
27	10	8	−2	−20 %
31	1	1	0	0 %
33	1	1	0	0 %
35	1	1	0	0 %
41	1	1	0	0 %
42	2	2	0	0 %
43	6	5	−1	−17 %
44	2	2	0	0 %
45	4	2	−2	−50 %
46	10	8	−2	−20 %
47	27	19	−8	−30 %
48	12	3	−9	−75 %
49	1	1	0	0 %
53	1	1	0	0 %
55	2	1	−1	−50 %
56	2	2	0	0 %
58	32	22	−10	−31 %
59	184	121	−63	−34 %
60	4	1	−3	−75 %
61	24	15	−9	−38 %
62	816	594	−222	−27 %
63	85	53	−32	−38 %
64	7	4	−3	−43 %
65	9	4	−5	−56 %
66	4	2	−2	−50 %
68	7	6	−1	−14 %
69	2	1	−1	−50 %
70	36	29	−7	−19 %
71	12	8	−4	−33 %
72	130	90	−40	−31 %
73	6	5	−1	−17 %
74	5	3	−2	−40 %
75	3	2	−1	−33 %
77	1	1	0	0 %
80	1	1	0	0 %
81	1	1	0	0 %
82	2	0	−2	−100 %

Table 9A.2　(continued)

Nace1	N Original (2006)	N suvived 2014	Change	Change%
86	13	9	−4	−31 %
87	3	3	0	0 %
90	11	10	−1	−9 %
96	2	1	−1	−50 %
	1525	1072		

Table 9A.3　*Sales development of the 2006 cohort of Swedish NTBFs*

Tkr	sal07	sal08	sal09	sal10	sal11	sal12	sal13
N	1069	1069	1069	1069	1069	1069	1069
mean	2786	3660	4080	4699	5745	6603	7267
p50	982	1144	1126	1096	1150	1103	1018
sum	2979120	3913343	4361625	5023547	6141868	7059320	7769331

Table 9A.4　*Employment development of the 2006 cohort of Swedish NTBFs*

Tkr	emp07	emp08	emp09	emp10	emp11	emp12	emp13
N	1069	1069	1069	1069	1069	1069	1069
mean	2.3	2.9	3.2	3.5	3.9	4.3	4.6
p50	1	1	1	1	1	1	1
sum	2544	3159	3460	3793	4195	4695	4998

Table 9A.5   *Growth in mean sales and median sales in different nace two digit categories*

Nace 26	sal07	sal08	sal09	sal10	sal11	sal12	sal13
N	18	18	18	18	18	18	18
Mean	1433	2487	1513	1781	2893	4981	3237
Change							126 %
Median	323	1278	515	590	912	1305	1074
Change							233 %
Sum	25794	44760	27235	32059	52074	89665	58262

Nace 47	sal07	sal08	sal09	sal10	sal11	sal12	sal13
N	19	19	19	19	19	19	19
Mean	2868	3093	2855	3751	4182	3894	3806
Change							33 %
Median	1294	1539	1334	1521	1514	626	656
Change							-49 %
Sum	54503	58774	54245	71283	79461	74003	72314

Nace 58	sal07	sal08	sal09	sal10	sal11	sal12	sal13
N	22	22	22	22	22	22	22
Mean	4121	4491	3700	4567	4992	5233	6936
Change							68 %
Median	1073	1488	1403	950	927	1044	1194
Change							11 %
Sum	90654	98800	81407	100464	109818	115116	152587

Nace 59	sal07	sal08	sal09	sal10	sal11	sal12	sal13
N	121	121	121	121	121	121	121
Mean	1893	2394	2637	3035	3508	3811	3433
Change							81 %
Median	850	983	951	923	825	819	775
Change							−9 %
Sum	229014	289630	319088	367228	424427	461106	415428

Nace 61	sal07	sal08	sal09	sal10	sal11	sal12	sal13
N	15	15	15	15	15	15	15
Mean	5065	14152	18086	23077	25955	31176	32115
Change							534 %
Median	862	1288	4469	8033	10560	11471	11140

Table 9A.5   (continued)

Nace 61	sal07	sal08	sal09	sal10	sal11	sal12	sal13
Change							1192 %
Sum	75979	212285	271297	346150	389332	467642	481722

Nace 62	sal07	sal08	sal09	sal10	sal11	sal12	sal13
N	594	594	594	594	594	594	594
Mean	3017	3822	4198	4884	6222	7020	7976
Change							164 %
Median	1177	1228	1296	1245	1339	1301	1185
Change							1 %
Sum	1792216	2270345	2493381	2900988	3695947	4169817	4737546

Nace 63	sal07	sal08	sal09	sal10	sal11	sal12	sal13
N	53	53	53	53	53	53	53
Mean	1681	2638	2600	3270	4119	3903	4481
Change							167 %
Median	533	779	738	950	764	638	767
Change							44 %
Sum	89086	139826	137774	173290	218310	206876	237479

Nace 70	sal07	sal08	sal09	sal10	sal11	sal12	sal13
N	29	29	29	29	29	29	29
Mean	2075	3605	4059	3968	4285	4033	3968
Change							91 %
Median	910	1069	838	830	1154	1103	1051
Change							15 %
Sum	60164	104533	117707	115082	124272	116958	115074

Nace 72	sal07	sal08	sal09	sal10	sal11	sal12	sal13
N	90	90	90	90	90	90	90
Mean	914	2228	3154	3535	3732	4299	5175
Change							466 %
Median	265	425	546	470	438	364	297
Change							12 %
Sum	82284	200556	283844	318150	335903	386942	465736

Table 9A.6   Growth in mean employment and median employment in different nace two digit categories

Nace 26	emp07	emp08	emp09	emp10	emp11	emp12	emp13
N	15	15	15	15	15	15	15
Mean	2	2	2	2	2	3	3
Change							41 %
Median	1	1	1	2	2	2	2
Change							100 %
Sum	29	33	30	33	37	39	41

Nace 47	emp07	emp08	emp09	emp10	emp11	emp12	emp13
N	16	16	16	16	16	16	16
Mean	2	2	3	3	3	2	3
Change							48 %
Median	1	2	2	2	2	2	2
Change							100 %
Sum	29	39	43	45	43	38	43

Nace 58	emp07	emp08	emp09	emp10	emp11	emp12	emp13
N	21	21	21	21	21	21	21
Mean	3	4	4	4	3	4	5
Change							52 %
Median	1	2	2	2	1	2	1
Change							0 %
Sum	63	79	74	81	69	85	96

Nace 59	emp07	emp08	emp09	emp10	emp11	emp12	emp13
N	100	100	100	100	100	100	100
Mean	2	2	2	2	3	2	2
Change							23 %
Median	1	2	2	1,5	2	1	1
Change							0 %
Sum	188	233	233	249	281	234	231

Nace 61	emp07	emp08	emp09	emp10	emp11	emp12	emp13
N	14	14	14	14	14	14	14
Mean	3	6	7	10	11	12	13
Change							370 %
Median	1	2	2	3	4	4	4

Table 9A.6   (continued)

Nace 61	emp07	emp08	emp09	emp10	emp11	emp12	emp13
Median	1	2	2	3	4	4	4
Change							300 %
Sum	40	80	95	133	148	171	188

Nace 62	emp07	emp08	emp09	emp10	emp11	emp12	emp13
N	528	528	528	528	528	528	528
Mean	3	4	4	5	5	6	6
Change							110 %
Median	1	2	2	2	2	2	1
Change							0 %
Sum	1612	1930	2192	2430	2686	3131	3389

Nace 63	emp07	emp08	emp09	emp10	emp11	emp12	emp13
N	46	46	46	46	46	46	46
Mean	2	3	3	3	4	4	4
Change							110 %
Median	1	1	1	1	1	1	1
Change							0 %
Sum	91	139	134	136	173	193	191

Nace 70	emp07	emp08	emp09	emp10	emp11	emp12	emp13
N	25	25	25	25	25	25	25
Mean	1	3	3	3	3	3	3
Change							100 %
Median	1	1	1	1	1	1	1
Change							0 %
Sum	33	71	73	67	72	68	66

Nace 72	emp07	emp08	emp09	emp10	emp11	emp12	emp13
N	69	69	69	69	69	69	69
Mean	3	3	4	4	4	4	4
Change							70 %
Median	1	1	1	1	2	1	1
Change							0 %
Sum	176	212	244	277	296	296	300

Table 9A.7a *The number of firms that are classified as high-growth firms if a firm has shown high growth in previous period according to combined OECD and kink-point approach*

	OECD and Kink HGF 0609 =1 (n=24)	OECD and Kink HGF 0710=1 (n=50)	OECD and Kink HGF 0811=1 (n=45)	OECD and Kink HGF 0912=1 (n=41)
OECD and Kink HGF 0710=1 (n=50)	18 firms (75%)	–	–	–
OECD and Kink HGF 0811=1 (n=45)	10 firms (42%)	36 firms (72%)	–	–
OECD and Kink HGF 0912=1 (n=41)	6 firms (25%)	21 firms (42%)	33 firms (73%)	–
OECD and Kink HGF 1013=1 (n=37)	3 firms (13%)	16 firms (32%)	23 firms (51%)	30 firms (73%)

Table 9A.7b *The number of firms that are classified as high-growth firms if a firm has shown high growth in previous period according to combined Autio et al. approach*

	Autio HGF 0609 =1 (n=10)	Autio HGF 0710=1 (n=24)	Autio HGF 0811=1 (n=13)	Autio HGF 0912=1 (n=10)
Autio HGF 0710=1 (n=24)	2 firms (20%)	–	–	–
Autio HGF 0811=1 (n=13)	0 firms (0%)	7 firms (29%)	–	–
Autio HGF 0912=1 (n=10)	0 firms (0%)	3 firms (13%)	7 firms (53%)	–
Autio HGF 1013=1 (n=10)	0 firms (0%)	0 firms (0%)	1 firms (8%)	1 firms (10%)

Table 9A.8   Temporal distribution of high-growth periods for different definitions of high growth (1= firm qualifies as a high-growth firm in a period)

	OECD_ emp_ higr_09	OECD_ emp_ higr_10	OECD_ emp_ higr_11	OECD_ emp_ higr_12	OECD_ emp_ higr_13
Firm 1		1	1		
Firm 2				1	1
Firm 3	1	1			
Firm 4				1	1
Firm 5				1	1
Firm 6				1	1
Firm 7				1	1
Firm 8			1		1
Firm 9			1		1
	Kink_ emp_ higr_09	Kink_ emp_ higr_10	Kink_ emp_ higr_11	Kink_ emp_ higr_12	Kink_ emp_ higr_13
Firm 1	1	1			
Firm 2	1	1			
Firm 3	1	1			
Firm 4		1	1		
Firm 5			1	1	
Firm 6	1	1			
Firm 7		1	1		
Firm 8		1	1		
Firm 9			1	1	
Firm 10		1	1		
Firm 11				1	1
	Autio_ emp_ higr_09	Autio_ emp_ higr_10	Autio_ emp_ higr_11	Autio_ emp_ higr_12	Autio_ emp_ higr_13
Firm 1	1	1			
Firm 2			1	1	
Firm 3	1	1			
Firm 4		1	1		
Firm 5			1	1	
Firm 6		1	1		
Firm 7		1	1		
Firm 8		1	1		

Index

Printed and bound by CPI Group (UK) Ltd, Croydon, CR0 4YY

23/04/2025

14660963-0001